Governors State University
Library
Hours:
Monday thru Thursday 8:30 to 10:30
Friday and Saturday 8:30 to 5:00
Sunday 1:00 to 5:00 (Fall and Winter Trimester Only)

DEMCO

# BLACK MASCULINITIES
# AND SCHOOLING

# BLACK MASCULINITIES AND SCHOOLING
## How Black boys survive modern schooling

Tony Sewell

**Trentham Books**

First published in 1997 by Trentham Books Limited

Reprinted 2000

Trentham Books Limited
Westview House
734 London Road
Oakhill
Stoke on Trent
Staffordshire
England ST4 5NP

**British Cataloguing in Publication Data**
A catalogue record for this book is available from the British Library
ISBN 1 85856 040 3

Designed and typeset by Trentham Print Design Ltd., Chester and printed
in Great Britain by Bell & Bain Ltd., Glasgow.

# Acknowledgements

I am indebted to many people for their support, encouragement and advice: I would like to thank Morwenna Griffiths for her guidance and wisdom and all the staff and pupils at Township school. A special note of thanks goes to Adele Williams who showed the utmost care and patience. Thanks also to Gillian Klein and the staff at Trentham Books.

To Zindzi and all the boys at Township

# Contents

## List of Tables

# Introduction

Black boys are Angels and Devils in British (and American) schools. They are heroes of a street fashion culture that dominates most of our inner cities. On the other hand they experience a disproportionate amount of punishment in our schools compared to all other ethnic groupings. This book seeks to explain why this has happened. This experience of being the darling of popular youth sub-culture and the sinner in the classroom has led to the formation of a range of behaviours. How do African-Caribbean boys in particular respond in a school that sees them as sexy and as sexually threatening? These responses are what I call masculinities. They are linked to how the boys perceive themselves as males and how others perceive them.

At the heart of the book is a thesis which asserts that teachers in primary and secondary schools cannot escape the wider perceptions that exist about Black boys. Indeed many of their actions in my research show a belief in the myth that African-Caribbean boys present a more serious threat to society.

This work is not a naive defence of the 'essential innocence' of Black people. It acknowledges the positive and negative force of peer group culture in the schooling of these children.

What drives my thesis is the evidence of how representations of Black masculinity have made African-Caribbean boys in Britain too 'sexy' for school. I use the word 'sexy' as a positive *and* negative force. Negative in its narrow perspective which sees Black males only in the context of sport, music and crime. Positive in their talent as makers of positive identity for both Black youth and White. In too many cases African-Caribbean boys were burdened with a representation that they all had to carry. It was centred on the 'body' and not on the mind. The most important factor was how it became anti-school.

The book therefore presupposes that school cannot be understood in isolation; both teachers and pupils come to the institution with wider perspectives acquired outside the classroom. It is the perspectives on Black masculinity that I want to explore. What are the teacher perspectives and how does this determine their actions in school? What are the messages coming from the popular Black culture that exists outside of school and how does this inform the peer and individual perspectives of African-Caribbean boys in school?

For the researcher looking at the complex interactions between teacher and Black male pupil, a surface reading will often hide a more problematic understanding of these relations. This potent mixture of race and sex cannot be explained by simplistic notions of teacher racism. What has been overlooked in too many studies is the complex interplay of racism, sub-cultural perspectives and schooling. It is an acknowledgement that in the field of 'real' schools life is very messy. As Rizvi puts it:

> Racism is an ideology which is continually changing, being challenged, interrupted and reconstructed, and which often appears in contradictory forms. As such, its reproduction in schools, and elsewhere, can be expected to be complex, multifaceted and historically specific. (Rizvi, 1993a p15)

Traditionally the discussion of gender and education has centred around girls. In the late eighties with the explosion of men's studies (e.g. Askew and Ross 1988; Heward 1988; Connell 1989 and Skeggs 1991) there was a growing interest in the links between masculinity and schooling. This was given added weight by government concern over the apparent academic gap between boys and girls.

When it comes to African-Caribbean boys however, the evidence for a conflict with schooling goes back to the early 1970s. Writers like Coard (1971) showed how Special schools had been systematically used as a dumping ground for Black children (mainly boys) who did not conform to schooling. The Swann Report (1985) also failed to address the particular issue of the experiences of Black boys in school and ended up talking about cultural deficits. The national interest in this area seems prominent only in the search for causes of juvenile crime. This was evident in police and media interest:

It is a fact that very many of the perpetrators of muggings are very young Black people, who have been excluded from school and/or are unemployed. (Paul Condon, Commissioner of Metropolitan Police, July 1995)

Outside of the literature on Black underachievement, little has been written on the 'total' range of Black male experience in school and particularly the role of their sub-cultures in school.

In his study of masculinities, Mac an Ghaill (1994) talks about how in ethnographic studies a certain incident captures the essence or kernel of one's research. This happened to me when I showed a video of a programme by Lenny Henry to a group of 15-year-old African Caribbean students, in which Henry plays the feckless Delbert who makes his living by doing scams. This was their response:

TS: Why does Delbert have to keep using 'scams' ?

Michael: It's the only way he, as a Black youth, can survive.

Donald: Check it, no one is going to give him a job, he has to do a bit of illegal business or else he's going to go hungry.

Michael: Most Black kids do scams.

TS: Why?

Dennis: It's how we are – we have to go crooked because the system is like that.

TS: What do you mean?

Dennis: The police and employers, let's face it, they don't like Black people.

Allan: I don't think it's just Black kids that pull scams. Loads of white boys always do it. They just do it differently.

TS: What do you mean?

Allan: Yes, the Black kids do it right up front and they don't care.

TS: Do you think that the white boys are more clever with their sneaky scams?

Allan: No way, the white boys are just pussies, they haven't got the balls like a Black man, most of them go on as if they are batty men (homosexual).

TS: Do you all agree with that?

There is universal agreement.

It was then that I realised that something had gone seriously wrong in the way that these group of boys were conceptualising 'race', masculinity and schooling. The incident pointed to the need to look at other categories of African-Caribbean boys and explore the connection between the unstable categories of 'race' and masculinity in the context of school life.

It is in school that ideas of sexual/racial 'desire', 'fear' and 'internalisation' have most subtly been played. My concern in this study is how these racialised/ sexual discourses have influenced the performance, both academic and social, of African-Caribbean boys. The intense focus on the lives of these students is not to position them as 'victims' or 'perpetrators' but to reveal two aspects of their relationship to schooling. The first is how the school, through its institutions and teacher attitudes supported by peer group cultures, acts as an agency for racialised/sexual oppression. The second is the different response routes that African-Caribbean boys choose to survive their context.

## Racisms and sexuality

I am aware that such complex and difficult terms as sexuality and racism appear frequently in this study. There is a need to locate their definitions outside the often casual use of such words. I use the word 'sexuality' in its identity formation context. In this sense it is linked to Foucault's (1979) ideas that sexuality underlies the whole truth about a person and is a strategic site for the regulation of populations. It is the policing of sexuality, both institutional and self-imposed, that is relevant to this project.

Theories on sexuality and its links with racism has had a tradition with the writings of Hall (1991), hooks (1992) and Mercer (1994). All these writers point to the need to balance a theoretical rejection of essentialism, objectivism and universalism with a commitment to non-oppressive, democratic and pluralistic values. Therefore 'living identity through difference' recognises that we are all composed of multiple social identities, and thus any attempt to organise people in relation to their diversity of identification has to be a struggle that is conducted positionally. According to Hall (1991):

> We are all complexly constructed through different categories, of different antagonisms, and these may have the effect of locating us socially in multiple positions of marginality and subordination, but which do not yet operate on us in exactly the same way. (1991 p57)

It is in this complex and contingent sense that I see racism operating. Racism must be defined within particular historical and social contexts where the old ideologies of racism can appear alongside new developments. Therefore in this book I see racism not as a monolithic concept but as varied and historically situated.

Race remains a vitally important part of contemporary life and politics, but it is neither separate from other factors (class, gender, sexuality, disability) nor is it always the most important characteristic in human experience and action. Race may be more or less important to the same person at different times in different contexts.

The racism that is of importance for this study is what has been called 'cultural racism' (Fanon, 1967). The historical context is Britain in the mid-1990s under the leadership of John Major. It is a government still committed to 'One Nation Toryism' but it finds its greatest threat not just from Black communities within but from the fear of joining a united Europe. Before this the big issues of race and identity were in the headlines during Margaret Thatcher's administrations. This was epitomised by the closing of the anti-racism friendly Greater London Council, the propagation of the English nativism extolled by Ray Honeyford and the passing of the 1988 Education Reform Act. Les Back (1992) sums up this new 'cultural racism':

> Here culture, rather than pigment, became the key referent. The texture of British identity, stripped of its Celtic and regional components, is dominated by a cultural aesthetic of 'Englishness'.

At the beginning of the new decade, the Conservative Member of Parliament, Norman Tebbit appeared on the BBC's programme 'Newsnight' and warned that: 'Many youngsters leave school totally confused about their origins and their culture.' It is this period in the history of English racism... Its focus is the defence of the mythic 'British/English way of life' in the face of attack from enemies outside ('Argies', 'Frogs', 'Krauts', 'Iraqis' and within ('Black communities', 'Muslim fundamentalists'). (1992 p6)

This book argues that the English landscape is a complex one where the traditional prejudices have been used as an ideological tool to confirm a particular form of nationalism. It is also a vision that regulates the sexuality of Black men, in terms of hyper-sexuality or as a vision of 'castration'. The terms and conditions for a Black male to enter or survive new Britain is one of denial of race/sexual identity or as an exaggerated phallocentric. It is in the institution of school that the Black boys in my study 'played' to these extremes.

## Ethnicity and Exclusions

African-Caribbean students are consistently over-represented in exclusion data. In 1988 the now abolished Inner London Education Authority (ILEA) first published details on the ethnic background of 'suspended and expelled' students. Caribbean students accounted for almost 14 per cent of the secondary school population, but made up more than 30 per cent of all 'suspensions' (ILEA, 1988, p9). That is, more than twice as many 'Caribbean' students were suspended than would have been predicted on the basis of their representation in the school population. In Nottingham, between September 1989 and April 1990, 'Black' (i.e. African-Caribbean and 'mixed-race') students made up 6.7 per cent of the secondary school population, but accounted for 24.8 per cent of those 'involved in exclusion procedures' (Nottinghamshire County Council, 1991, p21). In Lewisham 'Black Afro-Caribbean' students have been consistently over-represented in published exclusion figures, ranging from three and a half times the predicted level (in 1990-91) to around double the predicted number in 1993 data. (Lewisham, 1993)

This exclusion picture for these local authorities represents the picture nationally. The only published figures on permanent exclusions across England and Wales (from the NEFRS) reports that over 8 per cent of permanent exclusions were of 'Afro-Caribbean' students (DFE 1993 P4). This must be compared with an estimate of under 2 per cent of the overall school population in 1993. This means that, nationally, four times as many African-Caribbean students were permanently excluded than would have been predicted, all things being equal. The overwhelming proportion were young boys.

In Township School (the name I have given the school that I studied) the figures on exclusion reflected these national percentages. What I add to this focus are figures on attendance, which reveal a disproportion of good attendance by African-Caribbean boys. This phenomenon was used by teachers to give their different perspectives on African-Caribbean motive and attitude.

## Fieldwork

Much of the material was gathered through semi-structured interviews and observations. I interviewed teachers and students as individuals and in groups. Detailed notes were taken and written up daily. I used classroom observation but in the interest of grounding my student perspective, I 'hung around' the playground and was regularly present in the student common room areas. Although this study does look at the teachers' perspective, I was aware that only a handful of studies had seriously taken on the African-Caribbean student perspective in any great range and detail. This was observed by James Baldwin (1965) in the sixties:

> I entered or anyway I encountered the white world. Now this white world that I was encountering was, just the same, one of the forces that had been controlling me from the time I opened my eyes on the world. For it is important to ask, I think, where did these people I'm talking about come from and where did they get their peculiar school of ethics? What was its origin? What did it mean to them? What did it come out of? What function did it serve and why was it happening here? And why were they living where they were living and what was it doing to them? All these things that

sociologists think they can find out and haven't managed to do...
(1965, p121)

It seems appropriate at this point to declare that I am a Black male
(aged 35 at the time of writing this book). By taking the school as the
main level for analysis, I wanted to work within a context that was not
dehumanising. Inevitably my presence as an African-Caribbean male
would have some implications on my work in the field. Would white
teachers reveal as much to me as they would to a white researcher?
Would I be too sympathetic to the points of view of African-Caribbean
boys? Would the school see me as a political threat in terms of the
politics of racism?

In order not to avoid these issues, I have used what can be called an
emancipatory research method, where I saw the research method not as
a process of 'them' and 'me' but as more of a collaboration. I allowed
the respondents time and space to reflect and comment on my own
analysis. This was achieved by having more than one interview with
the same respondent.

An important factor that underpinned my collaboration with the
students was a tension which came from their perception of me as one
of them – and yet I was older and part of the teachers' world. I used
this as a positive positioning. It gave me enough 'critical distance' so
that I was not just a mouthpiece for their perspectives. On the other
hand the students felt an affinity with me, not just as a Black male but
because I would often 'chill' (relax socially) with them or engage them
in topics that I knew would be of interest.

## Categorising Black masculinities

This book seeks to challenge essentialist notions of Black masculinity.
I see masculinity in a plural context, which is not fixed but fluid and
can only be understood by a series of complex interactions. The boys
in this study manifested a range of masculinities in which categories
can only act as 'benchmarks'. I have tentatively labelled them: 1
Conformists, 2 Innovators, 3 Retreatist, 4 Rebels. These broad brushstrokes clearly hide many sub-categories and contradictions, which are
key features of African-Caribbean masculinity and attitude.

## What this book is about

The book opens with a chapter called Raising the Issues. It is a preliminary study based in a mixed school (gender and race), which I used as a dry-run before my main study. The data generated from talking to teachers and students produced the key issues for a more in-depth study of the second school. It pointed to the powerful position of African-Caribbean subculture as a myth and a reality in forming powerful discourses in school. Moreover it pointed to the way teachers were socialised to defend their institution even when it operated social injustice.

In chapters three to six the range of student responses are examined, from Conformists to Rebels. Chapter seven traces the historic development of Black British sub-cultures. The question posed here is: to what extent are Black boys paying a high price for dominating popular culture? Do Black boys only provide the fuel for an industry (music, fashion etc.) that will simply exploit them? What are the images of Black masculinity that Black popular cultures' leeches draw on? How does this square with the passionate need for identity formation?

Chapter eight looks at how Black masculinities are regulated through disciplinary power into two caricatures. One is a humbled emasculated conformity; the other is a destructive rebel. I argue that too many African-Caribbean boys are forced to make this choice of two evils.

Chapter nine seeks some practical solutions for teachers and Black boys on the level of school policy, curriculum and racial identity development – so the factors that have been unravelled in this book, with their negative consequences for these boys' education, do not prevail.

# 1

# Raising the issues:
# The case of John Caxton School

*All Black men are more or less pissed off, and can you wonder when you look around our society?* – Mike Phillips

In carrying out the research for this study it was necessary to find a school where I could test out some of my concerns and questions on the topic of Black masculinity and schooling. I wanted to look at a mixed-school, which had a multiracial intake. It was at John Caxton School (not its real name) that big questions were formulated for the main study at Township School.

John Caxton has a racial composition of 30 per cent white, 30 per cent African-Caribbean and 30 per cent Asian. This is a mixed comprehensive, two-thirds of whose pupils are boys. It is located in an area which has high unemployment, poor housing and low income families. In 1991 there was a total of 700 children in the school. African-Caribbean boys made up only one third of the total school population. However, they represented 85 per cent of the total exclusions.

## Teacher attitude and practice
The work of Green (1983), Gillborn (1990) and Mac an Ghaill (1988) all conclude that African-Caribbean boys receive disproportionately larger amounts of control and criticism compared to other ethnic groups, who are often ignored when committing the same offence. They all place the blame firmly with teachers and the schooling process. Do the teachers in John Caxton agree with this analysis?

The perspectives of Ms Murray, a white Religious Education teacher and John Watts, an African-Caribbean Head of History, are surprisingly similar on the issue of African-Caribbean exclusions.

Ms Murray agrees that African-Caribbean boys are more likely to be excluded, but she denies that she operates any form of discrimination in her class. She believes in multiculturalism, mixed ability teaching, child centred learning and a pastoral approach. She describes herself as liberal. At first one could easily agree that her politics are not right wing. However, as Mac an Ghaill (1988) found in his study:

> The teachers' understanding of the students' response to academic work highlighted the way in which both authoritarian and liberal teachers assumed the neutrality of the dominant values of the school. Many of the teachers were critical of the students' lack of competitive spirit, especially among the Afro-Caribbeans. (1988, p59)

This sums up Ms Murray's perspective – she does accept that there are 'unfair practices in the school' but in the final analysis the 'blame' for academic and behavioural poor performance lies in the home, she says.

> Ms Murray: Some of the boys (African-Caribbean) come from unsettled family backgrounds. I remember one boy who was excluded four times within four months. He was also never settled at home, sometimes he lived with his mum, other times with his Dad. This wasn't to do with a 14 year old acting flash – it was something deeper.
>
> TS: Like what?
>
> Ms Murray: I blame the home. It can also be expectations. Because, on the other extreme, there are those who come to school from very strict backgrounds where they get hit. When they come to school the expectations are a lot lower.

Ms Murray perceives herself as 'liberal' but it is clear that she shares a similar perspective to the teachers who conform to an authoritarian typology. She works within the same educational paradigm as an Authoritarian, who defines the 'problem' of schooling Black youth in terms of the students themselves rather than the racial, gender and social class determinants of the school and wider society.

In contrast, John Watts openly attacks white teachers for being frightened of Black boys because of their size:

TS: Why are so many boys of African-Caribbean descent excluded from this school?

Mr Watts: There are some teachers, Black and white, who have no connection with the Black community. A boy of five feet nine inches is seen as a threat. I blame weak teachers who are clearly afraid of Black boys and over-react through fear. I hardly have any confrontations with Black kids.

TS: What makes your attitude work?

Mr Watts: I won't accept that because X amount of reports say that Black boys don't do well, so I won't try. I seem to be going against the tide because I expect them to do well.

However, John Watts' attitudes are similar to those of Ms Murray, in that he also blames Black boys for their lack of educational hunger and discipline:

Mr Watts: These kids haven't got the hunger we had in the fifties – we were hungry for education. Black children need to take a more long-term perspective on things – they have got to look to themselves and stop making excuses. I know racism is out there, but you can't just lay down and die. Education is still an important tool. We can't afford for our children to lose sight of this.

Both these teachers acknowledge the negative effect of the schooling process on African-Caribbean boys. More precisely, they both see that the racist perception by many teachers has meant that these boys receive a disproportionate amount of control and criticism. However, they refuse to shift the 'blame' from the culture and attitude of the boys themselves. This supports Mac an Ghaill's theory (1988) that teachers – no matter how 'liberal' they say they are – are socialised by the act of teaching to defend the dominant ethos of the school.

My sample of teachers both have 'ideal' pupils. For Ms Murray it is the Chinese girls in her class:

TS: Can you point to any groupings in your classes which work best?

Ms Murray: I have a group of Chinese girls who never give any trouble and their work is excellent. I suppose it's to do with their culture.

John Watts' 'ideal' student was an unseasoned (i.e. not influenced by Black Britain) Jamaican. Watts had the 'old traditional values' of hard work and a belief in the system of schooling irrespective of negative pressures. Watts blames the Black British students for the loss of the Caribbean tradition and the creation of an anti-school ethos:

> Mr Watts: A couple of years ago I had a boy straight from Jamaica. He came into the fifth form in November. I was told that he wanted to do the history exam in June. I took him on and he got a C in that year. I put it down to the Jamaican hunger for education. Later he went on to the sixth form centre – now he had become a 'Black Londoner' – He couldn't do his 'A' levels. He had fallen back – right into the groove of the kids around him.

The key word is 'groove'. In Watts' perception this has not been 'cut' by the school – the road to failure is clearly part of the culture and lifestyle of the boys. In looking at the way school affects the per-formance of African-Caribbean boys, I have noted that teachers are so wedded to the function of schooling that they will defend it irrespective of its failings. As the deputy head of the school said to me: 'I am just the executioner. I know I am having to exclude Black children because of bad teachers but what can I do?'

Watts and Murray were seen to be similar when their views were placed in the categories of home background, political attitude and ideal pupil. This leads to a new hypothesis: that teachers are socialised into believing that the faults of children can be explained by home and lifestyle.

Neither Murray nor Watts is overtly racist – in fact they acknowledge an unfair institutional practice. Their positions as class teachers tend to leave them in the micro world of their classrooms, unable to make the link with macro injustice. Even though Watts gives lip-service to bad teacher attitude, he feels that because there is no injustice in his classroom, there is no need to attack the wider institution of schooling. Therefore he ultimately blames the African-Caribbean boys for not trying hard enough. In the end Murray and Watts may not be disproportionately punishing these boys, but in terms of their socialised perspective they add to the 'criticism' by blaming the students and their background.

In analysing the performance of African-Caribbean boys, then, the teachers are 'socialised' to defend the school. What, then, are the teachers' attitudes to the lifestyle and culture of African-Caribbean boys? To answer this I looked at some critical incidents at John Caxton school.

For Mr Watts one such incident arose when an English teacher asked him to read a Jamaican dialect poem to his class. Watts describes how the children who would normally be asserting how they identified with Jamaica through its music reacted with embarrassment when they heard him reading. Most of them began laughing and treated the session as a joke. Watts was hurt by the experience:

> Watts: They don't want you to sit them down and teach them and say this is your 'culture' – in the context of school. All they want as culture is what they know and what they've created.

It would be wrong to say that Watts was totally negative to the cultural expressions of the children, but he was clearly 'disappointed' that for these children Caribbean culture – or more precisely Black diaspora culture – had been reduced to the mere rhyming chants of DJs. In fact, it is Watts who draws the stronger demarcation line between 'their' culture and school:

> Mr Watts: I have no desire to stop them from following the youth culture of the day. But there's got to be a line drawn between what goes on out there and what takes place in the classroom. I make sure that my children know where I am when it comes to Blackness and pride, but certain things belong in your own time.

John Watts was aware that even as a Black teacher he was not seen by the children as a peer who could teach them more 'culture'. He still represents the world of authority. Their own culture belongs to them and was used to challenge the school. In fact, he criticises the children for their lack of knowledge of Black history, thus again reinforcing Black culture within the norms of schooling.

In order to analyse teachers' attitudes to African-Caribbean youth culture, we can place Watts within the category of 'teacher legitimacy'. In other words, given the teacher's perspective, how much space will children allow teachers and how much will teachers give to students? Watts has made it clear that outside the context of academic rigour (e.g. Black history studies) he will not allow any overt expression of ethnicity. However, the students have equally locked him out of their space by rejecting his version of 'Jamaican' culture.

The new emerging hypothesis sees teachers as agents of social control who, in their attempt to promote self-esteem by using elements of the students' culture (e.g. dialect), induce a counter-action in which students adapt their culture, maintaining its illegitimate status as a culture of resistance. What Watts began to realise was that the children would not allow him to absorb the key elements of their culture which they could use to subvert his authority. Perhaps his biggest realisation was that his 'Jamaican' culture is not fixed but is ever-changing and re-adapting in new landscapes, with new generations.

Ms Murray admitted that she knew little – if anything – about African-Caribbean cultures. She agrees that African-Caribbean boys show greater displays of aggression and threatening behaviour. However, she does not want to make a wider political link between this behaviour and the way these boys are treated by the school. Instead, she deracialises the problem as 'adolescent' war games:

> Ms Murray: I see these boys simply as adolescents who are chest beating, but it isn't a particularly Black expression. Image is all right, but when it has to confront authority and other children, then it's different. it can be a confrontation issue. It's back to who's in charge.

Ms Murray's 'colour-blind' approach fails to answer why it is that 80 per cent of these 'confrontations' happen to African-Caribbean boys, thus leading to a disproportionate number of exclusions. There is enough evidence to argue that the school has a racial crisis that mostly affects African-Caribbean boys. What Ms Murray has done is hide it behind a power struggle and deny a racial element. Ms Murray had not seen any expression of ethnicity in political terms – only from an administrative point of view. Therefore the hypothesis derived from this discussion will state that teachers deliberately (or unconsciously) ignore the political implications of African-Caribbean boys' cultural resistance and turn it into a value-free technical problem. The category has changed to strategies, which in this case refers to an ideological strategy for depoliticising education.

## Summary

The analysis of John Caxton School shows that teachers in the survey displayed more control and criticism of African-Caribbean boys compared to other ethnic groups. It also shows that teachers react negatively to many displays of ethnicity from these boys. However, this is only a preliminary study and one cannot make general claims from such a small sample. What did emerge were several new themes, hypotheses and categories which need further detailed investigation. The first was that teachers are socialised to believe that the problems children have with school can be reduced to home and culture. This gave me a new category for analysis, namely 'teacher socialisation' – which helps us to understand how teachers who are seemingly 'fair' and 'liberal' still defend an institution which operates against African-Caribbean boys.

When it comes to ethnicity I found that even the most progressive Black teacher could not penetrate 'the culture of resistance' set up by the children. They would not accept the absorption of their culture by those who were agents of a system they wanted to challenge. The new hypothesis saw teachers as agents of social control who would always be resisted when they attempt to co-opt the pupil culture. This produced a new category called 'teacher legitimacy'. The last hypothesis was a political one, which noted that teachers ignored the political/racial implications of the African-Caribbean students' assertion of their ethnicity. Teachers would turn it into an issue of administration, in order to kill the political sting. This led to the category of 'strategies'; in this case a strategy to control ideas.

It is against this background that the teachers were socialised to defend their authority as a teacher. In so doing they contributed to a process of depoliticisation and deracialisation which, for the student, meant little differentiation in teacher attitude. As one student said: '...these teachers will always stick together. No matter if they know that another teacher is in the wrong.'

These teacher attitudes permit schools to function so that racial inequality is prevalent but nothing is done to address the issue. Worse still, even the most progressive of teachers operate within the same discourses as the more openly authoritarian ones. Finally, within their concepts of the 'ideal pupil' there is a criticism of African-Caribbean male youth culture as a destructive force in schooling.

## Student response: rejection and adaptation to schooling

In the second part of this study I will test two issues. The first looks at the strategy of Black girls and suggests that they have a different strategy to Black boys in coping with a racist schooling process. The second looks at the concept of 'racelessness'. This suggests that when entering school, Black students have to unlearn or at least modify their collective culture to suit the 'white' mainstream.

In her study on Black girls, Mary Fuller (1980) talks about how these girls developed a pro-education and anti-school position. They adopted a pragmatic approach to schooling: it was a means to an end. They could do this without investing much value in white teachers and a white curriculum. The cost of directly attacking schooling was too high for them. This was a strategy of resistance within accommodation.

In John Caxton School there was evidence that many of the boys also attempted this strategy. This is contrary to the literature that places African-Caribbean boys only as rebels. However, the evidence will show that even if they adopt the girls' approach the outcomes are still negative.

Martin, a third-year pupil, had just returned to school after being excluded because, according to him, his Art teacher had said that 'I was aggressive and I swore at her'. The rest of the class confirmed that the teacher over-reacted and punished the wrong boy. In fact, they felt so incensed by this punishment that they all signed a petition and gave it to the headmaster. This was ignored and Martin was excluded for one day. This was his third exclusion to date and he says: 'I am a marked man with a bad reputation. I always get picked on because I stand up for myself.' In this instance Martin did not flout authority but was treated as if he had.

According to Mary Fuller:

> A sub-culture emerged from the girls' positive acceptance of the fact of being both Black and female. Its particular flavour stemmed from their critical rejection of the meanings with which those categorisations are commonly endowed. Their consequent anger and frustration, unlike that of their Black male peers, was not turned against themselves or translated into an automatic general dislike of whites or the opposite sex. Rather their feelings and understandings gave particular meanings to achievement through the acquisition of educational qualifications. (1980, p81)

In the light of this, it would appear that Martin's response – which turns his frustration back on himself and his self-perception as a victim – is different to the girls in Fuller's study. However, he felt that the teachers were all-powerful and that to fight them was self-destructive: 'You ain't gonna win a teacher so you might as well go along with them. No one ever believes us, it's all one sided.'

It was clear that Martin was a complex character who was not happy being the anti-school rebel, nor was he happy taking on the persona of the 'one who stoops to conquer'. Martin therefore embodies resistance and accommodation. However, he belongs to no identified sub-cultural group in the school. In fact he actively resists it: 'I don't hang around any gangs in school. Although they might call me a 'goody-goody'. I know these boys will only bring you down.'

So Martin is not part of an anti-school sub-culture; in fact he is perceived by many of his peers to be a conformist. Yet he feels a victim of injustice and we are aware that teachers see him as 'disruptive' (this was the deputy head's classification when she gave me the sample pupils). He does not fit neatly into the typologies of extreme open resistance or accommodation of conflict, yet he also fails when he attempts to merge the two. This shows that Black girls have not got an exclusive hold on this coping strategy. What is different is that boys appear to find it less successful.

Graham does not support the schooling process uncritically. Like Martin he is unhappy with the lack of Black history in the curriculum. It was Graham who took the lead in presenting the petition to the headmaster which protested Martin's innocence before his exclusion. He said that he did not feel that his teachers were excessively critical:

> Graham: You see, unless it's something really bad, if they pick on me I just ignore them. It's the best way to get on. Some people think that it's pointless working because there's no jobs. I think if you work hard and really try you'll get a job.

Graham's response is closer to that of the Black girls in Fuller's study. Their desire for independence and a good career led them to value academic success as a means to an end. As Gillborn says:

> In fact the girls seemed to act deliberately in ways which distanced them from the 'good pupil' role and allowed them to minimise friction with peers of the same ethnic origin who did not share their commitment to academic success. On the other hand, their deviance was well measured so as to avoid serious conflict with other members of staff. (1990 p67)

Graham is aware of racism, but he will play the right role to keep his friends and teachers on his side. It was a balancing act that Martin was unable to achieve even though he understood what actions were needed for success. What must be stressed here is that Graham's management of all these negative forces on his schooling is not an argument for other students to do the same. His resort to 'survival strategies' must be seen in context of a schooling system that is unjust. If students are failing it is not because they lack the 'will' or 'courage' of Graham; it is the result of their peculiar social context.

Gavin is one of the most unusual students at John Caxton in that he appears to be unaffected by his peers' perception of himself. This 'mature' approach is apparent when he talks (as a 13 year old) about his life goals. Although he got top marks in his year for most of his subjects, he too was to be excluded. He also protests his innocence: 'I was joking with my friend using a mock-Nigerian accent. When Miss Achebe heard me, she said 'You are a rude boy, a racist boy!' We got in an argument and I was suspended for two days.'

Gavin complained bitterly about the exclusion policy. He felt that the school barred students on the most trivial of pretexts. He is also critical of the system of detentions whereby the whole class can be kept in because of a minority who do not want to work. He even feels that teachers are biased when it comes to race and gender: 'At this school some of the teachers are biased in favour of girls and white kids... You can see it'. Like the rest, he is acutely aware that the school does practise injustice, but his response is one of subtle adaptation. He says: 'I would only go so far with my mates. When I saw they were getting into serious trouble I would slip away. I am part of them and I am not, if you see what I mean.'

Gavin is the most self-conscious of the boys in this study – yet he still got caught out with an exclusion. This has not discouraged his belief in the schooling system nor his willingness to try and manage it for his own good. His flexibility challenges the hypothesis that the male response will tend towards a more open conflict with authority whereas the girls subtly learn to manage the system.

However, a serious charge which threatens to undermine my findings comes from Peter Foster (1990). He found in his study school that the students did not perceive racism to be a problem, with the exception of three students who 'complained without being asked about what they felt was racism from their teachers' (1990, p134). However, Foster summarily dismisses these accusations, locating them instead within the Black students' general, profound feeling of alienation from the school. He concluded that:

> Occasionally the hostility of Afro-Caribbean students was expressed using the vocabulary of 'racism', but such accusations rarely specified incidents that were racist in terms of the definition I have used. (1990, p136)

In other words Foster may well say that it is fine to look at the students' responses as examples of boys experiencing racist/sexist discrimination from their teachers. We still do not know for sure that we are getting the right interpretation from these students. After all, they are only echoing what many students feel about school irrespective of racism.

Intriguingly, it is Foster (1990) himself who almost unwittingly makes the case for race and gender discrimination by making uncritical observations. For example, he says:

> Interestingly, Afro-Caribbean boys were more likely to be seen as anti-school than might have been expected given their numbers in the year. (p131)

> There was a tendency for Afro-Caribbean boys to be less likely to be placed in the top sets than would have been anticipated given their numbers in the school. (p174)

> Afro-Caribbean boys were somewhat more likely to be seen as poorly behaved. (p146)

These observations of his remain wholly unrecognised by Foster as manifestations of racism in whatever form. Foster is forced to explain these differences in terms of their being facts ('this may have been because Afro-Caribbean boys on average in this particular year had less ability') (p174) or because 'Afro-Caribbean boys were somewhat more likely to present behavioural problems to the teachers' (p143). Foster has to retreat from dealing with the question of the education system to unfairly blaming Black students an analysis which is ultimately racialised.

The profound alienation of one group of children defined by 'race' needs explanation. It is not enough to say that this is the doing of society not school: is school not part of society? Is not society made up of people like teachers and the parents of children? So if 'society' is to blame it is important to see how that society is found in school. This study will show that alienation is not a simple substitute for racism. Foster has arbitrarily reduced racism to matters of insult or direct discrimination, but racism has so many other manifestations. It can be institutional as well as personal and in the context of school it is woven into notions of class and gender.

I am suggesting that we need to ask different questions about the experience of African-Caribbean boys, questions that deal with their coping skills in a context that was hostile to their gender and race.

We can conclude that the coping strategies of boys when confronted with racism in school can be the same as those of the girls. But the boys are less successful at making these strategies work. They showed limited resistance, which was carefully measured so as to avoid open conflict with teachers. However, all the boys in my study, to differing extents, were unable to avoid conflict.

The second concern is in relation to pupil response and comes from the work of Signithia Fordham (1988) who argues that the characteristics required for success contradict an identification and solidarity with Black culture. Students who feel the conflict between 'making it' and group identification develop a particular strategy known as racelessness: 'For many Black adolescents, therefore, the mere act of attending school is evidence of either a conscious or semi-conscious rejection of indigenous Black culture'. (1988, p57)

So to reinforce their belief that they are members of the Black community some students desperately hang on – through, say, using Black English – to stay 'in tune'. Conversely, there are those students who minimise their connection to the Black community and assimilate into school culture. This, Fordham argues, improves their chances of success:

> Students who assimilate seek to maximise their success potential by minimising their relationships to the Black community and to the stigma attached to 'Blackness'. These students attempt to develop a raceless persona in order to succeed in school and in life. Racelessness, then, is the desired and eventual outcome of developing a raceless persona, and is either a conscious or unconscious effort on the part of such students to disaffiliate themselves from the fictive-kinship system. (1988, p57)

Fordham's definition of a fictive-kinship system is applicable not only to the Black American communities but also to Britain. The term implies a particular world view of those who are Black not only in colour but in shared values; essentially it is a group loyalty which is culturally patterned and serves to delineate 'us' from 'them' – more so given the Black community's penchant for collectivity. The student who strikes out on an individualistic path can not expect any kind of support from his peers because succeeding in school is invariably associated with movement away from the community and is seen as a sign of having been co-opted by the dominant society.

It is this category of perspectives on peer groups which I want to use to see if there is a link between success in school and taking on a raceless persona. Graham has an ambivalent relationship with his peers. On the face of it he appears to be proud to be Black and aware of racism.

He says:

> Graham: I wouldn't stand up and say I'm British and I'm proud. Let's face it, if you're white you can be British – if you're Black you can't. I was really angry when our class got broken up because of bad behaviour. There are some Black boys who get into trouble and call me stupid because I don't hang around them and I get on with my work.

However, it is when he speaks of a racist incident which the school 'handled badly' that we see an allegiance with the Black community and against school:

> Graham: Last year there was a football match organised by the local police. During the game our school team faced racist abuse and then a fight broke out, one of our boys and our teacher got beaten up. The school handled it badly. They got the police to come and apologise but it was a big whitewash. The headmaster said he was going to take it further but it wasn't even in the local papers.

Graham is far from raceless but he believes profoundly in the schooling system. Indeed, he wants to be an English teacher when he leaves school. In this light his approach is individualistic and he has no strong Black peer group allegiances. He has managed to balance his racial pride and a belief in the dominant schooling system.

Gavin is unable to achieve Graham's fine-tuning. He openly puts down his own community. He says: 'I think that most of the people who cause trouble in this school are Black people. I know that my mother wanted me to go to a school with less Black kids.' His way forward in terms of achievement was to distance himself from his Black peers, justifying this by racially stereotyping other African-Caribbean students.

Among the boys in this study Martin has the strongest affinity to his Black community. He has even gone to meetings where he heard speakers talk about Black history and he would like some of these ideas incorporated in the school curriculum. Martin tries to have two lives – one for school and one for outside. He says:

> Martin: I don't hang around in school with no rebel youths. Anyway I have learnt my lesson, I will work hard and try not to cross any teachers because you can't win.

This is tough for Martin because outside school all his friends are African-Caribbean, yet in school he feels he has to shed them in order to 'succeed'.

Apart from Graham none of the students in this study 'achieved' without social cost. What high-achieving students often forfeit as they develop toward becoming raceless is their allegiance to their Black communities and peer groups. It can be said that the organisational structure of John Caxton School rewards racelessness in students and thus reinforces the notion that it is a quality necessary for success in the larger society. As a result the students are also led to accept a view of racism and discrimination as the practices of individuals rather than part of the policy of institutionalised schooling. There is evidence that a degree of 'racelessness' is characteristic of students who succeed. However, given the fact that all the subjects of this study were unable to avoid the negative aspects of schooling, a new hypothesis should state that the more race-conscious a student is, the harder it will be for him to succeed in school. In order to test this, we need categories for perspectives on shared values, perspectives on friendship groups and comments on other institutions like youth groups, the church and popular culture.

## Summary

In this study I have discovered many of the endemic tensions and conflicts experienced by African-Caribbean boys as they seek to define themselves within a system of schooling that challenges their ethnicity and gender. The key issue on teacher attitudes is that African-Caribbean boys receive a disproportionate amount of control and criticism compared to other ethnic groups. This brief survey and analysis at John Caxton bears this out.

Although the teachers at John Caxton School saw themselves as progressive, they did nothing to challenge a context in which African-Caribbean boys were subject to a disproportionate exclusion rate. These teachers were far from racist but they failed to see that by always defending the school (and blaming the home and sub-culture) they were actually part of the negative influence on these students.

The second issue on teachers' attitudes is that teachers react negatively to any display of African-Caribbean boys' ethnicity. The teachers were not openly hostile to the boys' sub-culture, but deflected its sting by either trying to co-opt it or refusing to see it in any political or racial context. A new label emerged called 'teacher legitimacy', which stated that teachers can never penetrate the sub-culture of young people because it is by very definition anti-school. This is a key hypothesis because it leads me into the next development of this thesis and that is the influence of the media (music, fashion etc) on the sub-culture of African-Caribbean boys. And in particular to what extent it is providing the rhythms and images of a culture that is used to resist schooling.

Gender has been a key factor in determining the response of students to racist schooling – the strategy of Black girls is said by some scholars (eg Fuller, 1980) to be different to that of boys. My study found no evidence for this and concluded the opposite – which was that boys had the same coping strategies as girls, namely limited resistance within accommodation. However, this did not shield any of these boys from exclusion or punishment. I was left, then, with a new hypothesis about coping strategies – which states that no matter how good the coping strategies of African-Caribbean boys they will always end up subject to negative discipline.

All the boys in my study had to pay the price of ignoring their peer-group, ethnicity and anti-school sub-culture in order to take the individualistic road of 'making-it'. This supports my second student response hypothesis – which states that African-Caribbean boys who want to succeed will have to resist identification and solidarity with Black culture and develop a strategy known as racelessness.

For African-Caribbean boys 'success' in schooling is clearly a hazardous and complex process whereby they are in many cases forced to 'present' themselves as having rejected their own community and peer group.

## The crisis of pluralism

One of the key observations to emerge from my study of John Caxton was the diversity in attitudes and backgrounds of the African-Caribbean boys in this school. It became clear that familiar, stable conceptions of race, class, gender and sexuality were no longer tenable in the context of a rapidly changing and cross-cutting interplay of fluid and contingent subject positions. This is shown in three ways: first, in their ambivalence to African-Caribbean groupings in the school, they distance themselves from their peers and in some cases share the teachers' stereotypes. But at the same time they feel they are part of the sub-culture that they have despised.

The second factor is the boys' experience of teacher racism in the school. There was no guarantee that a Black teacher from the Caribbean would operate within a less racist framework than a teacher who is white, middle-class and knew little of 'Black cultures'. This was seen in John Watts' approach as an older Black teacher. He idealises his Jamaican background and uses it against 'Black British' children whom he sees as culturally inferior. He then goes on to blame them for their own 'failure'. This leads to a discourse that is no different from that of many of the white teachers who defended the school and blamed the home and sub-culture of African-Caribbean boys for their 'underachievement'.

Moreover, John Watts got a rude awakening when he was asked by a teacher in the English department to read a poem to a class in Jamaican dialect. The African-Caribbean children all laughed and, to Watts' dismay, were not interested. This was a critical incident because it showed that the English teacher made incorrect assumptions about the relationship of these children to the Caribbean, which is in fact highly complex and has gone through much cross-cutting and re-inter-pretation. Therefore it may be that a poem written about Jamaica in Jamaican dialect (or nation language) has no particular relevance for African-Caribbean children from a diverse background.

Thirdly, there were processes at work in the classroom whereby, for example, African-Caribbean students might identify themselves as Black, 'Jamaican', 'Trinidadian', 'African', 'Black British', 'British' etc. At one point a student might be fiercely protective of a certain ethnic identity, at another he may reject teachers' (or researchers') attempts to classify him as a member of any particular group.

Any theory that attempts to examine and challenge racism in education must acknowledge this complexity. Previous approaches, which can be called pluralist and antiracist perspectives, do not adequately address the consequences of the de-centring of the racist subject. By subject I mean the person or group who is the victim of racism and also the 'subject' who perpetuates racist attitudes. There is a need to re-think the theory in the face of reality.

Richard Pring (1992), suggests that popular definitions of pluralism similar to that in the Swann report (1985) are oversimplified. He sees it as functionalist, as seeking participation, as working within a common framework of values. In this construction, education becomes a key element in shaping social order. According to Pring (1992) the problem with pluralism is inherent in its definition. Is it an ideological framework telling the world what should be or is it a descriptive framework? The main problem with the pluralist discourse is that it slips between description and prescription. For example, when pluralists say that there should be an equal opportunity for everyone to participate in society, there is an underlying assumption that they are against fragmentation and difference. To 'participate' actually means to leave the margins and join the rest of 'us'. The ideology of 'educa-tion for all' (Swann, 1985), and the recommendations it promoted need, as Troyna (1987) says, to be seen in this broader historical and socio-political context, one which is essentially reactive in its concern and pre-emptive in its goal. As the Swann Committee stated in their final report:

> We believe that unless major efforts are made to reconcile the concerns and aspirations of both the majority and minority communities along more genuinely pluralist lines, there is a real risk of the fragmentation of our society along ethnic lines which would seriously threaten the stability and cohesion of society as a whole (1985, p7).

## Education and pluralism

According to Swann, the prescription, or description, of a pluralist ideal can be achieved when opposing cultures get over their ignorance. The imperative for the education system, then, is 'to equip a pupil with knowledge and understanding in place of ignorance and to develop his or her ability to formulate views and attitudes and to assess and judge situations on the basis of this knowledge' (Swann, 1985). According to this ideological framework, education becomes a 'conversation' between teachers and pupils, and pupils and pupils. The problem with this is that if education is a conversation then it is first an elite one, which through its curriculum and market orientation has excluded many groups. It has been a Eurocentric conversation all the way from morning assemblies to curriculum content. And the school knowledge has failed to grapple with real differences that exist in terms of class, race and gender. Documents like the Swann report failed to take on how teachers and pupils have acquired normative perceptions of Black masculinity. What still needs to be taken into account is the legitimate right for Black boys to develop their own culture without being accused of being 'divisive' or 'aggressive'.

There is an arrogance within pluralism that assumes racism to be irrational. It fails to acknowledge that racist perspectives do offer a rational argument for racists. This can be seen in the racist arguments that linked Black immigration with unemployment. For some white working-class people this is a rational argument. Secondly, the pluralists assume that racists are easy to spot. This superficial approach assumes that there exists a common framework of values and that racism can be addressed within the normal existing structures. It is simply a case of making the rules of the game fairer rather than changing the game itself. Racism, in other words, is synonymous with prejudice in this ideological framework and the task becomes one of persuading different sections of the education system, and the state in general, of the educational efficacy of the orthodoxy, 'education for all'.

The attack on this 'naive' framework has come from both left and right. The most damning assault from the left came in the form of the Macdonald Report (1989), the inquiry into the murder of 13 year old Ahmed Iqbal Ullah by a white boy in the playground of Burnage High School in South Manchester. The committee of inquiry was composed of individuals with impressive antiracist credentials. However, in their report, they astonished some by attacking the antiracist policies at the school, which they said were divisive, ineffectual, doctrinaire and counterproductive. It was the most high-profile attack on antiracism outside reactionary comments from the new Right. It pointed to the problems inherent in what they called 'symbolic antiracism'. This perspective was seen as essentialist and reductive in its perception of other factors like gender as being of secondary importance. There was a naive assumption that racism was only practised by whites. There was a simplistic, binary opposition of Black and white, whereby Black people were perceived as the victims. The major criticism from the Burnage report was that this kind of antiracism based on a naive 'cultural pluralism' led to unnecessary polarisation in the school.

Research by the Runnymede Trust (1996) revealed that Black teachers were perceived as tending to punish Black pupils more frequently and for lesser offences than their white colleagues. The old pluralist framework would be inadequate to explain this complex phenomenon. It is something which I discuss about Township School, with its Black headteacher and deputy. Clearly, an approach is needed that allows researchers to have several handles on one issue.

## De-centring of the racist subject

The old pluralism was ill-equipped in theoretical terms to deal with the complex, contingent and contextual experience of the racist subject. It is to notions of postmodernist theory that I will turn, with its emphasis on 'difference', in order to formulate a new kind of pluralism.

The cultural homogeneity of the 1950s was challenged by the emergence of identity politics, which enabled marginal groups to assert the importance of their diverse voices and experiences. This was based on the assumption that there was an intrinsic and essential content to any particular identity which can be traced to an authentic common origin or structure of experience (Grossberg, 1994), and led to the development of the 'great collective and social identities' which, Hall (1991) observes, were thought of:

> as large, all encompassing, homogeneous, as unified collective identities, which could be spoken about almost as if they were singular actors in their own right but which, indeed, placed, positioned, stabilised and allowed us to understand and read, almost as a code, the imperatives of the individual self: The great collective social identities of social class, of race, of nation, of gender, and of the West (1991, p44).

Although these great collective social identities have not disappeared they can no longer be thought of in the same homogeneous form, as conceptual thought now focuses on their inner differences, contradictions and fragmentations. This has also led to an abandonment of the unproductive search for grand theories which specify the interconnections between social class, gender and race, and which are best constructed as historically contingent and context specific relationships. Consequently, the great collective social identities in relation to our cultural and individual identities are no longer the structuring and stabilising force (Denning, 1992) they once were:

> Race, class and gender are not the answers in cultural studies, the bottom line explanation to which all life may be reduced; they are precisely the problems posed – their history, their formation, their 'articulation' with particular historical events or artistic works (1992, p38).

The realisation of the impossibility of developing fully constituted, separate and distinct identities led to the emergence of the politics of difference and representation, which was based on the belief that the identity of any term depends on its relation to, and its difference from, its constitutive other. This shift in emphasis on identities and differences highlighted the importance of the connection between the fragments, as well as the articulations between the differences, and the challenge then became how 'to theorise more than one difference at once' (Mercer, 1992, p34).

This challenge was met by the emergence of postmodernism which involves the rejection of all essentialist and transcendental conceptions of human nature, and highlights fragmentation, particularity and difference. Whilst this position can be viewed as liberating in its refusal of certainty, and has provided us with the basis for a critique of the logic of identity which denies or represses difference, it can equally be seen as 'paralysing in its deconstruction of all 'principled positions'' (Squires, 1993, p1). An increasing number of commentators have expressed concern over the practical implications of using deconstruction as a method for exposing contradictions and assumptions within existing discourse. This is because the unending process of deconstruction and signification inevitably depends upon the continual repositioning of its differential terms. Consequently 'meaning in any specific instance depends on the contingent and arbitrary stop' (Hall, 1991, p51). However, Hall argues that in order to speak you have to be positioned somewhere even if you are trying to 'unposition' yourself.

Similarly, Anne Phillips (1993) argues that if theorists concentrate solely on the endless differences between people instead of the things we all share, they run the risk of losing the ability to talk of people as equal due to the complex diversifications that exist between them. Therefore we need to resist the temptation to step into an endlessly sliding discursive liberal-pluralism.

Nevertheless it is important for positioning to be viewed as contingent because dominant groups often appeal to bonds of common cultural experience in order to create new political identities. And although this may lead to their assertion of a seemingly essentialist difference, this challenge to one form of oppression may inevitably lead to the reinforcement of another. For example, whilst the political category 'Black' (as an essentialism) was extremely important in the antiracist struggles of the 1970s it had a way of silencing other dimensions ( i.e. gender, social class) that were positioning individuals/groups in a similar way (Hall, 1991). Therefore, 'although it may be over ambitious... it is imperative that we do not compartmentalise oppressions, but instead formulate strategies for challenging all oppressions on the basis of an understanding of how they interconnect and articulate' (Brah, 1992, p144).

> What is at stake here is not a rejection of universalism in favour of particularism, but the need for a new type of articulation between the universal and the particular... it should be possible to conceive of individuality as constituted by the intersection of a multiplicity of identifications and collective identities that constantly subvert each other (Mouffe, 1993, p79).

One of the key dilemmas of contemporary theorising is how to balance a theoretical rejection of essentialism, objectivism and universalism with a commitment to non-oppressive, democratic and pluralistic values (Squires, 1993). Therefore 'living identity through difference' recognises that we are all composed of multiple identities, and thus any attempt to organise people in relation to their diversity of identifications has to be a struggle that is conducted positionally. In Hall's words:

> We are all complexly constructed through different categories of different antagonisms, and these may have the effect of locating us socially in multiple positions of marginality and subordination, but which do not yet operate on us in exactly the same way (Hall, 1991, p57)

It is the move away from singularities of 'race' , 'class' or 'gender' as the main conceptual and organisational categories that has made scholars aware of the subject positions of other locations, which defy a simple category. This 'ambiguous reality' that locates identity both as a universal and a particular is not only the key to understanding positions taken up by feminists but also gives us the best understanding of Black masculinities in school.

## Conclusion: raising the key issues

John Caxton raised a number of issues concerning, first, teacher attitude and, second, the power of peer pressure and culture:

1. Teachers displayed more control and criticism towards African-Caribbean boys.

2. Teachers reduced the complex interactions with African-Caribbean boys to deficits in their home and culture.

3. Underpinning teacher criticism was the implication that African-Caribbean youth culture was a key destructive force in school

4. There were boys who did adopt the traditional Black girls' tactic of being pro-education but anti-school. But they found this balancing act too difficult in the face of teacher and peer group hostility.

5. There was a high price to pay for those who conformed to schooling. African-Caribbean boys felt they had to deny key aspects of their race and sub-culture in order to avoid negative discipline from their teachers.

# 2

# Teacher attitudes:
# Who's afraid of the big Black boy?

*The armed forces tend to recruit people who are quite well-educated. One set of people are good at one thing but not so good at another. Your Afro-Caribbean is a big chap, often very athletic and more interested in sport and music* – A Ministry of Defence spokesman

## Township School: historic and social setting

In this study I have drawn data from two secondary schools, one mixed and the other a boys' school. The first, John Caxton, acted as a preliminary study for the the major ethnographic work done at Township School. The boys I interviewed at John Caxton helped raise the key issues for my main study in terms of methodology and the research focus.

'Township' School is a boys' comprehensive school with a roll of 497. There is no sixth form. At the time of research there were 61 students of Asian origin, 63 of African origin, 140 of African-Caribbean origin, 31 mixed-race students, 127 white boys and 23 others. The school is located in one of the richest areas in England and is surrounded by several public schools which have achieved some of the best examination results in the national examination league tables.

However, Township School has all the characteristics of a tough inner-city school. A large percentage of the boys have free dinners, their parents are unemployed and many come from single parent homes. But

Township is not a 'community school'. Despite the claims in the school brochure, none of the boys come from the local catchment area and the school has little positive contact with the surrounding residents. In terms of geography, few boys actually live within walking distance of the school; most take the bus or train from the surrounding inner-city areas to come to a school located on the rich side of the borough. That is why I have called it Township School. There is a parallel with the townships in South Africa. Poor Black people travel to rich areas each day to work and then return home to their own neighbourhoods at night. And there is a secondary meaning to the word township, derived from the school's antagonistic relationship with the local community. To residents this school has the status of 'squatter' on their green and pleasant land. The local borough, in their eyes, has transplanted a slice of the township onto their 'respectable' domain. The difficulty facing the school as a result of its location is best expressed by the deputy head, Mr Arnold:

> It would be fair to say that it has not been considered a suitable choice by local parents when transferring their children to secondary school. Although two of the local primary schools recruit well, and benefit from the use of some of the school's facilities, none of this is translated into tangible outcomes when it comes to choice for secondary education. The school is also surrounded by successful and nationally renowned independent schools, many of the pupils of which make their way to and from school, sharing the public transport systems which serve the area. The interactions between our pupils and those in these neighbouring schools is generally negative. The school receives and responds to some 80-90 complaints each term about the behaviour of its pupils from local residents, shopkeepers and users of public transport serving the area.

There are many examples of the conflict between the locals and the school. The children are regularly accused of vandalism, brawling and bullying. The hostility of the residents was illustrated in a letter to the local newspaper, entitled, 'Homework?' The letter read:

> With reference to your article on 'Township School' (March 31) maybe nobody has included in the school roll the number of pupils

who appear to be taking extra-mural lessons at Township station and on its trains during school hours, having graffiti practice. Perhaps some of the parents could be persuaded to redecorate the station to its recently-refurbished standard, as well as their children's school.

## History of teacher attitudes to Black students

The school was built in 1954 and the early records show only white students attending. The school has always drawn on a local working-class population. The teachers who remember the early sixties speak of it being a tough school. In fact, they all say that in the earlier days the children were a lot 'tougher', before it acquired a majority Black population in 1974.

There is evidence of growing alienation amongst the African-Caribbean boys during the seventies. This is seen by the steady pattern of disproportionate exclusions. Ms Clark (white), who is head of Special Educational Needs, came to the school in 1974 and says she was appalled at the treatment of African-Caribbean boys:

> When I came there was a roll of nearly a 1000 pupils, with a large special needs department. I thought to myself – what a shower of a place. There were lots of pupils who were not getting a proper education. The special needs post at Township had been unfilled for two years. A large number of Black children in those days were in lower streams and were not thought of as students who were going places. There were a number of African boys in the sixth form, in those days we even did the Classics. However there were large groups of alienated African-Caribbean boys who were very hostile. Relations with the teachers and Black boys worsened as time went on. So if there was trouble anywhere they would all flock together. There was a kind of self-supporting network. They needed this because they weren't getting a fair deal. They didn't really have a antiracist policy and some members of staff were outwardly against Black people.

The third phase of development at Township was in the early eighties. It was the time after the Brixton and the inner-city uprisings that engulfed Britain in 1981. The local authority was keen to see antiracist policies operating in its schools. This coincided with the departure of many of the old staff at Township and the arrival of younger teachers who at least had to pay lip service to the borough's antiracist policy. It was also the time for a new headteacher, Mr Francis, who described himself as a 'humanist'. He quickly abolished corporal punishment and went on to relax the rules on school uniform. Commenting on Francis' headship, Ms Clark says:

> In the old days heads of year and the head caned and slippered boys. When this was abolished there was a significant reduction of conflict, particularly with African-Caribbean boys. Teachers were forced to work on their personality and classroom management.

However, it was during this time that the statistics revealed a sharp increase in the number of African-Caribbean boys excluded from the school. Township School also began to experience a dramatic fall in the roll, from 1,200 in the mid seventies to 500 in the early nineties. Mr Francis spent most of his last days fighting to keep the school from closure as it became hard to justify its continued existence economically.

The fourth phase is marked by the appointment of a Black headmaster, Mr Jones, after Mr Francis retired. But the same pattern of exclusions, with African-Caribbean boys experiencing a disproportionate toll, continued. The early nineties also saw a period of dramatic change in the sub-culture of African-Caribbean youths, which represented more than opposition to white middle-class culture – it was also a conflict with their parents' and grand-parents' generation as embodied in the values of the new Black headmaster.

## The failure of the schooling process

The OFSTED report (1994) on Township School said that the children 'received a barely satisfactory education'. This was after the school found itself near the bottom of the borough's league tables for GCSE passes. Only 10 per cent of the lessons were judged to be good, with the worst performance being in maths and science where standards have dropped since 1992. The school was criticised for failing pupils of average and above average ability in maths, since achievement was 'well below the national average'. The inspectors blamed several factors, including a high number of pupils with special educational needs, poor attendance, low expectations by teachers of pupils and poor reading skills among first year pupils. Budget cuts, including a £72,000 pound clawback, had hampered attempts at improvement.

The OFSTED report and the earlier borough report all attribute the school's poor performance to a failure in teaching and management. There is little mention of the sub-culture of Black or white students as the major cause for decline. This emphasis on poor schooling is important to note, given the weight that the headmaster and teachers give to African-Caribbean sub-culture as the cause for the failure of the school. It is this pattern of decline that the new headmaster stressed as his job to halt. He said:

> I want to help to move the school out of the pits. It is now in recession. The challenge is to start moving this school onto the road to recovery. This isn't what a school is supposed to be. There is a serious question mark about the quality of the teaching and the quality of the learning in this school. It is an extremely difficult school. As one member of staff put it, we have an overdose of disaffected children.

There is little evidence to support the notion that, academically, African-Caribbean pupils were disadvantaged any more than any other ethnic group. Table 1 below shows that in two out of three years African-Caribbean pupils got better results than their white counterparts.

**Table 1: Examination Results**

| Year | Pupils | Number Taking Exam | Average Score |
|------|--------|--------------------|---------------|
| 1988 | Caribbean | 45 | 11.3 |
|      | ESWI | 50 | 10.9 |
| 1989 | Caribbean | 20 | 6.0 |
|      | ESWI | 38 | 12.6 |
| 1990 | Caribbean | 13 | 12.6 |
|      | ESWI | 42 | 10.1 |

Source: Borough's inspectorate report 1992.
Caribbean  = African-Caribbean.
ESWI  = English, Scottish, Welsh and Irish origin.

This is important because the school has a disproportionate number of African-Caribbean pupils who arrive from primary school with a reading age of below 10.00. It suggests that Township school had a positive impact on many African-Caribbean boys to progress from reading disadvantage to exam passes. It could also mean that many white children did not bother to take exams.

However, the numbers of exclusions reveal an intense conflict between teachers and African-Caribbean pupils. The figures over a three year period reveal a steady pattern of African-Caribbean boys having the highest exclusion rates and in two of the three years they scored over twice as many as the white boys, although they only made up 30 per cent of the school population.

Another important set of statistics was the figures on fifth year after-school destinations. They showed a greater number of African-Caribbean boys than white boys going on to further education. Forty-one per cent of the white boys went straight into work, while zero African-Caribbean boys for that year went straight into employment. There were no available figures indicating how many of them tried for work as opposed to college. However, the available figures might point to the lack of job opportunities and contacts open to African-Caribbean boys. They may also indicate that in spite of the exclusion rate, education still remained an important mechanism of economic and social progress for African-Caribbean boys.

At the time of this study there were 30 teachers on the staff at Township School. In their response to African-Caribbean sub-culture in the school they can be divided broadly into three categories: 'supportive', 'irritated' and 'antagonistic'. As I stressed in the introduction, the term 'African-Caribbean culture' is an essentialist category which this study will deconstruct. As Cornel West (1993) has said:

> Distinctive features of the new cultural politics of difference are to trash the monolithic and homogeneous in the name of diversity, multiplicity, and heterogeneity; to reject the abstract, general, and universal in light of the concrete, specific, and particular; and to historicise, contextualise, and pluralise by highlighting the contingent, provisional, variable, tentative, shifting, and changing (1993, p19).

These postmodern features form the theoretical underpinning of this study. When I speak, therefore, of an 'African-Caribbean sub-culture' I am referring to a cultural expression which, although diverse, is specific to a group of boys of African-Caribbean descent that live in a certain area of a big city. What are the main features of this expression? First, it draws its ideas from the Black diaspora – namely America, Jamaica and London. Second, it is complex and ambiguous – e.g. its politics are both reactionary and progressive. Last, it has evolved through various stages, linked in different ways to the pattern of white/Black capitalist development. This cultural development, according to critics like bell hooks (1990), has formed a phallocentric style of Black masculinity. This is supported by Mac an Ghaill (1994) in his study on masculinities:

> In order to enhance and amplify their own masculinity, the Black and white Macho Lads were overtly sexist to young women and female staff, and aggressive to male students who did not live up to their prescribed masculine norms. They adopted a number of collective social practices in their attempt to regulate and normalise sex/gender boundaries. The Black Macho Lads were particularly vindictive to African-Caribbean academic students, who overtly distanced themselves from their anti-school strategies. (1994, p87)

The majority of teachers in Township School were convinced that the cultural expressions that came from the boys most deeply involved in this sub-culture adversely influenced their schooling.

The teaching typologies are categories based on the teachers' perception of themselves. These categories were constructed on the basis of interviews with, and observations of, all the teaching staff. The danger in constructing these ideal types is that some teachers' behaviour and attitudes are far too complex to be housed in these categories. In addition, some teachers could be placed in more than one category, given the changing nature of their job.

Therefore my three categories can only be broad brushstrokes which are useful in understanding in general terms the prevailing teacher attitudes to African-Caribbean boys' culture. This meant approaching the teachers response on two levels – first an impressionistic one, based on a first reading of their response. This is what I call pre-heating the oven. It is at this point that I label the teaching staff. I then move on to a more intensive interrogation of the data that involves putting the categories through the 'heat' of 'triangulation' – making comparisons and importing observations in the search for either sub-categories or a completely new main category. This will help to test the main research question of whether African-Caribbean sub-culture is the major factor in the performance of African-Caribbean boys in school.

In his study on masculinity, Mac an Ghaill (1994) divides his teachers within an ideological typology, which he calls: The Professionals, the Old Collectivists and the New Entrepreneurs. Although this approach is useful in trying to understand teachers' positions on education and their social world views, there are two reasons why it would not work for this study. Firstly, I wanted an 'emotional' response to what these boys presented, which in many instances cut across the teachers' political standpoint. In this ethnographic study I perceived the teachers and students as 'actors' using survival strategies to get through the day. I am concerned to articulate the individual 'voices' of these teachers. This is in order to challenge the notion that teachers are not critical of their own practice, and to reveal the extent to which teachers remain powerfully articulate about their own understanding of their profession. This also illustrates the ways in which teachers, like pupils, are active subjects within their lived experience.

Secondly, too many teachers just did not fit Mac an Ghaill's categories. In fact he says of his own work (1994):

> It is important to emphasise that these ideologies are not always found in pure form; nor is it possible simplistically to allocate teachers to one or other of the categories. Social reality is more complex. So, for example, I was unable to place several teachers (about 12 per cent) who straddled the categories, and during the research period teachers adopted shifting discourses. Fullan (1982 p127) adds an important qualification to the labelling of teachers, that it may: '...run the risk of reifying what is a loose classification system and implying that teachers may not change from one orientation to another.' (1994 p18)

The 'social reality' in Township School was such that 88 per cent of the teachers straddled Mac an Ghaill's categories; his classifications were too inflexible for this study. I am not saying that teachers do not bring with them ideologies that affect their relationship with students. The new teaching culture of accountability and quantifying achievements has also brought new forces into teaching – namely, the marketplace. However, the teachers in Township School demonstrate a clear sense of the significance of the social construction of identity. As they struggled with the impossible task of making the boys conform to their expectations, the challenge was more than just responding as a 'traditionalist' or 'liberal' – it was about the deconstruction of 'self'. These teachers were forced to question themselves through other cultural positions. It was a task that also fell to Black teachers. Therefore the interaction with African-Caribbean students called into question not only their politics or their response to institutional inequalities. It was an experience which asked teachers to confirm their own identity, not in rationalist political slogans but in terms of their own personality.

Why teachers felt that African-Caribbean children, more than other pupils, should make these demands on them, is one of the fundamental questions of this study. In this chapter I look freshly at teacher interaction with African-Caribbean pupils in order to confirm or reject this analysis. In addition, I have placed the teaching staff into my three categories and after interrogating the data, I want to see if any new categories will emerge. In the following chapter I will look at the results of this process by discussing it in the light of some key schooling issues. These categories are based on the teachers' response to the amalgam of African-Caribbean sub-cultures that exist in Township School – expressed in relation to music, hair, dress and attitudes. An ideal type of each teacher group would read as follows:

## Supportive

Mr Avril (White)
Mr Lewis (White)
Mr Howard (African-Caribbean)

## Irritated

Ms Williams (African-Caribbean)
Ms Clark (African-Caribbean)
Mr Walsh (White)

## Antagonistic

Ms Kenyon (White)
Ms Allen (White)
Mr Sutton (White)
MS Glasgow (White)
Mr Arnold (African-Caribbean) Deputy headteacher
Mr Jones (African-Caribbean) Headteacher
Mr Frances (White) Ex-Headteacher
Ms Brooks (White)

## Supportive

There are ten per cent of teachers who could be said to be supportive of African-Caribbean sub-culture. These Supportives want African-Caribbean boys to see him/her as a mentor. This teacher, in or out of class, will always try to enhance the cultural expression of African-Caribbean boys. Mr Lewis (white) ran the school basketball team, and for him it was invaluable time to have out-of-class interaction with the boys.

Mr Avril (white), along with Mr Lewis, was able to have 'informed' discussions with groups of African-Caribbean boys on topics of their interest. They gave them space to do this at the beginning or end of their lessons. These two teachers would also support the boys' perspective during staff meetings – when staff would implicitly attack the cultural expressions of the boys. In one staff meeting, Mr Avril defended a group of African-Caribbean boys who were under attack for arriving late to lessons, announcing that he could not understand what the fuss was about because these same boys arrived early for his lessons. He went on to imply that perhaps the curriculum and classroom management of those who were complaining could be the reason for the boys' lateness. His support is rooted in his successful relationship with the fourth year 'Posse':

TS: How do you relate to the group of African-Caribbean boys known as the 'Posse'?

Mr Avril: I get on with them a treat. This was because I was able to build a relationship with them. I would always have time for a chat with them. I knew Lenny was a key player in that group – if I could build a decent relationship with Lenny, he would influence the others to make sure they do as I wanted. Lenny valued his relationship with me so much that the others came in line. So the word went around that I was a nice bloke to chat to, so they couldn't get into my room quick enough to chat to me.

As in Mr Avril's case, Supportive teachers tended to get on best with the students tainted with a bad reputation. These were teachers who had good classroom management skills and could create an environment in which the boys felt secure. Mr Lewis points to bad classroom management as a reason for the high rate of African-Caribbean exclusions, rather than the culture of the boys:

Mr Lewis: I think we've gone overboard with exclusions that are from physical contact between pupil and pupil and pupil and teacher, when there are other reasons. We have to look to the build-up to the incident, the lack of consistency in the classroom to start with – We don't get a lot of physical contact in the playground or on duty. It is in the classroom where the boys don't know where they stand because there has been no consistency laid down by the member of staff.

The Supportive teachers were aware, and critical, of the teacher racism in the school. Mr Howard, a Black Section 11 support teacher, was outraged at the racism he saw among the staff:

TS: What kinds of problems do the boys complain about?

Mr Howard: Essentially, racism and much of it out of school. I have had boys in years 8 and 9 coming into school distressed because they have been abused by the police on their way to school. Therefore when a Black child comes to this school and teachers get abusive – they appear to be police without uniforms and the Black child will react to that.

The key universal concept that shaped this Supportive category is that all the teachers feel that their strength as teachers comes from having empathy with the African-Caribbean boys who are disaffected with schooling.

## Irritation

The teachers in the Irritated category form the majority – making up 60 per cent of the staff. The term refers to their frustration with students and the school, which they blame for falling standards of behaviour. They are antagonistic to some African-Caribbean cultural expressions but there are others which they support. There is also a tendency to have an assimilationist perspective and to deny that teacher racism was a problem. For these teachers the main issue was 'discipline'. African-Caribbean boys were allowed to cause mayhem because the school lacked authority, discipline and control. This is seen in the frustration of a Black teacher, Ms Williams:

> TS: Are there any specific groups in the school that tend to give discipline problems?

> Ms. Williams: The Black pupils act in a particular way. The way they challenge authority is very different to the way white pupils challenge authority. They do it in a particular style. It is the same way they relate to each other and this comes out of their sub-culture.

She then goes on to attack the school for its lack of discipline and the teachers for their bad classroom practice:

> We as teachers have also contributed to the discipline problems that face Black children. We have not made these kids and their parents accountable. This is through bad practice which allows the children to get away with murder.

There is a tendency amongst these teachers to deny that racism has a significant influence on the performance of African-Caribbean students. Instead they make reference to the high number of Black pupils or paint a picture of racial harmony in a multicultural school. These teachers cannot be classified as a coherent ideological entity because they display a variety of political convictions. What sustains them is a desire to survive the day in the face of children who oppose them and a support structure which is too weak. They have the capacity to be supportive of the boys' culture but see too much in it that they find objectionable – ranging from sexism to a perceived challenge to authority.

## Antagonistic

Antagonistic teachers fall into two camps and make up 30 per cent of the staff. There are those who are overtly racist and feel that the cultural displays of the boys are a negative-essentialist characteristic of all African-Caribbean people. This was evident when some Black boys became aggressive because they had missed their school lunch and a teacher remarked, 'Well, Black kids tend to worry about their food more than white ones'. The other type believes, on political, moral and cultural grounds, that the sub-culture of African-Caribbean children is harmful to their social and academic progress. In addition there are teachers who they believe have identified characteristics of these boys' culture and perceive it as a threat to the authority of the school.

## School ethos

Many researchers see schools as basically closed institutions designed to make those within them 'conform'. According to Cohen and Manion (1981):

> They are miniature societies governed by their own special norms and values. As closed systems, they have been compared with 'total institutions' such as prisons, military units and mental hospitals. At first sight this might appear a somewhat odd parallel. On reflection however, there are similarities. A pupil is no more able to leave the school which he is legally obliged to attend than a prisoner is at liberty to quit the goal to which he is confined. ...Waller goes even further, describing the teacher-pupil relationship as a 'form of institutionalised dominance and subordination ... (in which) children are defenceless against the machinery with which the adult world is able to enforce its decisions; the result of the battle is foreordained. (1981, p325 )

This may be an exaggerated picture of the role of schooling, but it stresses the conflict model of teaching which involves the promotion of conformist behaviour. Developing these ideas, Paul Corrigan (1979) sees school as an 'imposition' on the children's culture. He goes back to its nineteenth century roots and suggests that teachers were seen as a substitute for the failing working-class parent. He points to four key factors that help to define schooling ethos: 1, The provision of useful bourgeois facts and theories; 2, The substitution of bourgeois morality for working-class culture: the failure of the working-class family; 3, The creation of a disciplined labour force; 4, The creation of a national hierarchy based upon education. It is these forces that confront working-class children who have a different lifestyle and face different material conditions. Corrigan (1979) says:

> Education is still about changing individuals; it is about challenging some of the 'bad cultural traits' of sections of the population. Nowadays such discussion takes place in terms of the failure of the family – a failure highlighted in the nineteenth century... It seems clear from the historic account that schools are relating to the children despite the major material experiences of their background; that there is a powerful strand within state education in this country which sees its role as transforming what is created by those material experiences... Therefore there are strands within the education system that are divorced from the material relationships of the children and are in actuality trying to change the children's culture and ideas. It is hardly surprising under these circumstances that school is experienced as imposition. (1979, p 43-44)

This analysis is supported by Pierre Bourdieu (1976) who talks of the functioning of school and its role as a socially conservative force:

> Teachers are the products of a system whose aim is to transmit an aristocratic culture, and are likely to adopt its values with greater ardour in proportion to the degree to which they owe it their own academic and social success. How could they avoid unconsciously bringing into play the values of the milieu from which they come, or which they now belong, when teaching and assessing pupils? (1976, p34)

Mr Arnold, the deputy head, perceives the ethos of Township as providing a much-needed 'conservative force' in the lives of boys who desperately need formal structures in their lives:

> Mr Arnold: What you've got to understand about our children is the lack of any formal structures in their lives. They have no concept of the family because in many cases their fathers have fucked off. Gone are structures like the Scouts or Sunday school. That is why particularly African-Caribbean children enjoy coming to school because they encounter adults who are willing to instil some discipline and routine in their lives. That's why I don't come down to their level in my teaching style. It's not that I don't like them. It's what they expect of me. I am probably the only male adult in their lives who is consistent.

Cornel West (1992) laments the breakdown of formal structures for African-American children, which in this case includes school:

> ... we see the decline in popular mobilisation and the decline of political participation and the decomposition more and more of the institutions of old civil society, especially of old Black civil society in the context of shattered families and neighbourhoods, and voluntary associations, with the market-driven mass media as the only means by which a person becomes socialised. I think, in fact, one way of reading rap music is as an attempt by certain highly talented cultural artists to socialise a generation in the light of the shattered institutions of Black civil society; the families no longer do it, the schools can't do it. 'How do I relate to other people? Tell me.' And so they listen to Salt-N-Pepa who provide some moral guidelines as to how to relate to other people. They used to get it in Sunday School thirty years ago. (1992, p45)

I am not saying that every teacher wants to change their students into models of white middle-class virtue, but the nature of schooling ethos must be understood as a culture that not only reflects State control but also individual control. It is a schooling culture that makes teachers, often unintentionally, reinforce certain norms around race, class and sexuality. Skeggs (1991) uses Foucault to show how the norms around sexuality produce dominant discourses in education:

The first [method of regulation] Foucault (1979) identifies as the internal discourse of the institution. Historically, he argues, the organisation of education was predicated upon the assumption that sexuality existed, that it was precocious, active and ever present. The second method of regulation involves the process of inclusion and delegitimation of certain forms of sexuality alongside inclusion and control of others... The third mechanism of regulation involves the prioritising of masculinity as the norm through the organisational structure and pedagogy of education. Taken together the processes of regulation and normalisation provide an interpretative framework of discourses of sexuality around a grid of possibilities which students draw from and are located within. (1991, p128-129)

It is the 'imposition' of these values on African-Caribbean boys which is the concern of this study. What is the relationship between the school ethos and the teacher typologies in Township School? In what ways did the ethos at Township confront the sub-culture of African-Caribbean boys? Mr Jones and Mr Arnold had a passionate desire for 'formal structures' in the face of what they saw as the collapse of 'Black civil society' – this is what determined a conservative school ethos. The problem was that they did not consider that the interpretation of such an ethos resulted in many African-Caribbean boys experiencing institutionalised racism, as well as the undermining of many positive aspects of their sub-culture. However, as Skeggs (1991) has pointed out, the main arena for this conflict is in the way race and sexuality interconnect. The perceived physical threat of African-Caribbean boys can be located within stereotypical notions of Black masculinity in the white male psyche. This was seen in the studies of Les Back (1994) and Mac an Ghaill (1994), which point to the 'physical' admiration that many of the African-Caribbean boys received from working-class white youths. This was supported by the sexual physical threat, perceived by the teachers, that was located within their Raggamuffin culture. In both instances teachers and white students feared and admired the physicality of African-Caribbean boys.

At the time of this research the Antagonistic teacher typologies were dominant amongst Township staff. A number of factors were in operation at the time which explained why teachers who were previously 'ambivalent' became Antagonistic. The major concern of the staff at the time was the budget crisis facing the school. Mr Jones had inherited a budget deficit when an accounting error by the school left it owing large sums to the local council. Coupled with a falling roll, the only way the school could repay the money was by staff cuts.

The teachers were left not only insecure about the future but cynical about their jobs. In interviews many of them spoke of the pressures of dealing with a school that was poorly financed and children who were academic failures. There was no motivation to do anything extra for the children because the teachers felt that both the council and the children had lost respect for them.

The low morale of the staff expressed itself in a number of ways. First, there was criticism of the headmaster and of senior management. They wanted a 'man of steel' who could crack down on bad discipline. Their main criticism was that the new headteacher was not dynamic and lacked the personality to deal with inner-city children. Ms Williams, a Black teacher, describes the problems created by this allegedly weak leadership:

> Ms Williams: Heads of year are not really pulling their weight. The deputies may as well be not at school; apart from covering lessons they have become invisible. Mr Jones' style is not what we need here. When he first came he gave the impression of being someone who was a disciplinarian. In schools – where you're dealing with power – staff and pupils expect a strong head. I don't think he really is. He has lots of good ideas but I don't think he creates the right vehicles and environments for those ideas to take root and be used positively as he intended.

These comments need to be put into the context of the micro-politics of all schools (Ball, 1987), where the head teacher is perceived as a manager who is never fair or competent. Township is thus no different to many other schools where the staff are highly critical of the leadership.

Secondly, from my observation, many teachers did very little preparation for lessons and operated a policy of containment. One teacher would simply photocopy worksheets for each lesson – minimising the amount of interaction he would have with the pupils. There was a lack of motivation to implement important school policy decisions. I frequently observed boys standing in corridors after being sent out of class. This even happened on days when Mr Jones had told staff that morning not to send boys out of their lesson. The children spoke regularly of members of staff who were too scared, or could not be bothered, to deal with serious discipline issues.

Thirdly, there was little contact between staff and students outside lessons. There was a basketball club which was run by Mr Lewis (supportive) and a Steel band run by another teacher. The majority of the staff did not want any social contact with the children, for two reasons: they perceived school as a 'prison' from which they wanted to escape and, secondly, they blamed the students for their lack of enthusiasm and interest in anything extra-curricula. Mr Cohen (white) head of drama, had never put on a full production at the school. When asked why, he said:

> Mr Cohen: Our kids can just about get up in the mornings. They just haven't got the discipline and energy to work at a school production. If we had a better intake then it might work. But the only acting our kids are good at is mucking around in class. It's sad, but I've got to be honest.

However, the Supportives did not agree that the children were at fault. They felt that the staff were using this as an excuse for their lack of commitment to the boys and a lax attitude because of weak leadership. Mr Lewis (supportive) was particularly critical of the staff:

> Mr Lewis: You look at the car park in this school at 4 o'clock – it's almost deserted. There's nothing going on in this school after 3p.m. In this school we will not grasp the nettle. The head says no boys should be put out of their lessons, yet teachers don't take any notice. Mainly because we went through a *laissez-faire* regime where people did as they pleased. Mr Jones has come in and he's got a can of worms. I'm not sure he knows where to start.

In Township the 'antagonistic' teachers were the ones who most readily supported Corrigan's model of a bourgeois schooling ethos.

This was led by the headteacher's Caribbean-rooted 'idealism'. However, as in the case of Mr Lewis, there were many Supportive teachers who shared this traditional vision as explained by Corrigan, but were not in opposition to the sub-culture of African-Caribbean boys. This is seen in the attitude of Ms Clark (irritated) when she criticises the 'liberal' schooling ethos of the sixties in primary schools:

> TS: Why are there more concerns about the reading of African-Caribbean boys in the first year?
>
> Ms Clark: When you see a whole population handicapped in that way, it's got a lot to do with teaching in the primary school. At the same time that more and more Black children entered the primary schools there was also a change in the approach to teaching reading. The move to child-centred learning in open-plan classrooms became the norm. I feel if the child is coming from an unstructured family background into a free-for-all, then some children aren't going to get taught – that liberalism all round did a lot of children no good.

The Supportive teachers did not see African-Caribbean boys as particularly anti-school or deviant, unlike the teachers in the other categories. They point to the weaknesses in the institution or teacher racism as the reason for these boys rebelling against the school. The Supportives perceived African-Caribbean boys as needing 'consistency' and 'security' from their teachers. Corrigan (1979) implies in his study that the schooling culture attempts to transform the working-class culture of the children. The Supportives felt that many of the African-Caribbean boys in Township actually welcomed and shared many of the values which Corrigan says are bourgeois. This is illustrated in detail in the chapters of this study which look at the boys' response. It is also acknowledged in the Policy Studies Institute report by Catherine Shaw (1994):

> The report shows that young people from the most disadvantaged backgrounds value education very highly. They recognise its importance to their future chances. This together with the limited job opportunities now available to school-leavers means that most 16 year olds are now opting to stay on at school or college after their compulsory education has finished. (1994, p8)

The school ethos must be understood in terms of a school culture. It was more than transmitting alien middle-class values to working class children. There was also a quality assurance problem within Township: the children realised that because of inadequate resources and teacher apathy they were receiving a low standard of education. What many teachers had done was to point to African-Caribbean sub-culture as the scapegoat for their own inadequacies and the failure of the institution.

## Teacher racism

There have been two dominant theoretical perspectives regarding teacher racism. One locates racism mainly in biased individual actions, which in turn are assumed to stem from ideas and assumptions in people's minds: prejudiced attitudes, stereotypes, and lack of information about (for this study) Black people. Viewing racism as prejudice and misconception assumes 'that racist attitudes are very rarely rational. Even in those cases where the attitudes are regarded as rational, they are not considered to be in the interests of the person expressing them'. Wellman (1977, p14).

By contrast, a structural analysis views racism not as misconception but as a structural arrangement among racial groups. Racist institutions, according to Frederickson (1981, p32) are controlled by whites, who restrict the access of non-whites to 'power and privileges' in order to regulate 'a reservoir of cheap and coercible labor for the rest of the country.'

The concept of institutional racism is of great importance: it establishes the simple but crucial fact that a rule which is applied to everyone is not automatically fair or just. This is important when looking at schools with a multi-ethnic intake where teachers may reject crude, popular racism but will act in ways which are, in their effects, discriminatory. Gillborn (1990) suggests that it is better to use the term 'ethnocentrism' to describe the more complex reality in schools. Ethnocentrism describes the tendency to evaluate other ethnic groups from the standpoint of one's own ethnic group and experience.

These definitions have led some antiracists to invoke the Racism = Power + Prejudice formula in their analyses. This was used as the basis of race awareness training in America and is now considered flawed. It was found that this formula, like institutional racism, was a crude oversimplification. In the words of Gurnah (1984):

> Though at first sight this formula appears useful, various difficulties arise as soon as one starts to probe it. For example, when Blacks have prejudice and power does that make them racist? Does it mean that every time a powerful white dislikes a Black, that is racist? What if a powerful white man dislikes a Black man because of the perfume the Black wears, does this make a white racist? What if the same white man despises a Black woman because of her gender? (1984, p12)

Critics such as Cohen (1992) and Rattansi (1992), in their attack on the cruder elements of antiracism, point to what they call the impoverished understanding of the concept of racism. Rattansi (1992) shows that 'teacher racism' is a circulation of complexity and ambivalence.

Troyna (1993) stressed that many antiracists had refined their theoretical and analytical concept before and after this postmodern critique. He acknowledged the weaknesses in some antiracist literature but criticised Rattansi for being selective:

> The important point to make here, however, is that these analyses have been superceded by more sophisticated theoretical and empirical accounts of the complex ways in which 'race' enters into the social life of working-class communities. In this respect, Cohen's own work with working-class youth in London has been highly significant and acknowledged as such in the literature on antiracist education (1993, p127)

Troyna (1993) points to the work of McCarthy (1990) to provide a more specific concept of the way in which 'race' operates within the institutional setting of schools:

> McCarthy recognises the intersecting and relational impact of class, gender and 'race' in the production and reproduction of educational inequality. He goes on to argue that the articulation of these structural characteristics is fraught with 'tension, contradiction and discontinuity in the institutional life of the school

setting' and should not be conceived in a 'static and simplistically additive way' (McCarthy, 1990). (1993, p123)

From this perspective Troyna declares that racism must be seen as a 'contingent variable'. He points to the work of Mac an Ghaill (1989) as an empirical demonstration of McCarthy's thesis, highlighting the way Mac an Ghaill interlocks race, class and gender as the restrictive features on the performance of Black youths in school. Troyna (1993) is right but teacher racism is even more complex than this. (This is further developed in Chapter 8.)

Studies on teacher racism in schools (Mac an Ghaill 1988, Gillborn, 1990, Mirza, 1992) have only offered a partial, albeit extremely important, insight into teacher-student interactions. Students' direct contact with teachers is only a small proportion of their schooling experience. There is also the interaction with peers. The experience of racism in Township was part of a package of interactions that involved not only student-teacher relations but also student peer-groups. The way in which the students adopt teacher stereotypes as part of their own 'reputation' within the peer-group is one example of how racism takes on a life of its own.

## School policy on racism

According to the local authority inspectorate Township's antiracist policy was big on theory and small on practical implementation. Its report made five recommendations: 1, The school should review its policy on race and establish a clear structure to implement it; 2, The school should define a mechanism for identifying and monitoring racial incidents; 3, Departments needed strategies for challenging racism in both the overt and the hidden curriculum; 4, Staff development strategies should provide for the specific in-service training needs of the Black teachers; 5, Systems should be established to monitor and record the progress of bilingual learners.

Township failed to respond to all but the last of these recommendations (help was given to bilingual learners). Many of the teachers at Township felt that the antiracist policy of the school was there for administration purposes only, so that it could be shown to whoever needed to see it. There was a consensus that there was no racism in the school and that if you were a racist in the popular sense of the word then you would not work at Township. This was the feeling of Mr Francis when I asked him about the school's antiracist policy:

> Mr Francis: I haven't had a complaint from a student about the curriculum being racist. The equal opportunity criterion is essential when making teacher appointments. The teachers know this is a multi-ethnic school. I know we have a small proportion of Black teachers but there aren't always enough Black candidates coming forward. I know that equal opportunities is working in this school because the teachers have a high expectation of Black students. I did a survey recently where I asked teachers of the present year to give me a rough estimation of how their students would perform in the exams. I broke the figures down ethnically. When it came to expected exam results African-Caribbean students had proportionally better expected results than any other group.

Mr Francis undervalued the purpose of having an antiracist policy by denying the existence of racism at Township. There was a sense in Township that antiracism was not for 'here' or for this time. It was for the late seventies and early eighties when radicalism was 'on the rates'. Mr Lewis (supportive) turns this myth on its head, when he points to the 'covert racism' that exists among white students in Township:

> Mr Lewis: I think there are certain problems in this school with certain boys which we never tackle, such as covert racism. I think this is far more serious a problem than is made out. It doesn't happen so much in year 7 and 8, but when they get to year 9 and 10 it subtly comes out. That's when you get the racial divisions. It's definitely here in this school. I'm sure it's there for the boys to see – the slurs and the casual violence which goes on.

The size of the Black population was used by teachers as an explanation for the high levels of African-Caribbean exclusions. This explanation also helps to mask the levels of white racism that continues to exist at Township. This is not addressed by an antiracist policy which is just for administration purposes.

Paul Gilroy (1990) is one of many critics of 'municipal antiracism', pointing to the flaws in its various conceptions. He criticised local education authority policies (to which Township subscribes) for being rooted in a 'coat of paint' theory of racism.

The limitations of equal opportunities policy at Township reveal a deeper problem of how teachers engage in a classroom context where there are differing cultural positions and multiple discourses of power. The school and the local inspectorate worked within an essentialist and reductionist view of 'difference', demonstrating rationalist beliefs about the translation of policies into practices. The reasons for most of the exclusions of African-Caribbean boys involved some sort of violent or abusive conflict in the classroom. It is here that teachers reveal their true selves. As Ms Kenyon said, when asked to compare the headships of Mr Francis and Mr Jones:

> Ms Kenyon: There is a marked difference in the style of the individuals rather than policy. I see very little difference in what is going on in the classroom. It's almost that it is irrelevant what style or policy the head has – the lessons go on in their own way. To change the attitude of the boys in the classroom is very hard.

This is a very revealing comment because it shows that teaching often takes on an emotional aspect, where teachers and students come to the classroom with certain presuppositions and compete for space. It means that equal opportunities will always remain reified or irrelevant if the policy does not operate on this social psychological level, where teachers are ready to deal with the wider social context of their students' lives. It is about the testing of the 'self' and the strengthening of one's own identity as a teacher. The gestures to inclusion of Black content in the curriculum is not the ground on which Township should seek to solve its multicultural and antiracist issues. Rather the solution lies in the ability of teachers to engage in the complex social formation of their students and constantly to review their practice. To quote Rattansi (1992) in his critique of 'some of the main underlying oversimplifications which have informed educational practices in the field of 'race' and education':

...we do ourselves no service if we neglect to ask fundamental, difficult questions about our understanding of some of the key issues and terms involved; if we ignore contradictions in our underlying discourses; if we fail to grapple with the limitations of our assumptions about pedagogy and how subjects and subjectivities are formed; and if we fail to notice how economic, political and cultural differentiations are undermining older fixities around the ethnic, class and political identities of the minority communities. (1992, p41-42)

Only a minority of teachers at Township were prepared to admit that they had a key role to play in the social formation of African-Caribbean students and that this role could often determine the students' performance. It is also at this level that you can engage the boys with their own racism and sexism. When Ms Allen says she is the 'ringmaster' and the children are the 'animals', it is hardly surprising that she had one of the worst records of conflict with students.

## Racism and the curriculum

All the teachers at Township School had had experiences of developing antiracist and antisexist curricula. What was interesting were the ways in which they reflected a growing re-evaluation of some of those ways of thinking about equal opportunities curricula. There were three types of responses: First were those teachers (about 45 per cent) who still believed in an assimilationist perspective. As far as they were concerned, all the children should be treated in the same manner (i.e. as though they were white and middle-class) and we should not 'create' differences. Second, there is the tokenistic approach (about 45 per cent) where the antiracist curriculum is based on a concession – such as teaching about slavery in history. The last category is what I call emancipatory teaching, which allows the pupils to understand better where they are 'coming from' and gives them the means to be critical about what influences them.

Teachers like Mr Sutton (white and antagonistic) poured scorn and ridicule on the whole concept of a non-Eurocentric curriculum by recalling the days when he said he was a victim of an antiracist witch-hunt. He once taught in a so-called 'radical' borough and was glad that those days had gone:

> TS: What do you think about those who say, including the children, that they would like to have more Black history in the curriculum, particularly pre-slavery?

> Mr Sutton: Well, that's interesting because in my last school, we did this. It's a joke! If you look at the Benin empire, they were a load of bastards who enslaved their own people. They did the same as the Europeans. What are we suppose to say: This is Africa wow, this is your history. This is wonderful, let's forget about the slavery business. That's why we've got all this talk about Egypt.

I put it to Mr Sutton that there were many books, including novels, which do not romantically glorify Africa but give a rounded picture. Mr Sutton was head of English and I asked him if he had ever heard of the book *Things Fall Apart* by Chinua Achebe. He said he had never heard of the author or the text. This is not an obscure work and there were several copies in the school library.

Ex-headteacher Mr Francis took a more tokenistic approach, talking about how the library had been purged of all the out-of-date books which might have reflected overt racism and sexism. It was these gestures that he counted as examples of the school's equal opportunity policy within the curriculum:

> Mr Francis: We try on many levels to produce a multicultural curriculum. In English I have read *Miguel Street* by V.S. Naipaul and I know in history they cover the slave trade. And of course we do have the steel band!

Mr Avril (supportive) has a more inclusive vision of antiracism and a non-Eurocentric curriculum and is critical of tokenistic and assimilationist approaches:

> Mr Avril: Well. I'm very suspicious of some of the multicultural exercises that used to go on in some schools. In the end I thought it was at best patronising. I find it laughable that in some exam questions a few Asian names are thrown in to make sure the school appears 'multicultural'.

TS: Can it be done seriously?

Mr Avril: Well, it seems to be that when we have essays on racism, in English or History, it's always in schools where there is a large multiethnic population. Yet if you go out to the 'white' Shires, it's considered not an issue because they don't have Black kids. This is wrong. I think if multicultural education is to be taken seriously then everyone should do it. Children in the countryside have a right to know what is happening in inner-cities. There is a need for a national approach. Teaching Black kids about racism is teaching them what they already know.

Township must be looked at in the context of a post-antiracist era. Troyna (1993) pinpoints this trend as beginning in the 1990s as part of the Conservative attack on liberal education practices. Developing a thesis by Connell (1987), McCarthy (1993) talks of the need for schools such as Township to adopt a curriculum that promotes difference and heterogeneity:

> Connell's arguments for reconstructing the curriculum from the standpoint of those 'carrying the burdens of social inequality' (Connell, 1987 p17) are well founded. A critical multicultural curriculum, which emphasises antiracist and anti-sexist change and social reorganisation and utilises the points of view and experiences of oppressed minorities and working-class women and men as the primary bases for a core curriculum, would constitute a fundamental step in the direction of preparing students for democratic participation in a complex and differential school. (1993 p301)

The teachers on the whole resisted any 'imaginative' attempts at producing a critical multicultural curriculum. Many teachers at Township felt that in order to 'survive' they needed to establish authority, particularly over the learning process. There was a contradictory feeling, between understanding that as white/Black middle-class teachers they could be in the line of fire from Black children angry about racism inside and outside school – and feeling the need to keep in check any degeneration into anger. This meant that progressive ideas in the curriculum were marginalised, shelved or not risked in case the balance of power went to the children.

This was expressed most clearly by Mr Sutton, who limited discussions on racism to America and South Africa but avoided England:

> Mr Sutton: In year 9 we've been looking at the issue of race in America and South Africa, not so much in Britain. I've done a similar thing in year 11 in their Personal and Social Education lesson. In these classes there was a lot of anger, which I allowed because it was creative. Children were voicing their views on a sensitive issue. I did a survey of the kids and they all, including the white kids, thought that it was important to look at racism.

It was the practical problems inherent in risking even more anger from the students that stopped the teachers from venturing into a more creative curriculum – as exemplified by the teachers who continually photocopied worksheets for each lesson. At Township there were teachers who were frightened of potentially confrontational situations with the children. A conception of teaching that involved the opening of a dialogic relationship in the classroom was resisted. The danger was that it demanded the teachers to confirm their own identity. Cultural dissonance which strains the social relations of the classroom – including discourses of racism, sexism, homophobia etc, as they inhabit the classroom – is seen as problematic. This means avoiding any intervention that would challenge inequalities by getting involved in such classroom discourses.

In Township this meant cutting through the ways in which children would 'curse' each other, using the language of racism, sexism homophobia etc., and also adopting certain conventions around words, looks and body posture. All this formed part of a powerful game that governed the lessons in the classroom. The teachers failed to develop a curriculum that would challenge the negative aspects of the pupils' sub-culture. The teachers treated these matters as disciplinary issues but little was done to look at the boys' language critically or in particular at the relationship that African-Caribbean sub-culture has with capitalism. Admittedly, many of the teachers did not understand these social processes, but they still had to find some way of bringing their cultural understanding into play with those of the dominant (African-Caribbean) sub-culture. This conflict is most intense around the issue of sexism. Ms Glasgow (Antagonistic) moves from being outraged by the boys' sexist remarks to a point where she develops a racist discourse:

> Ms Glasgow: I think the language of many African-Caribbean boys is particularly offensive and it comes from their community. I think it is very widespread in the school and is not been taken up.
>
> TS: Surely boys will use fruity language at this age. What is so bad about the talk at Township?
>
> Ms Glasgow: It shows a total disrespect for women. It is becoming worse and it is becoming endemic. Everyone does it right down to the new first years. Being a woman in this school, I imagine is on the same level as a Black person hearing racist abuse all day. They think that because it is not directed at me, I shouldn't be upset.
>
> TS: What strategies do you use to deal with this problem?
>
> Ms Glasgow: I confront it. It does mean a lot of extra effort compared with a male teacher.
>
> TS: Why do you point to African-Caribbean boys?
>
> Ms Glasgow: Because they tend to be more lively and challenge authority more strongly. I feel that the sexist attitude and the lack of respect comes from their culture. You only have to listen to the music they like to see how it can have a negative influence.

Many teachers in Township resolved the conflict inherent in the idea of developing a radical curriculum by blaming African-Caribbean male sub-culture. They perceived the energy in these boys as being too high and unsteady to allow them to engage in creative learning. So they resorted to a curriculum and practice that was depolitised and deracialised. The radical curriculum responsibilities were denied and the boys' sub-culture became the 'bogey man'. The teachers preferred to continue with what one year 5 student called a 'mind blow', which would keep them safe from a sub-culture that was thought to be destructive to schooling and teachers.

## Teachers' response to a varied Black community

It is true to say that teachers at Township School had little contact with the community where the African-Caribbean boys live. But did this make them racist? And does it really bear any relation to their attitudes to the boys? When researchers remark that teachers have been at a school for many years but do not identify with the Black community (Mac an Ghaill, 1989), the implication is that white, middle-class teachers must make some effort to identify with an 'alien' Black working-class. When researchers talk about 'the Black community' it must be made clear which one, of many, they are talking about. At Township the African-Caribbean boys came from backgrounds as varied as the Pentecostal church, Rastafarian, middle-class, lone-parent, Conservative and Black activist.

There were teachers at Township like Mr Sutton who were hostile and patronising to the parents of African-Caribbean boys. I asked him about a boy named Errol, who had not attended school for a long time:

Mr Sutton: I've really tried hard with Errol but he's a bloody waste of time.

TS: What about his parents?

Mr Sutton: Well, you only have to look at his Dad to see what home he comes from. He comes into school very cocky dripping with gold chains and a flash car.

TS: What do you mean?

Mr Sutton: Well he looks like a gangster or drug-dealer.

TS: How would you describe your relationship with the parents of African-Caribbean boys?

Mr Sutton: I have talked to many parents who share my cultural values.

TS: Which are?

Mr Sutton: They believe in courtesy, they believe in looking smart, working hard, ambition, accepting authority, enjoying themselves not at the expense of others. Sadly, there are other parents who don't share these values and it shows in the behaviour of their children. These parents usually get aggressive when the school punishes their child.

Mr Sutton can only deal with parents and children who conform to his stereotype of having 'good' values. If they pass his culture test then they are good parents whom he can respect. He has assumed Errol's Dad does not share his values of hardwork and honesty because he has gold chains and a 'flash' car. The rest of the staff at Township might not have been this extreme in their views but there was a consensus that parents and in particular African-Caribbean parents were failing. This was most strongly voiced by the headteacher Mr Jones:

> TS: What impact does the home background of these children have on their school performance?
>
> Mr Jones: Most of the boys I have excluded come from single-parents. These boys are up until four in the morning – going out to raves. The parent is struggling hard to impose their authority on their lives. Some of these young men exploit their mums. I've had parents who have said to me; 'I don't know what else to do' or 'I've got a life to live myself'. You've got relatively young mothers – who could easily pass as big sisters. I am disappointed, I would have thought we'd have moved on – people still don't realise the demands of family.

There was no mechanism for the parents of African-Caribbean pupils to make a positive contribution to the school. It was far away from where they lived. Moreover, what contact they did have with the school was superficial – teacher-parent liaison consisted of a response (poor) to the Summer fête or perhaps a meeting when their son was about to be excluded. The school, to its credit, initiated a programme of teaching parents how to teach their children to read. But Township staff remained critical of the parents' culture. This was never said overtly, but staff made comparisons with Asian family background in relation to which the African-Caribbean family clearly fell short.

The most open hostility to Black community members was expressed in the comments given about the two Black school governors at Township. They sat on the exclusion panel and many teachers (both supportive and antagonistic) claimed that they were mischievous in blocking some of the exclusions of African-Caribbean boys. Mr Sutton in particular held this view:

TS: Do you think that all the exclusions in this school are fair?

Mr Sutton: Of course they are. In fact I would say if it wasn't for the two Black governors we would have a lot more.

TS: What are their views?

Mr Sutton: They want to make matters political. Every Black kid that comes up for exclusion – even the most villainous ones – they always make it a 'them' and 'us' situation. The other day Dennis Morgan who was caught red-handed stealing a teacher's bike, was up before the governors and they blocked his exclusion. It's ridiculous!

The objections to the Black governors disguised a deeper racism – the 'chip on the shoulder' stereotype that many teachers held of the Black community. They forgot that the governors are meant to represent pupils as well as staff. The teachers' attitude revealed a suspicion of the Black community, whom they caricatured as being paranoid about racism. To this extent the teachers shared the 'popular racism' that is part of the wider society.

The Supportive teachers were critical of the school's reluctance to make more connections with the Black community. They were surprised that Mr Jones, as a Black headteacher, had not done more to bring in Black role models into the school. According to Mr Lewis (supportive), this would help to boost the self-esteem of many African-Caribbean boys:

TS: Do you think the school has made good links with the home communities of the African-Caribbean boys?

Mr Lewis: No, this point was brought to me by a Black mature student teacher who used to work here. He said that the major problem with many Black boys in this school is that they have no respect for themselves. They've got no role models, no goals, no targets; they are being suppressed by their overall culture. They have no positive aims and they feel as if they're failures. This has to do with the environment in which they live, which is grossly depressed. They don't see any way out. You hear kids coming out with trite comments like 'I want to be a drugs dealer because that means money'.

TS: Can the school address this problem?

Mr Lewis: We should address this and show the children that there is more [to life] than just the mean streets. The kids feel this because their horizons are so narrow – they don't see beyond the inner-city. What we need is a major input of people coming in – not just saying work hard and be successful – but just trying to guide them and show that there is a future.

Mr Arnold (Antagonistic), who demonstrated a good knowledge of local politics and cultural issues that face many Black people, questioned the role of Black role models in the school. He was a Black senior manager at Township but still felt his 'Blackness' was not particularly significant. His vision of success is based on an individualistic ethos – where collective values are opposed to the ones espoused in school. If children are to succeed they must do what he did, that is, have the courage to break from the 'group', be that your 'peers' or your own 'community':

TS: Do you feel any additional responsibility as a Black teacher?

Mr Arnold: I have never in my teaching experience played the so called 'ethnic card.' It is true if you are Black and you're in a position of authority you may appear to other Blacks as someone who will give out favours and treat them leniently. I've always worked on the basis that I have no mandate from the Black community – they never put me here. I've worked hard and it's been through sheer grit that I am here. I couldn't be seen to be more favourable to any group.

TS: Do the children feel more confident with you around?

Mr Arnold: If I were a Black kid and I had Black adults as my managers I suppose it would remove an element of alienation. There is now a lot of Black media about with more successful role models. They need not rely on us (Black teachers) for role models.

I don't think they will behave any differently because of the existence of Black teachers.

TS: Do the parents feel the same?

Mr Arnold: Only some parents see me as a good role model; usually it is those who value what I am doing.

Mr Arnold sees no need to make any special effort to identify with the home lives of the African-Caribbean boys. He talks about keeping his 'distance' from the children who, he feels, always take advantage if you become too relaxed with them. Mr Arnold also feels that he 'owes nothing' to Black people; his vision is an individualistic one. He subscribes to the dominant ethos of the school, which demands that children forego the 'collective ethos' of the community and stand on their own. It is a perspective on social mobility that has been contentious in America – as expressed in the work of Signithia Fordham (1988):

> Increasingly, however, today's Black Americans are rejecting the older generation's attitude toward social mobility: they do not view the accomplishments of individual members of the group as evidence of the advancement of the entire group; instead they more often define Black achievement in terms of the collectivity (Dizard, 1970). Success now means that Blacks must succeed as a people, not just as individual Blacks. In other words, contemporary Black Americans are opting for a more inclusive view of success. (1988 p54)

America, like Britain, has been split on the issue of the place of role models and the need for those who are successful to give back to the 'community'. The late tennis star Arthur Ashe (1993) was critical of this 'inclusive' view of success and shares Mr Arnold's perspective that often 'community' loyalty becomes an obstacle rather than a help:

> The discipleship of student to professor, which is the principal method by which deep learning is passed on, so that experts nurture experts, became nearly impossible; how could a proud young Black man subject himself to a white figure of authority? Finally, in increasingly wide circles among teenage Blacks,

learning itself became discredited. To study hard, to aim for good grades, has become to 'act white', which is supposed to be the gravest charge one can level at a young Black man or woman today. However, since the best students in the United States increasingly are Asian, perhaps 'act Asian' should be the charge; in which case the element of colour disappears. (1993, p171)

The inclusive notion of success, which comes from many in the 'Black community', is also criticised by Signithia Fordham:

Yet, given the Black community's penchant for the collectivity, what kind of support from peers can be expected by Black adolescents whose behaviours and values in the school context appear to be at odds with the indigenous social organisation of Black people? At Capital High School there is not much support for students who adopt the individualistic ethos, because succeeding in school is invariably associated with movement away from the community and is seen as a sign of having been co-opted by the dominant society. Hence, even those high achievers who camouflage their efforts at academic excellence are viewed with suspicion and are tested constantly by their less successful peers... Unfortunately, this constant surveillance of the behaviours of members of the school community – both high and under achieving – drains the energy of students which might be devoted to the pursuit of academic excellence and other creative endeavours. (1988 p56)

There is also a danger that Fordham's concept of 'racelessness' – based as it is on the notions that the Black communities oppose an individualistic ethos – is, firstly, American and, secondly, essentialist. As Mr Jones correctly points out, there has been a Caribbean tradition which sees 'education' as a means of social and economic advancement. This has not been totally lost on many African-Caribbean children born in England, as noted by Mr Walsh, when he talked about the gang or 'posse' who always get into trouble:

Mr Walsh: 'You must remember that the minority I mentioned are not necessarily anti-school; they do come to school and enjoy coming to school. The truancy rate amongst white children is much higher than amongst Black children. On the whole, badly behaved Black children keep coming to school.

TS: Why?

Mr Walsh: The white children, in a failing culture, are brought up to be anti-school. I suspect that the Black children from a similar background have a greater respect for education. It is an anti-personal success culture.

Mr Walsh is right to point out the pro-schooling characteristic of Black British communities. Additionally, he points to the ambivalent attitude of the 'Posse', who consistently attend school (though keeping to their own agenda) but also display an anti-school attitude. He fails to see that one of the reasons why the 'Posse' may feel ambivalent about school, is no different to the way their parents and their home communities may feel about any white institution.

On the other hand Black communities have been depicted as 'innocent' particularly by Afrocentric scholars. I use this term innocent as in Rousseau's concept of Africa, and with it all things 'Black', as once perfect but corrupted by white racism. In their attempts to shift the balance away from those earlier writers who presented a distorted picture of pathologically burdened community, these scholars may well have lost sight of how complex and diverse the so-called Black community has become.

I also use the term 'innocent' as Stuart Hall (1992) uses it when he talks about 'the end of innocence or the end of the innocent notion of the essential Black subject' (1992, p254). It is a recognition that 'Black' is a politically constructed category and that there is an immense diversity in the experiences of Black subjects.

When we talk about teachers making an identification, we cannot be sure that this guarantees anything in terms of how they will go on to relate to African-Caribbean pupils. I am not saying that ignorance is bliss. There were teachers at Township who were racially hostile to the Black community and believed that no good could come from there. However given the complexity of teacher-community relations, any thorough analysis will examine both teacher attitude and community pressures, not as good versus evil, but in light of changing discourses.

The key ideas include the insistence of the situatedness of human thought, the impossibility of discovering a neutral transcendental reason or autonomous self-legislating self. This subjectivity is in a state of change, as it positions and repositions itself in terms of (at least) gender, race and class, and reacts to and is changed by the changing discourse.

## Racism as stereotype

In examining teacher racism it is also important to look at how teachers at Township constructed stereotypes around African-Caribbean boys. What were the teachers' dominant social images of the African-Caribbean students at Township School? There was a tendency by some teachers, both Supportive and Antagonistic, to see Asian students as being highly able and socially conformist. This contrasted with their view of African-Caribbean boys as antagonistic to authority rather than less able. This is an important point. At Township, in contrast to the studies of Wright (1985) and Mac an Ghaill (1988), there is no evidence that white teachers thought that Black students were less able. There were, however, many teachers who felt that African-Caribbean boys were instinctively against authority while Asian boys were the complete opposite:

> TS: What are your views on the high numbers of exclusions of African-Caribbean boys?
>
> Ms Kenyon (Antagonistic): Well you've got to remember that over 50 per cent of this school is African-Caribbean. I actually think that generally the African-Caribbean boys are louder. I do believe they are more volatile. I don't know if more African-Caribbean children come from single homes and so are left to their own devices. Maybe there is a feeling in the home of not being wedded to this society; therefore a feeling that the school system here hasn't got anything to offer them.
>
> TS: Is this the case with other students?
>
> Ms Kenyon: I don't think I have any more conflict with African-Caribbean children, but I do have less conflict with Asian kids. It is something to do with their culture, not to put themselves in a

position of conflict. This is ingrained in them. They are not so concerned about their rights as African-Caribbean children and indigenous whites. Asian kids, I find them seldom in a position of conflict.

Ms Kenyon has failed to differentiate among the African-Caribbean boys at Township. They are lumped together as one working-class anti-school mass. This construction was prevalent in Mac an Ghaill's (1988) study school:

Also, the teachers working within a culturalist perspective which assumes a class homogeneity of the Black community is of central significance in maintaining the teacher stereotype of the 'passivity' of the Asian students. In particular, teachers tend to extend to all Asian students the conformity of the middle-class Asian boys. (1988, p111)

This perspective is extended even further by Ms Brooks (white and Antagonistic) who thinks that Asian boys are more ambitious than African-Caribbean ones:

Ms Brooks: The Asian kids are brought up in a different way, as far as I can see. There is a lot of parental pressure to succeed. When I am doing the work experience for fourth years with the careers teacher all the Asian kids put down lawyers, doctors, accountants and when you ask them why, they say, 'Well my brother is an accountant and my older brother is training to be a lawyer, so I want to be the estate agent in the family'. They appear to have higher aspirations.

Ms Kenyon and Ms Brooks both overestimated the number of African-Caribbean students. They in fact represent a third, not the majority. This seems to support the notion that many teachers did not see African-Caribbean boys as a varied grouping and distinct from those of African origin or mixed parentage. However, Ms Kenyon later did indicate in the interview that she had some grasp of the politics of difference:

Ms Kenyon: Quite a few bright Caribbean boys don't succeed because of the sub-cultural groups that they identify with – this does not relate well to school and work. They are more interested in being the leader of their posse or the life on the streets or in their block of flats. I don't think the rest of the school is pulling them away from learning. I think they've already been drawn elsewhere.

If I look at year 10's (fourth years) top English set, the brightest West Indian kid at the moment is not turned on by work. Their natural interest is elsewhere. Whereas the brightest African boys, whose parents tend to be middle-class, are completely on task. With the individual African-Caribbean boys I'm struggling to keep their interest because what they're really interested in, is the life out there.

This response is an important one; Ms Kenyon could be seen as engaging in a 'racist' discourse. She talks about African-Caribbean boys' 'natural interest' – this is of course an essentialist perspective because African-Caribbean boys at Township came from varied backgrounds with equally varied interests. However, she does make a distinction between 'African boys' and 'African-Caribbean boys', which she feels might suggest a class distinction. She is also prepared to acknowledge that African-Caribbean sub-culture is not all 'innocent', and for her this is the biggest factor in the performance of African-Caribbean boys in school. This is a good illustration of Troyna's (1993) point, that racism is a 'contingent variable' and Rattansi's (1992) – that it can be contradictory. Ms Kenyon is able to convey a racist discourse while also being aware that not all Black people are the same.

Gillborn (1990) asserts that white teachers in his study school constructed stereotypes because they believed in the 'myth of an African-Caribbean challenge.' According to his analysis teachers were working on the assumption that African-Caribbean boys represented a more frequent and severe threat to authority. Secondly, any clash between these boys and white teachers was seen in this 'racialised' context; it was not simply a clash of individuals. He gives the example of a student, Paul Dixon, who was judged by his looks:

Teacher: He always (Paul Dixon) looked away from me when I was speaking to him. You could see him thinking: 'what right do you have, a white, to tell a Black man what to do?' (Gillborn, 1994a notes from seminar)

Gillborn (1990) points to three elements in the teachers' construction of this stereotype. The first is to do with physicality; Black boys are seen as bigger and therefore more threatening. The second element is about sexuality – Black boys can not be trusted because of their excess sexual appetite. The third is a local dimension whereby these stereotypes become part of the local culture of the school. To what extent did the teachers at Township subscribe to the 'myth of an African-Caribbean challenge'?

Some teachers at Township did make a link between the size of African-Caribbean boys and a perception that they were therefore more threatening. Ms Brooks makes a stereotypical comparison between Asian physical weakness and African-Caribbean toughness, after making another distinction about career aspiration, which associated Asian students with the 'professions' and African-Caribbean boys with a lack of ambition:

> TS: Would you say there was a difference in behaviour between African-Caribbean and Asian boys?
>
> Ms Brooks: Well, you tend to find that African-Caribbean boys tend to be bigger. This gives them a more big, butch image. The African-Caribbean boys tend to be larger built than the Asians. To put it into schoolboy parlance the Asian kids look more weedy and so are easier to pick on. Whenever I see any tensions, it tends to be between the African-Caribbean boys and the Asians. The white kids tend to keep themselves to themselves and there's no real conflict with Black and white.
>
> TS: Do you think you are perceived differently by African-Caribbean boys?
>
> Ms Brooks: Yes I do. I've had kids who, when I told them to wait until the bell goes say: 'Let me go you white bitch!' I've never had that kind of talk from the Asians, although I do accept they are using the fact I am white to try and get at me.

Ms Brooks conforms to the dominant social image of African-Caribbean boys as potential trouble-makers because of their size whereas Asian students are described as victims of African-Caribbean aggression. This is a racist discourse, which is linked to the racist images of the wider society and informs the racial structuring at Township.

In August 1994 there was massive media outrage at the killing of a 15 year old white boy, Richard Everitt, by a gang of Asian youths. This went against the media stereotype of the Asian as 'conformist' and 'victim'. However, as London magazine *Time Out* (1994) reported, Asian gangs have been operating in Britain for years:

> The best estimates suggest that there are around 30 gangs in London, split between Bengalis, Pakistanis, Punjabis and Sikhs. Ali is member of a gang, or posse which draws its members from Wembley, Harrow and Stonebridge Park in north-west London. 'We hang around the streets because we've got nothing better to do. Most of the youths have fallen foul of the police, feel let down by the system and are now living life by their own rules'. (1994, p16)

Ms Brooks is seen to confirm racial stereotypes with her comments on the difference between Asian and African-Caribbean boys. However, she then contradicts herself by saying that she saw nothing wrong with the sub-culture of these boys, after implying they were sexist, racist, aggressive and lacked ambition:

> TS: Do you think that the sub-culture of African-Caribbean boys is competing with their interest in education?

> Ms Brookes: I don't think it makes a great deal of difference. We had a similar attitude when we were at school. The only thing that has changed is the music, clothes and hairstyles. They are all into rap music and we were into Donny Osmond. I see nothing wrong with it; we were all like that at some stage.

There is another point here, about teacher expectation – the notion that students respond to the teacher expectation of their ethnic group. There was evidence at Township (which I will show in chapter 8) of African-Caribbean boys realising that teachers feared them on a physical level and then using this knowledge to be resistant to schooling. The same can be said of Asian boys who tended to adopt a covert anti-school practice – what can be called the 'invisible form of resistance.' At

Township teachers would excuse the behaviour of many Asian students on the grounds that they had language difficulties. I observed a group of students from Vietnam who would disrupt lessons and challenge their teachers. I asked Mr Walsh (ambivalent) why these students were behaving so badly:

> Mr Walsh: It is really frustrating with these students. It is clear to me that even if they were in Vietnam they would be a problem to teachers. As they learn more English and get more confident you can see that they are no different than many other naughty children.

What Mr Walsh has realised is that the practice of linking teacher expectation with ethnic groups is wrong. He had to 'unlearn' his stereotypes of Asian boys.

## Summary

The 'myth of an African-Caribbean challenge' was rooted in the ethnocentric assumptions of teachers as they attempted to survive the everyday 'stresses' of school life. Belief in the myth existed in Township and must go some way to explaining the disproportionate exclusion rates. However, these attitudes were not without contradiction and context, which left teachers in all the categories responding ambivalently. The 'supportives' indulged in the same sort of essentialism as the 'antagonists' by failing to acknowledge the diversity of the African-Caribbean boys.

At Township 'stereotypes' were created by teachers who linked their assumptions of the boys with perspectives from outside. However, this was not one sided. The boys in many instances saw themselves and others in stereotypical constructs. Township is not a world of 'evil' racist teachers and 'innocent' African-Caribbean pupils. It confirms Rattansi's (1992) point that racialised discourses are always articulated in context:

> An appreciation of contradiction and context, combined with a sensitivity to the variability of discourses among teachers and their practices also puts into question simplistic models of the process whereby (uncontradictory) teacher stereotypes of Black pupils are supposedly translated into discriminatory practices that lead to unequal outcomes (1992).

The predominant focus on student-teacher relations within the ethnographic to which I referred (Wright, 1985, Gillborn, 1990), has had the effect of inhibiting a more detailed investigation of the complexity of racism as it articulates with other discourses on gender, age and class and how, as a consequence, it finds expression across a number of contexts in an inherently contingent and contradictory manner. I have argued that within the confines of a focus on student-teacher relations, such work has constructed a closed and uniform experience of racism for Black and Asian students that belies the complexity of social reality.

For the teachers at Township it is not simply that racism is an external set of beliefs that they consciously or sub-consciously draw upon in their dealings with Black and Asian students. Rather, it represents a set of discourses that come, over time, to structure the way they think about the world, themselves and others. It is therefore embedded in their personal experience, how they come to act and how they perceive themselves. The key point here is that, in looking at the process of teaching in challenging contexts, teachers demonstrate a clear sense of the significance of the social construction of identity. Teachers at Township did not just simply throw the stone of racism at African-Caribbean boys. It was a process that detoured in order to cut across a number of discourses. This was clearly seen with Mr Jones, whose middle-class Caribbean ideal resulted in a racialised discourse.

The dynamic and complex expression of African-Caribbean sub-culture at Township demanded a response, even if this response was to ignore it. The challenge was more profound than a simple acceptance or rejection of stereotypes about African-Caribbean boys. It was about the 'deconstruction' of themselves, the questioning of self through other cultural positions.

Nevertheless, there was enough wrong in the process of schooling at Township to justify African-Caribbean students displaying resistance. What we need to know in this study is the place of African-Caribbean sub-culture in this resistance. Did this cultural expression help or hinder their educational outcomes? Were the teachers exaggerating its influence and using it as a scapegoat for their own weaknesses and racism?

## Conclusion

The majority of teachers at Township saw teaching as an act of 'survival', with little support from the headteacher and senior management. They pointed to African-Caribbean sub-culture as the main reason why the schooling process was not working. However, the teachers who had less conflict with African-Caribbean boys realised the staff's key role in the social formation of these boys' attitudes and the wider social context that informed them. This was not a simple Black versus white conflict. The Black headteacher, irrespective of his idealistic motives, engaged in a racialised discourse with his inflexible assault on African-Caribbean sub-culture. Although teaching styles and policies are important, the source of the disproportionate exclusions for African-Caribbean boys came from their conflict with teachers in the classroom. The 'survivalist' attitude could, and did, also lead to a racist discourse, in that it is a doomed mission with teachers failing to see the complexity of the students in front of them. Asian students are perceived to be more passive than African-Caribbean students, but what about the conformist African-Caribbean students and the rebel Asian boys? Are there differences in the way cultural groups 'subvert' the class? Their 'survivalist' attitude meant that teachers did not spend any energy questioning the formation of their own cultural position in relation to their students.

On the other hand, we cannot ignore the tough questions that the teachers ask about the influence of African-Caribbean sub-culture. Additionally, Mr Jones and Mr Arnold point to the fact that for many African-Caribbean boys school provides the only 'formal structure' in their lives.

**Table 2: Ethnicity Distribution in School**

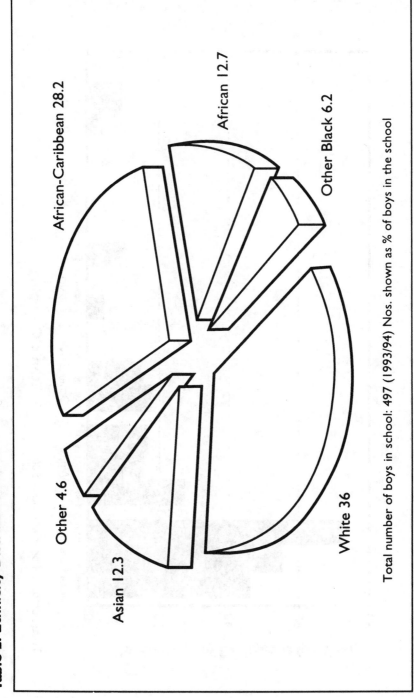

African-Caribbean 28.2

African 12.7

Other Black 6.2

Other 4.6

Asian 12.3

White 36

Total number of boys in school: 497 (1993/94) Nos. shown as % of boys in the school

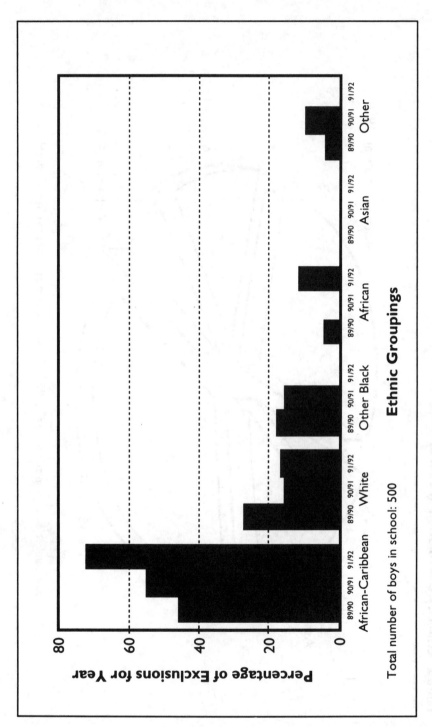

**Table 3: Ethnicity/Exclusions for Township School**

**Table 4: Ethnicity Distribution in Year 4**

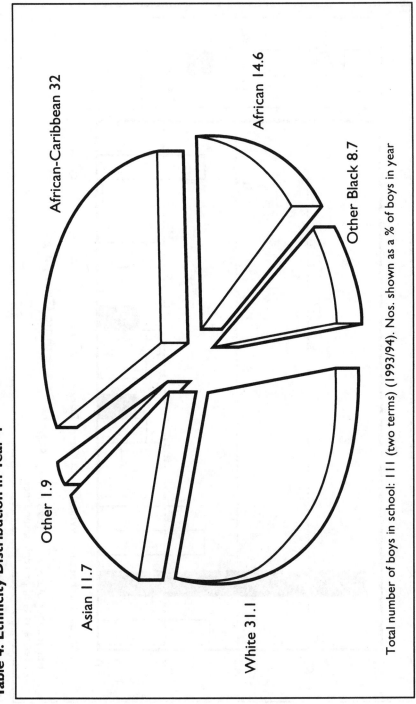

African-Caribbean 32

African 14.6

Other Black 8.7

Other 1.9

Asian 11.7

White 31.1

Total number of boys in school: 111 (two terms) (1993/94). Nos. shown as a % of boys in year

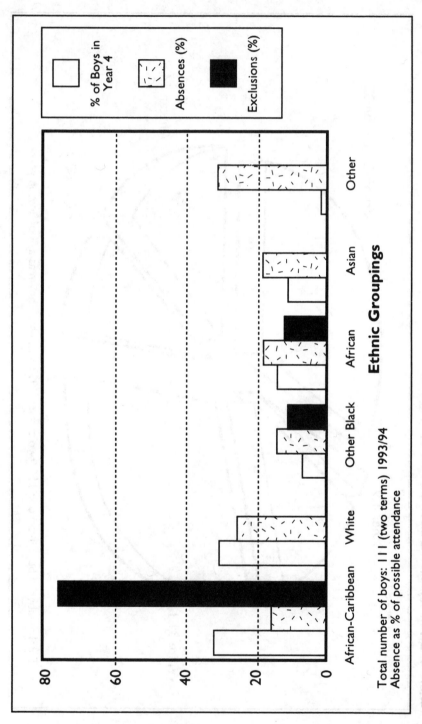

Total number of boys: 111 (two terms) 1993/94
Absence as % of possible attendance

**Table 5: Ethnicity/Absence/Exclusions Year 4 School**

**Table 6: Holborn Reading Ages on Entry**

| YEAR 7 | NUMBER IN YEAR | READING AGE 12.00—13.9 | READING AGE 10.00—12.00 | READING AGE BELOW 10.00 |
|---|---|---|---|---|
| African | 13 | 2 boys — 15% | 2 boys — 15% | 9 boys — 69% |
| African-Caribbean | 34 | 6 boys — 18% | 3 boys —9% | 25 boys — 74% |
| Whites | 52 | 10 boys — 19% | 5 boys — 10% | 37 boys — 71% |
| Asian | 23 | 7 boys — 30% | 2 boys — 9% | 14 boys — 61% |
| Other | 12 | 1 boy – 8% | 3 boys – 25% | 8 boys – 67% |

Year 1993

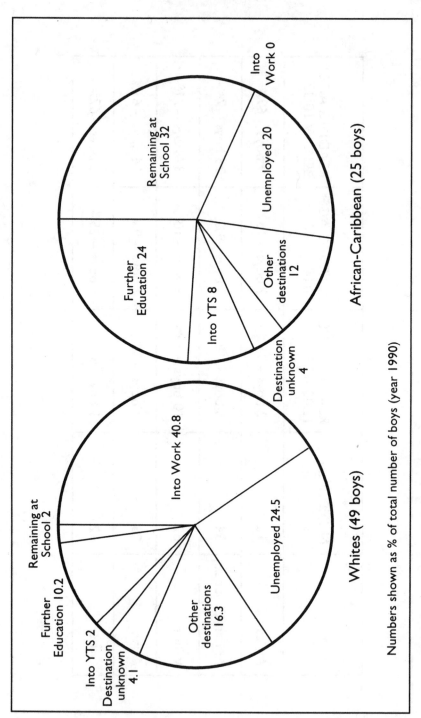

Remaining at School 32

Into Work 0

Further Education 24

Unemployed 20

Into YTS 8

Other destinations 12

Destination unknown 4

African-Caribbean (25 boys)

Into Work 40.8

Remaining at School 2

Further Education 10.2

Into YTS 2

Destination unknown 4.1

Other destinations 16.3

Unemployed 24.5

Whites (49 boys)

Numbers shown as % of total number of boys (year 1990)

**Table 7: After-school Destinations (Fifth Year Only)**

# 3

# A range of student responses: Conformists to Rebels

*Since men are born into male bodies, but not into the successful accomplishment of culturally appropriate versions of masculinity, becoming a man is a complex process of learning and doing within shifting sets of social constraints* – Holland et al (1993)

Too much of the literature on African-Caribbean children's response to schooling has concentrated on the children who are visibly resisting the schooling process: Dhondy (1974), Cashmore and Troyna (1982), and Mac an Ghaill (1988). The exception has been Gillborn (1990), who described the responses of these students in terms of 'a range of adaptational styles and sub-cultures'. In Township School, the African-Caribbean fourth year gang called the 'Posse' had a disproportionate influence on teachers and pupils. However, it would be an over-simplification to say that this was the only sub-culture that operated in the school and that members of the 'Posse' were only committed to a single response to schooling. The picture is far more complex – of boys having a range of adaptations to schooling – from Conformists to Rebels.

Merton's (1957) typology gives a range of adaptations which can be applied to a cross-section of social contexts and institutions. First, he points to culturally defined goals held out as legitimate objectives for diversely located members of the society. Second are institutionally prescribed means for reaching these goals. He proposed five major modes of adaptation to social order based on combinations of acceptance and rejection of official goals and means:

---

1. Conformity        (acceptance of both means and goals)

2. Innovation        (acceptance of goals, rejection of means)

3. Ritualism         (rejection of goals, acceptance of means)

4. Retreatism        (rejection of both)

5. Rebellion         (rejection of both but with replacement)

---

The Merton model presupposes that student behaviour can be regimented into these fixed categories. I have argued to the contrary, that students are de-centred subjects changing their social identity depending on the context and their role(s) within it.

Moreover, the 'goals' in Township School were never really 'known'. They were ambivalent and contradictory – sometimes there appeared to be a policy goal of containment and at other times the school was led by idealist (unrealistic) aspirations.

Finally in this critique of Merton, it was impossible to distinguish the goals from the means used to achieve them. An example of this was Mr Jones' ban on certain Black hairstyles. Is he giving the boys the goals or the means to succeed? In this case the two are linked. A student who had excellent results in his school work and behaved impeccably could still be in trouble if he had patterns in his hair.

There is a need to look at positions around different discourses and cultural forms and to regard Merton's categories not as fixed entities but as rooted in positions that come from an acceptance or resistance to the various discourses and cultural forms of the school and the boys' sub-culture. A re-worked model would look like this (see opposite).

There are important limitations in using models or typologies like Merton's: they often mask the complex meanings that are hidden behind the oversimplified types. However, they are useful as a heuristic device to highlight the range of responses in Township School. What is more useful is a 'grammar' of principles that would account for the different kinds of relationships that students have with school and how

---

**Positioned**

(Discourse and cultural forms of the school and the way they are perceived as goals and means)

**Position themselves**

(Communities and sub-culture; producing discourses of acceptance or resistance)

**Categories**

(From a multiplicity of axes for the production of possibly conflicting subject positions and potential practices and interactions)

---

these relationships are produced. In his work on deviance, Aggleton (1987) uses a framework to examine different types of 'resistance' and 'contestation'. Resistance means a challenge against 'relations of power structuring relationships between groups'. An example of this would be a boy who decides to leave the (macho) anti-school group where he is positioned by his peer group as a rebel and identify with a pro-school group who are perceived in feminine terms. Contestation means a challenge against 'principles of control within a particular setting'. An example of this is a rebel student adopting a Black phallocentrism in order to contest the dominant white male, or Black conservative power structure.

It is impossible to talk of 'goals' and 'means' without first unpacking the cultural influences or relationships available to different students. The 'categories' then become the result of different discourses and cultural forms and the way individuals are positioned and position themselves in relation to them.

Post-structuralism has relied strongly on spatial terms of reference, and the reconceptualisation of identity politics. I have reworked Merton (1950) so that it is possible to appreciate an understanding of familiar categories of identity like class, nationality, ethnicity, gender or (as in this case) behavioural type. These categories become positions we assume, or are assigned to:

> The post-structuralists' deconstruction of the subject-as-agent allowed an understanding of the subject as a position within a particular discourse. This meant that a subject was no longer coterminous with the individual. Rather, the power/knowledge relations which produced a subject-position implied that there was no necessary coherence to the multiple sites in which subject positions were produced, and that these positions might themselves be contradictory. (Henriques et al, 1984 p203)

How, then, are we to understand the 'positionality' of these boys if there is no 'coherence'? The sites are 'multiple' and they may even be contradictory. Liz Bondi (1993) answers this problem and it is this theory which I have applied to 'position' the boys in this thesis:

> The point is that if they are to retain their potency, the geographical metaphors of contemporary politics (education) must be informed by conceptions of space that recognise place, position, location and so on as created, as produced. Then the positionality of identities can be deployed imaginatively and creatively to construct a politics that, in Donna Haraway's words, can 'embrace partial, contradictory permanently unclosed constructions of personal and collective selves and still be faithful and effective' (Haraway, 1990 p199). (Bondi, 1993 p99)

These student categories were constructed on the basis of interviews, observations and group discussions held with 100 students. The only category that these young men used to describe themselves was 'rebellion'; the others were created for them. Roughly 41 per cent of the students surveyed were termed 'conformists', 35 per cent of these students were classified as 'innovators', I found zero per cent in the 'ritualism' category; six per cent in the retreatism category and 18 per cent were classified as 'rebels'.

# 4

# Conformists: A cultural sacrifice

*You don't know anything except what's there for you to see. An act.*
*Lies. Device. Not the pure heart, the pumping Black heart. You*
*don't ever know that. And I sit here, in this buttoned-up suit to keep*
*myself from cutting all your throats.* – 'Dutchman' Leroi Jones

*I am no Uncle Tom, I love my people* – Frank Bruno

In Township School the Conformists were the largest category (41 per cent) and their defining characteristic in terms of social identity was an opposition to 'community' and the embracing of 'individualism'. Weis (1985) in her study of an Urban Community College in America argues that conformist Black students felt they had to learn the dominant culture as if they were:

> ...someone from France coming here and having to learn to speak English. This implies that the individual has to adopt a totally new culture from that which he or she knows. It must be stressed here that the form the collective culture takes in the college works against this. Success, therefore, involves a break from the collectivity, and a willingness and ability to adopt a new cultural style. While the majority of students may enter the institution as individuals with this goal in mind, it is only a very few who remain outside the collective culture that is produced in the college and accomplish this end. It is these students who have access to a disproportionate share of faculty time in that they are defined by the faculty as the 'one or two who will make it.' Thus the sense

**79**

among the graduates that faculty spend a great deal of time with them is not incorrect. (1985, p9)

In the case of Township School the majority of students saw themselves as conformists. It was decided to institutionalise success by creating what I call the talented thirteen. Mr Jones was under pressure not to let the school score poorly in the league tables of exam results. He decided to introduce a mentor system and give special help to thirteen students who were capable of getting five GCSEs in their fifth year. The rest of the students in that year were placed on a scale ranging from 'mediocre' to 'a lost cause'. The policy was to contain these students and prevent them from interfering with the talented thirteen.

On the basis of research conducted in a secondary school in England, Keddie (1973) has argued that pupils who are perceived as most able in a streamed school reach top streams. There are those who have access to or are willing to take over the teacher's definition of the situation. They display what can be called 'appropriate' behaviour. In other words it is middle class students who are most likely to have access to teacher categories, thus ensuring their relative success in school. According to the school's measurement the criteria of free school meals and parental unemployment designated it a Social Priority school. There is little evidence in Township to show that African-Caribbean Conformists had a different socio-economic background to that of the Rebels. The only significant difference was in the occupation of the parents of African students, which revealed a link between their background (professionalism) and students who were conformists. In fact, even on a sub-cultural level many of the African-Caribbean Conformists shared the same music and out-of-school interests as the Rebels. Ricky Melvin is a year 11 student who shares much of the sub-culture of the Rebels but has a strong individualism which is characteristic of Conformists:

TS: What kind of music do you like and how do you spend your weekends?

Ricky: I like ragga music and most weekends I like going to ragga raves and dressing up with mates and just looking good.

TS: Do you ever hang around with the 'Posse'?

Ricky: No way! I think they're stupid. I don't know what they're doing in the school anyway. They just come to school to bully little kids and muck about. I think they all should be thrown out of the school.

TS: What contact have you had with them?

Ricky: None, I stay well clear. Anyway we in year 11 can't stand them mainly because they also bully year 11 boys – especially the small ones.

TS: Is there anything you dislike about this school?

Ricky: I think there are not enough strict teachers. Yesterday I had to take a note to the Head because a student had punched a teacher for no reason.

Ricky is a good example of how the Conformist student sees the world from the teachers' perspective. This difference is not only about 'obeying' rules and 'disobeying' them. According to Keddie (1973), what marks out the Conformist is 'an ability to move into an alternative system of thought from that of his everyday knowledge.' Therefore the students who cannot or will not learn standard English, for example, cannot succeed in school. This went a stage further at Township. Most of the African-Caribbean boys had some knowledge of Caribbean nation languages (patois) but they operated in a Black English inner-city dialect. The main difference between the Rebels and the Conformists was the ability of the Conformists to 'verbalise' in 'good' standard English. A characteristic of the rebels was an inability or unwillingness to communicate on the same level as their teachers.

Conformists tended to have a mixture of friends from different ethnic backgrounds, unlike the exclusively Black peer group of the Rebels. Some of these Conformists tended to go to the extreme in their break from the collective, so much so that it borders on a racialised discourse. Kelvin, who is a third year student, gives this 'individualistic' perspective as the reason why he has avoided exclusion:

TS: Do you belong to a gang or a posse?

Kelvin: No because my mum says I shouldn't hang around students who get into trouble. I must take my opportunity while I can.

TS: What students in this school do you avoid?

Kelvin: They are fourth years, you can easily spot the way they walk around in groups, they are mostly Black with one or two whites. They're wearing baseball hats and bopping (Black stylised walk).

TS : Don't you ever 'bop' ?

Kelvin: Sometimes for a laugh, but it's really a kind of walk for bad people. I might walk like this at the weekend with my mates but not in school in front of the teachers. It sets a bad example.

Kelvin has not only linked group or community dynamics with bad behaviour, but is also using a racialised discourse. It is this perceived anti-school sub-culture of African-Caribbean fourth years that Kelvin links with 'bad people'. It is also an act of self-degradation because he shares these boys' 'stylised' walk at weekends, but in school he links it with being offensive to teachers.

Fordham (1988), as I said in the first chapter, describes the kind of collective identity that Kelvin resists as 'fictive-kinship'. In her study of Black American children she looks at how this sense of 'brother-hood' and 'sisterhood' affects their attitude to schooling. This desire to flee from the Black collective and cut an individual path is not only shown in attitudes to work but in music and cultural tastes. In Fordham's study, the students who conformed to the schooling process also felt they could not share the same music as the students who were anti-school. Kelvin echoes this in his comments on Black music:

TS: What music do you like?

Kelvin : I like UB 40 and Meatloaf.

TS: What do you think of rap and ragga music?

Kelvin: It's not my favourite because some of the rappers are offensive to women and cuss. It makes you want to dance to the beat, but the words about women are bad. It's not fair.

TS: What do the rest of the kids in your year think about your musical tastes?

Kelvin: They think I'm weird, but I say to them 'I don't have to listen to the same music or dress up like you'. I am my own person. My mum told me to be my own person and not copy other people. I just follow that.

The group UB 40 is a white reggae band and Meat-loaf is a well-known white rock band. Although he condemns rap and ragga as sexist, Kelvin does not mention other Black music genres that are not controversial, such as soul music. However, despite his verbal claims of not wanting to be part of a 'Black' category in school, he has a strong sense of a Black identity which is supported by his parents. He gets extra lessons at home in literacy and Black history and his parents remind of him of the power of racism as a means of motivating him to work hard at school:

TS: What advice does your mother give you about school?

Kelvin: She says this is a white man's country and if you want to get anywhere in life you have got to pull yourself together. There are no favours in England if you're a Black man.

TS: What does your Dad say about school?

Kelvin: He's like my mum, but says it more strongly. He would say that my great great grandad was a slave. So you have to prove to the White man that you're not a person who takes rubbish from them, but you have to even give orders. I really believe this.

Kelvin shows an ambivalence: he distances himself from any Black cultural expressions in school but at the same time he shows a profound awareness of racism and race pride. Weis (1985) notes this ambivalence when she argues that being a Conformist is more than just an act of individual will:

The ethic of co-operation is deeply rooted among the urban poor, and individuals do not break these ties easily. While individualism may be a desired goal, it may be impossible to live out in a context of scarce resources. It must also be stressed that the desire for

> dominant culture embodies its own contradictions: while dominant culture may be desired on one level, it is white, not Black. Given that student cultural form at Urban College acts largely to reproduce the urban underclass, success in school represents a severe break with the underclass community. Since the collective offers the only security students have, the individual must carefully weigh his or her chances for success against the loss of security that the community provides. (Weis, 1985, p125)

There are strong indicators that Kelvin wants to dissociate himself from the fictive-kinship system prevalent in the Black community. However, it is expressed on the basis not of 'acting white' but of 'acting elite'. This kind of 'elitism' allows Black people to retain the elements of their culture that will help them progress within white institutions and eject the things and people who refuse to conform. Inevitably it involves some form of racist discourse, but for them it is a price worth paying in order to succeed. An emerging sub-category for 'conformists' becomes 'elitist'.

Although this elitism is a widespread characteristic of the Conformists, there were those who did share African-Caribbean cultural expressions. However, they still wanted to dissociate themselves from the 'group', even at the risk of being ostracised from it. Their frustration lies in the failure to persuade teachers that they are individuals and are not part of the anti-school group. Stephen Carter is a fourth year boy who hovers on the periphery of the anti-school gang. He finds it difficult to fine-tune the balance involved in keeping his distance and at the same time staying 'in' with his friends:

TS: Have you ever been excluded?

Stephen: No, I have been sent home once when a group of boys in the toilets were smoking cannabis and my name was on the list saying I was with them, which I wasn't. I was out of my lesson and because of that I was accused of being in the toilets.

TS: What was the punishment?

Stephen: I was given a letter to say that Mr Jones wanted to see my parents.

TS: What was your parent's reaction?

Stephen: Anger and disbelief, because I also suffer from asthma. My parents smoke but they can't smoke around me. When they saw Mr Jones, all he said to them was that I could be innocent and I could be guilty. I was out of my lesson and the teacher saw me in there. So it was my word against the teachers'.

TS: How did you feel about being in trouble because of the actions of other fourth years?

Stephen: I'm not very happy because I don't really hang around with that group. I think some teachers do see me as part of that group.

TS: Why?

Stephen: Because I use to hang around with this group a few years ago.

TS: What makes you different from the 'posse'?

Stephen: When I'm in lessons I don't mess around. I get on with my work.

TS: Tell me about the kind of mates you hang around with in school.

Stephen: They don't mess around: they're like me.

TS: Are they mostly Black?

Stephen: No, a mix of different boys.

TS: And outside of school. Do you hang around with the same people?

Stephen: Yes.

TS: What music do you like?

Stephen: I like rap music, ragga and a bit of soul.

I verified Stephen's exclusion story and the teacher admitted that it was a case of mistaken identity. Stephen received no apology even though his parents asked for a letter from the school to put the record straight. In class he sat away from the anti-school cliques and he regularly completed his homework in maths and English. His teachers had high expectations of him and he was continually mentioned as being a 'bright and mature student' by his English and maths teachers. Stephen felt that he always had to take the punishment for others; it was when he asserted his individual rights above those of the group that he encountered most conflict. This was illustrated most graphically when someone from his maths class beat up a first year student. Stephen was forced to do a week's detention with the rest of the class for something he knew nothing about. When he protested his innocence the teacher threatened to give him alone a further week's detention.

Stephen was determined not to be linked with the 'Posse' but his teachers were not prepared to separate him from the group when it came to punishments. This was confusing for him because his teachers would tell him he was bright, but their actions in the class denied this. Stephen shows some similarity to Gillborn's (1990) student, Paul Dixon:

> Like the members of the clique discussed earlier, Paul Dixon recognised and rejected the negative image which some staff held of him. Rather than reacting through a glorification of that image within a culture of resistance, however, Paul channelled his energies into succeeding against the odds by avoiding trouble when he could and minimising the conflicts which he experienced with his teachers. (1990, p63)

Like Paul Dixon, Stephen was too often perceived as being in the same category as the anti-school students, despite his efforts to claim individual ground. This individuality was also challenged by his peer group and, most strongly, by the fourth year 'Posse':

TS: What do the 'Posse' think of you?

Stephen: I think they think I'm part of them, even though I'm doing my own things now. When I go to my class and they bunk off, they will say to me I'm a goody-goody. But I turn to them and say that when I get in my flash car and you're begging for money, then you would wish you had behaved liked me.

TS: What do they say when you tell them this?

Stephen: They call me a pussy.

Being called him a 'pussy' Stephen suffers the ultimate attack for being a Conformist, which is a charge against his masculinity. Being pro-school cannot be reconciled with the machismo of the sub-culture. Mac an Ghaill (1994) comments on how some anti-school African-Caribbean boys have linked academic achievement with being gay or effeminate:

> The Black Macho Lads were particularly vindictive to African-Caribbean academic students who overtly distanced themselves from their anti-school strategies. In response, the Black Macho Lads labelled them 'batty men' (a homophobic comment). As Mercer and Julien (1988 p112) point out, a further contradiction in subordinated Black masculinities occurs, 'when Black men subjectively internalise and incorporate aspects of the dominant definitions of masculinity in order to contest the conditions of dependency and powerlessness which racism and racial oppression enforce'. Ironically the Black Macho Lads, in distancing themselves from the racist school structures, adopted survival strategies of hyper-masculine heterosexuality that threatened other African-Caribbean students, adding further barriers to their gaining academic success. (1994, p87- 88)

There were two types of conformist student at Township School. The first was the elitist student, who saw academic success in terms of a break with the fictive-kinship of the Black community. But they do not conform to Fordham's notion of 'racelessness' since they did not fully reject Black identities. However, they would sometimes indulge in a 'racist discourse', for example, by stereotyping their Black peers. The second emerging sub-category was what I call 'accommodation'. This was the attempt to, first, keep an individual pro-school personality while being confronted by negative teacher attitudes that perceive all African-Caribbean students as anti-school and, second, to 'accommodate' the pressure from the clique in the anti-school sub-culture that links academic success with being effeminate. What links these two new sub-categories is the desire by Conformist students to see academic success not as collective but as individualistic.

## One Teacher's perception of CONFORMISTS
### Mr Jones: Caribbean idealism versus the new Raggamuffin

The appointment of Mr Jones as head was met with hopes that he would be a leader who would impose a firm hand on the children. It was the first time in the history of the school that the two top posts (the deputy head Mr Arnold was African-Caribbean) were filled by Black teachers. This contrasted with the number of Black classroom teachers. At the time of the new head's appointment there were only three full-time Black teachers. Mr Jones' comments reveal that he shared many of the perceptions of Mr Francis, most notably his refusal to admit that teachers' attitudes were the reasons for the disproportionate number of African-Caribbean exclusions.

Mr Jones, like his predecessor, perceived the positive action of good attendance as a 'problem' for African-Caribbean boys. It is this reason, along with the charge that an anti-school sub-culture operates, that Mr Jones gives for his record exclusion rates:

TS: Can you tell me, in the year that you have been here, what percentage of the boys you have excluded have been African-Caribbean?

Mr Jones: I have excluded 53 boys so far and all have been African-Caribbean.

TS: Can you explain this pattern?

Mr Jones: Well, this has been the situation since I was teaching 20 years ago and nothing has changed. These are African-Caribbean youngsters who have lacked the type of domestic curriculum (which they need). These boys have got to a stage where they feel very bitter, very angry. So they have engaged themselves in a sub-culture of anti-authority, anti-work, anti-academic prowess.

TS: So are they worse behaved than white kids?

Mr Jones: No. The mere fact that as a group they are not known to truant, sets them up into circumstances where they are going to run into the authority of the school. What tends to happen is that African-Caribbean children come to school very regularly. What they do while they are here is open to question. The indigenous white kids tend to truant; they do this with the acceptance of their family. You will have kids who are 13 and 14 who are working with their cousins and uncles; Black youngsters haven't got that socio-economic network.

Mr Jones saw himself as a classic role model for African-Caribbean boys. His attack on aspects of the sub-culture of African-Caribbean boys was linked to his own Caribbean conservative notions of conformity to school. Township School may have had its first Black leader but a new hegemony prevailed which, ironically, saw a more blatant attack and denial of African-Caribbean youth culture than under the leadership of the retired white headteacher. Conformists Black students were therefore expected to share these values.

One big difference between Mr Jones and Mr Francis is in the way in which Mr Jones points to African-Caribbean culture as the reason for African-Caribbean performance; whereas (middle-class, white) Mr Francis is unaware of many of the changes in Black popular culture and talks of a general 'alienation' or 'kicking against authority'. In this sense Mr Francis appears to be more sympathetic to the boys' sub-culture but this is only because he knows little about it. His wider 'liberalism' will only attack it from a distance and in general terms, whereas Mr Jones knows it and sees it as an evil. It is for this reason that he is categorised as Antagonistic.

To understand the ideology of Mr Jones, one must come to terms with his cultural background in Jamaica . Mr Jones' way of thinking reflects his early upbringing in Kingston, Jamaica, where he spent most of his youth with his two brothers and sister under the strict control of his grandmother and a huge extended family which he came to cherish. His parents left for England during the early fifties and he recalls the strict discipline to which he was subjected in their absence:

> Mr Jones: They were very strict disciplinarians and, in my view, it was the female members of the extended family who held the family together in terms of discipline.

> I came to England when I was 11. For all of us who came over in the early sixties going to school here was a very traumatic

experience. I don't think our parents fully appreciated the anxieties and traumas that their children had to go through.

TS: What were your parents' hopes for you?

Mr Jones: They thought that the sky was the limit, more or less.

The reality for Mr Jones was very different; he found that both the quality of education and the level of discipline in English schools were 'sub-standard':

Mr Jones: For the first time, I was mixing in a classroom with kids who had little manners or respect for teachers. That was an eye opener for me. Worse to come was the racism. In the Caribbean I went to school with Chinese, Syrians and Jewish people, but I never had any problems. The question of colour was never in my psyche, so I didn't know how to react. I tried to speak to my father about it but got very little help from him. He would always say, 'This is England, boy! I haven't sent you to school for anyone to like you. If the teachers tell you that two plus two equals four, I want you to write it down.'

Out of this background comes Mr Jones' firm belief that education is still the key force in Black social mobility. It was the only one offered to Black people in the Caribbean and he passionately believes that education will once again free African-Caribbean children because it worked for him. This view was recognised by educationalist Gus John in a conference on Black achievement at schools (March 5, 1994):

In order to understand low performance in our urban education system we must acknowledge that for years the British education system was designed to socialise white working-class people into having low aspirations. Our experience in the Caribbean was different. Even the most illiterate farmer would expect his children to succeed in the education system so that they could better themselves. When we came to Britain we found that there was a fundamental difference. It is clear that we have moved away from what education originally meant for us. We now have a generation of Black parents who were failed by the education system and are not sure what direction they see for their children in that system.

The idea that the Caribbean offered a meritocracy to Mr Jones' generation has to be seriously questioned. Gus John (1994) goes on to point out that there was a framework of thinking that said that 'A good education would take you out of poverty'. However, the reality was different. These education systems were elitist and designed to cream off a certain percentage of high-achieving pupils who would then run the country. The vast majority did not – and do not – have access to the quality of education enjoyed by this elite class. As Gus John says:

> Blackness isn't a guarantee of anything. The issues of class, gender and greed are actively at play in Britain as they are in other places. We can't see the Caribbean and Africa in a romantic view, which has been static for a hundred years. These societies are susceptible to greed and capitalistic accumulation systems – we need to de-romanticise Africa and the Caribbean. (1994)

This view is supported by Austin (1987) in her study of Jamaican class and ideology, where 'education' helps to reproduce class divisions:

> The Jamaican notion of education, so intimately involved with the politics of that nation, addresses not only formal qualifications, but ability in public affairs, social competence and a proper socialisation. It is a notion which in the colonial context stood for equality, in opposition to notions of colour which stood for an essential inequality. Moreover, in a quite concrete sense for many Jamaican leaders higher formal education has been a transport to success and greater service to the nation. Education in 'proper' behaviour and formal qualifications has been the means by which many Jamaicans in the post-war era propelled themselves from the insecurity of working-class life into the modest security of a middle-class position. (1987, p55)

She goes on to say:

> However, educational institutions have also played a role in Jamaica as instruments of division. The 'dual system' of education, part inherited from the British, has made education in the past, and still to a great extent in the present, serve the logic of Jamaica's class relations. (1987, p56)

The ideology propounded by Mr Jones defines education almost exclusively in terms of enculturation. He identifies education as not only a means of getting work but as a civilising agency against the barbarism of the African-Caribbean culture of the street. Within this discourse 'school' is an institution to socialise the boys in the face of a chaotic and often immoral environment.

Mr Jones' ideology is rooted in this idealistic vision of Caribbean education. It is from this perspective that he attacks the boys' sub-culture, which he perceives as anti-school. He is not unaware of racism, even in his school, but he places the major weight of achievement on the shoulders of the boys themselves:

TS: Do you think the new music and sub-culture of African-Caribbean boys helps their self-esteem?

Mr Jones: Too many of our young people prefer a Raggamuffin life because it lacks discipline and is easy. You don't get anything for nothing, and if they think by living this loose ragga type of lifestyle they're going to get anywhere – well they're wrong. Eventually you're going to have a family. How are you going to feed them? They've got to hold onto something that is concrete, something that has substance.

One of the practical steps Mr Jones took to show the boys that ragga culture must be left outside the school gates, was to ban the wearing of patterns in the hair. This caused a storm, with many boys complaining that the policy was racist because it only affected Black boys. This hairstyle was popular when Mr Francis was headmaster but he never objected.

TS: Why have you banned Black boys from having patterns in their hair during term time?

Mr Jones: What I am trying to do is to get them to create an atmosphere and image in the school which is not like anywhere else. We live in a society, whether you be white or Black, where certain dress styles are stigmatised or certain types of behaviour will be associated with that dress code. Whether it's right or wrong it's there. I want the kids in this school to use me as an example. I want to equip them with skills to manoeuvre their way through society and get to the pinnacle. As far as I am concerned it applies to their outward image as well as what comes out of their mouths. To me the whole thing comes as a package so [what I am saying to them is] use me as an example and I'll guide you through so that you can get on in society.

Mr Jones' rule on hairstyles brought staff into cultural conflicts that few were able to resolve. In one incident a boy I had been working with came up to my room and said that he no longer wanted to be in Mr Cole's class. He was very pro-school so it was unusual to see him in such distress. He was crying. This student had come to school with what he thought was a great hairstyle. It was not a patterned cut so technically it was allowed. The style was a short weave, made by extensions. He said that the teacher had told him that he should not come to his lessons with that kind of hairstyle and that he should take out the extensions. I later asked Mr Cole (white), what objections he had to this hairstyle:

> Mr Cole: I told this student that his hairstyle was not allowed. It was bad discipline and he should get those twists out of his hair. They are not natural so he can put them back in during the weekends.

> TS: I thought the rule said that the children were not allowed to make patterns in their hair.

> Mr Cole: I know it's confusing, but from what I understood there were to be no ethnic hairstyles. It was the same in my old school. The headmaster would wait at the gate and any boy with an ethnic haircut would be sent home.

> T.S: Did you know he was very upset?

> Mr Cole: Well, he would be. He can't have it his own way. Those are the rules.

Another teacher who heard our conversation, and had been at the school only a term, said that this was the first time she had heard of the rule. These teachers were undoubtedly confused. Mr Cole was going to make no distinction between the various styles of haircuts available to

Black boys – anything that looked 'ethnic' would be deemed to be in breach of school rules. He also had no idea that the type of hairstyle that this student displayed takes about three hours to style, at a cost of about £40. It was never going to be a practical option to put it in just at weekends. What was worse was that the new teacher exposed the ambiguity of rule-making in Township; she was unaware that Mr Jones had made this rule. She also pointed out to me that Mr Jones had given this student a 'merit' in the morning and made no comment about his hairstyle. The murky ground of legislating over hairstyles left many teachers having to make interpretative decisions which exposed them to accusations of cultural bias.

In terms of categories Mr Jones would probably see himself as 'antagonistic' in his opposition to the sub-culture of African-Caribbean boys. He sees himself as a role model who upholds values which African-Caribbean children are in danger of losing. This view was supported by some African-Caribbean pupils. They thought his tough rhetoric was good for the school and an improvement on Mr Francis' attitude.

The staff were less generous and criticised Mr Jones for having the same weakness as Mr Francis. They pointed to an inability to make his staff carry out his policy. In staff meetings, Mr Jones demanded that staff be vigilant about the wearing of school uniform, that they did not put disruptive pupils outside their class, and that they made sure that boys got to their lessons. In all these areas the staff not only failed but in some cases were defiant about not co-operating. For the staff little had changed; there was no management mechanism to ensure that the teachers obeyed orders.

Stephen Ball (1993) notes the importance of leadership styles for headteachers' performance. He identifies three basic styles of leadership: interpersonal, managerial and political. Mr Jones conforms to the 'political' style and within that to the sub-category of adversarial leadership, which Ball (1993) describes as a public performance:

> ...the emphasis is upon persuasion and commitment. The ideological dimension is often strong, with debate being devoted to questions about 'what we are doing with the kids' and 'have we got

it right?', rather than administrative... The accomplishment of the adversarial style relies very heavily upon the ability of the head to cope with the uncertainties of relatively unorganised public debate. That is, to deal with attacks, to persuade waverers, to provide reasoned arguments, to employ stratagems and devices where necessary. (1993, p 104)

Mr Jones was accused by the staff of lacking 'the stratagems and devices' to realise his vision. The perception of Mr Jones by the staff soon became one of a 'soft' headmaster, who was no different to the last one. This problem is not peculiar to Mr Jones. According to Ball (1993), most headteachers will experience 'grand social dramas' when going through a leadership succession:

...the investigation of succession is also an opportunity to explore opposition and conflict. The focus on the headteacher serves as a vehicle to raise other issues. As Miskel and Owens points out, 'it is during the pre- and post- arrival phases that old resource allocation decisions are argued again, that suppressed ideological divisions over goals and performance are raised for revaluation and that job responsibilities are redefined. (1985, p25)

This point was illustrated in Township School when the teacher favoured most by the staff failed to get the headship. Both staff and pupils had expected that Mr Arnold, the current deputy-head, would become the new headteacher. The local authority thought otherwise and appointed another African-Caribbean teacher (Mr Jones) from outside. It was said that Mr Arnold was the best man for the job but that he needed more academic training to run the school. The staff of Township reacted on different levels to the appointment of Mr Jones. First, they resented that an 'insider' was not given the post. Second, there was a desire to have a headteacher who would be tough on discipline – unlike Mr Francis – and, third, they were suspicious to the point of being racist at the prospect of having a Black headteacher. In other words, if they were going to have a Black headteacher then they would have preferred one that they already knew.

This was best summed up by a Black teacher, Mrs Wells, who observed all the prejudices at work and yet was still critical of Mr Jones:

TS: What are the main problems which face the new Head?

Mrs Wells: In the case of the Head it is like giving him a sinking ship. Mr Jones needs more support, which was given to Mr Francis.

TS: Why did Francis get the support and not Jones?

Mrs Wells: It is really politics. There is a bias against a new head and he receives little support. I think, like the kids, some of the teachers expect him to fail. Francis was too patronising with the kids. I don't think they liked the way he would talk down to them. In my view Mr Arnold would have been my choice. The boys need a tough leader to look up to.

Most of the teacher interviews suggest that little had changed under Mr Jones' headship. Therefore Mr Jones' image as a new Black role model worthy of respect falls short because his ideas were not having their desired effect. His major impact on the children was his decision to make school uniform compulsory. It was a positive step and 'intellectually' had the support of children and staff. However, the confrontations with staff and the rate of exclusions remained at the same level. There was a management crisis in Township because Mr Jones' adversarial style of leadership nevertheless lacked the bite to motivate a reluctant staff.

Mr Jones was, instead, passionately 'antagonistic' to the current African-Caribbean sub-culture. However, he could not be taken seriously by the children unless he was an effective manager. The myth or reality of an African-Caribbean challenge must be seen in the context of a crisis of management. Had African-Caribbean boys become the scapegoat for issues that had nothing to do with their sub-culture? They were certainly confronted with a new leader who refused to blame the management, personnel and structures within the school and who, instead, led an assault on the sub-culture of African-Caribbean boys.

The basis of this attack is rooted in the history and cultural make-up of Mr Jones. His ideal of motivating children through his older Caribbean perspective illustrates this clearly. Their concept of the Caribbean is twofold. They are either not very interested or they use it as a means of bolstering the machismo-sexism of their sub-culture. This supported Mr Jones' perception that in the sub-culture of the boys role models were worshipped that were irresponsible and destructive:

TS: What do you think about the African-Caribbean boys' attitude to women?

Mr Jones: During a Social Education class, we were talking about children's reading books and we were trying to identify stereotypes. I told them I had 10-year-old twins, one boy, one girl, and my wife and I decided we would not create this gender divide in the twins. Then one of the boys in the class said to me: 'You've only got two kids sir? '

I said: 'Yes, that's right.' He then asked: 'What about the others back in Jamaica?'

I said: 'I've only got two children.' He said: 'Well sir you're not really a true Yard man!

The term 'Yard man' is a reference to Jamaicans who are from 'back home' or affectionately the 'back yard'. He is linked with a street 'hard-man' life style and he is notorious for fathering many children with different mothers and taking no responsibilities for his actions. Mr Jones is convinced that unless the boys adopt a different cultural model they will not progress. There is a missionary zeal in his vision of African-Caribbean youth culture as the major obstacle to progress in schooling:

Mr Jones: The Asian students exploit the education system. When you go into universities you see them and you see our African-Caribbean people in minute numbers. Every time you ask a Black child what they want to do they say they want to go to college, to do re-takes or a B-Tec. How many of them say, 'I'm going to University?' The reason why they don't say that is that it goes against the 'street-cred' which going to university, for them, has not. They are misguided.

Mr Jones points to an expression of 'fictive kinship' as the major reason for African-Caribbean conflict. He will not concede that poverty and class as well as poor schooling are more significant factors in school performance than the street sub-culture:

> TS: What would you say to those who would say that Mr Jones has good ideas but really he's trying to impose middle-class values on working-class children?

> Mr Jones: It isn't about class – this comes from the heart. I have to refer back to my earlier days of my development in Jamaica. I came from a poor family – we were very poor but it still didn't mean that we should lead a Raggamuffin type of life.

His response not only idealises the Caribbean but also presupposes that African-Caribbean boys need to break away from the group and become individualised:

> ... an individualistic rather than a collective ethos is sanctioned in the school context. Black children enter school having to unlearn or, at least, to modify their own culturally sanctioned interactional and behavioural styles and adopt those styles rewarded in the school context if they wish to achieve academic success. (Fordham, 1988, p55).

## Summary

The refusal by both headteachers, notwithstanding their different styles, to accept that schooling can undervalue African-Caribbean boys puts them in the same category. They both shared a misconception about African-Caribbean boys. Mr Francis undermined their desire for formal schooling structures, such as school uniform – which many of the boys wanted. Mr Jones went to the other extreme and attacked the boys' sub-culture because it did not conform to his middle-class Caribbean individualism. Both Mr Francis' and Mr Jones' perception of schooling can be located in what I call an 'idealism'. The idealised perception of the Caribbean drove Mr Jones to launch an attack on the pathological nature of the sub-culture of African-Caribbean boys and to fail to acknowledge the shortcomings of the schooling process on these children. Both headteachers also expressed a paternalism in regarding the school as a second family for these boys. For Mr Francis it was a safe haven from a hostile world and for Mr Jones it was the ladder to becoming successful and middle-class.

It is the new category of 'idealism ' that helped to form the dominant ethos in Township School. The 'idealism' of these teachers is based on a 'conservative' and 'pastoral' perception of Black culture. It feels most threatened by a changing youth culture, that no longer adheres to the values which perceive school and its structures as a means of social mobility. This emerging category supports my thesis that teacher conflict is at its sharpest when it confronts the sub-culture of African Caribbean boys. The category of 'idealism' is a means of defending the schooling process from the perceived enemy of African-Caribbean sub-culture.

Can we see from the emergence of the new category of 'idealism' that Mr Jones has complex motivations? Does this mean that we can excuse him from being categorised as operating a racist discourse? It could be argued that Mr Jones is responding to Black culture by using a racist discourse: his belief that his culture is superior, is an unintended bias against African-Caribbean boys, even though he himself is Black. I would say that in suggesting that certain cultural expressions of African-Caribbean boys are anti-school, such as hairstyles, he is a promoting a racist discourse. Those who argue that the ethos of school is about uniformity are not justified in this context, because the ruling was open to teacher interpretation and was perceived by the boys as racist. White boys in Township were allowed to cultivate their own culture. There were, for example, a group of white boys who wore pony tails, but Mr Jones did not consider this hairstyle to have a negative effect on their schooling.

However, his discourse is not totally racist. He points to the 'weakness' in some of the boys' cultural perception of academic success as a white person's prerogative. This strand of Mr. Jones' attitude attacks the boys' rejection of Black academic success, which he feels to be counter-productive.

Mr Jones places little emphasis on teacher racism and ineffective schooling. It has emerged from the data that he operates within the idealist category which has left him engaging in a racist discourse. But his criticism of African-Caribbean male culture must still be taken seriously despite evidence of bad schooling and teacher racism. His analysis of 'individualism', the role of music and the need for formal structures raises important questions about the place of Black sub-cultures in Township School.

# 5

## Innovators and Retreatists
## Learning to balance the books

*The history of the American Negro is the history of strife... The Negro is a sort of seventh son, born with a veil, and gifted with second sight in this American world. It is a peculiar sensation, this double-consciousness, this sense of always looking at one's self through the eyes of others, of measuring one's soul by the tape of a world that looks on in amused contempt and pity. One ever feels his twoness – an American, (a Briton) a Negro; two souls, two thoughts, two unreconciled strivings; two warring ideals in one dark body, whose dogged strength alone keeps it from being torn asunder.* – W E B Du Bois

The second largest grouping (35 per cent) of African-Caribbean boys surveyed came under the category of innovation. This category accepted the goals of schooling but rejected the means. The origins of their pro-education values are mostly parental. Frank Sinclair is a fourth year student and a key member of the clique in his year called the 'Posse'. He was expelled from two schools before coming to Township on grounds of violent behaviour outside of school. He has already had five short term exclusions since he has been at Township:

> Frank: I got excluded the other day. I had an alcohol bottle with me and Miss caught me drinking. She tried to pull it from me and I cut my finger, so I pushed her. She then said I must go home. I told her to 'fuck off' and ran out the class and told Mr Jones what happened.

TS: Are you a member of the 'Posse'?

Frank: I suppose so; most of the people in this group I knew before I came here. So I ended up hanging around with these guys. When the teachers see us together they think we're in a gang. They reckon we're getting up to no good.

TS: According to the register you have not missed one day of school for the last two terms. Why do you come to school so regularly?

Frank: Well, I come every day because I want to learn, whereas others I know come to get jokes in the class. But then again, if we're all in the class and the lessons are boring we will tell jokes and make noise.

His good attendance is supported by his parents, who believe in the 'Caribbean' ideal of education as the only ladder to success:

TS: What did your mum say when she found out about your latest exclusion?

Frank: She just sent me to my Dad's house. And my Dad would talk long, long, long.

TS: What did he say?

Frank: He says it would be harder for me to get a job than a white man. He's always talking about this; it's like when he starts he can never finish. Most of the time I go up on Saturdays, get my pocket money - I only want to speak to him. He would just keep on about education. Then as I'm about to go he would get a book out and I would have to sit down and do some weird maths. And if I can't do a sum he would start getting mad.

TS: Do you think it is worth coming to school?

Frank: Yes, I have some friends who are about 21 and they're just loafing around. I just want to go to college do a B-Tec National and go and work in a bank.

Frank Sinclair is representative of many boys at Township School who were positive about education but rejected the schooling process.

These boys were unable to fine-tune these two opposing instincts in order to avoid open conflict with teachers. This is in contrast to the findings of studies done on Black girls. Fuller (1980) has shown how the Black girls in her study managed subtly to resolve this dichotomy. She describes their attitude as 'pro-education and not pro-school'. They managed to distance themselves from Conformists (keeping themselves close to their peer groups) and yet achieve academic success.

It is this pragmatic attitude that academic success is a means to an end which the Innovators in Township failed to grasp – the cost to their 'masculinity' was too high. Unlike the Black girls in Fuller's study and some of the boys in John Caxton, they could not operate some sort of limited resistance which was sufficient to satisfy the needs of their peer group and simultaneously to avoid open conflict with teachers.

The majority of 'innovators' were unable to carry through their desire for education into the schooling context, where they needed to obey rules or avoid conflict. We are thus brought back to the power and pressure of the peer group that desires a hyper-masculinity. The children invented their own word for this machismo, 'Raggu', a corruption of Ragga:

> TS: Are there any differences between white and Black youths in this school?
>
> Roger: Yeah, some of them are not as Raggu as Black youth. At the end of the day a Black person's got more bottle than a white person.
>
> Stephen: Some white boys try acting like they're Black but they should stay as they are. They have a different way. We Black youths have to pull these skanks because we're poor, whereas the white youths get their money from their mum.
>
> Roger: I agree. Black people have to work twice as hard to get anywhere.
>
> Stephen: We're coming from a lower class and they're coming from a higher class.

TS: But surely in this school there are many poor white students?

Roger: No, I am saying that a Black person in the past had to suffer slavery.

TS: But what about now?

Stephen: Well, now it might not be slavery but we have a stricter home life than they do.

This exchange reveals a belief by many of the 'innovators' that the cultural difference between Black students and white is on the level of machismo and money. The sub-culture helps to feed the stereotype that African-Caribbean boys are more openly aggressive/rude than their 'weak' white counterparts. Academic success is still regarded as a 'mental' activity and therefore is not linked with being tough. There does appear to be a contradiction here. How can boys who are pro-education link academic success with being anti-masculine? The answer lies in the ambivalence that stems from the culture of these boys. There is a pro-education culture rooted in the Saturday School movement and the Caribbean traditions of their parents. This is contrary to the demands of the peer group, the fictive kinship that demands a loyalty that is frequently anti-school. This explains why the 'innovators' declare themselves pro-education whereas their actions are in fact anti-school.

The nearest equivalent to Fuller's (1980) Black girls were a minority of students who took advantage of the weaknesses in the discipline structure and were clever enough not to get caught. David Nelson was one such boy, a year ten student who operated as a peripheral member of the 'Posse'. David was in the top set for most of his subjects, but his head of year told me that 'he would always be seduced by the anti-school behaviour of the 'Posse'. However, we never have enough evidence to catch him. He is 'slippery like an eel'. David had developed the art of avoiding trouble at school, not because the teachers were after him, but, in his own words, because he was 'sneaky and I find it too easy to get away with things.' One incident I observed was when the 'Posse' were smoking cannabis in an empty classroom at breaktime and the classroom was raided by a group of teachers. David had his work spread out on his desk as if his only reason for being there

social mobility. This may be one reason why African-
boys have much better attendance figures than their white
s. The other 'safe haven' factor is racism. This is borne out
er of African-Caribbean boys who were stopped by police
school or brought back in police cars. I observed one
r school, where a mixed group of boys from Township
owdy at the back of a bus. The driver stopped the bus and
minutes the police arrived. The first thing the officer said
l the coloured boys get off the bus.' He was quickly
Black woman passenger, who said that she was going to
he boys gave me a catalogue of similar stories of
ich they encountered when walking the streets. These
iew school as perfect but clearly felt that it was an
hich protected them from a hostile world. This, of
ontradiction. It protects at the same time as it turns a
demeanours for which it is then criticised by David and
giving it approval because it is safer than the streets.

vid see school as valuable on their terms only. They
gree of autonomy. They are not passively accepting a
e that serves the imperatives of capital and the state.
ll accept school they do so only on the basis of their
d gendered subjectivities. School becomes a 'safe'
n which to continue their social activities without
Weis (1985) argues that although the purpose of
eate students who are compliant to the capitalist
y and division of labour, the actual culture of the
effective agent of social control. In Township the
sub-culture on a Black collectivist anti-school
onsumerism and phallocentrism was more
ng them into roles destined by capitalism than
Therefore they accepted the goals of schooling,
eir terms and through meanings distributed not

s that Township is neglectful because he can get
ts, he means that he expects the school to fulfil
te and discipline him. For him the school has no

was to do his homework. He 'got away with it' while the others got into trouble. I asked him about how he saw himself as a student at Township:

TS: How would you improve this school?

David: Some teachers should be changed. I'm saying some teachers don't know how to handle the lesson, so they get taken for a ride. They don't know how to handle kids socially.

TS: What do you mean?

David: If a child is being rude, they don't know how to handle it. They can only teach – that's it.

TS: Which headmaster do you prefer – the new one or the old?

David: I prefer Mr Jones. Mr Francis was an idiot. The kids could get away with murder.

TS: Did he exclude you?

David: No, he couldn't because I'm a bad boy. I do bad things but I never get caught.

David has contempt for the institution of Township, not because he is experiencing teacher racism but because the classroom management and discipline of the teachers is so poor. There is almost a sense of regret that he is allowed to be a 'bad boy' and not brought to book for his actions. He has devised his own way through Township, even though he has rejected the prescribed means of reaching these goals. David falls into the category of innovator, to the extent that he accepts the formality of schooling and what it should be but rejects the poor methods used to achieve these goals. In most cases, students who fall into the innovation category are those who reject the prescribed 'means' of a school because they are too demanding or formal. For example, a child who passes all his exams despite doing very little in class. In the case of David, he accepts the goals of schooling but rejects the means because they are too 'slack' and not formal enough:

TS: How come you're not wearing school uniform?

David: The problem in this school is that it's too easy to dodge the rules. Look at me. I'm wearing multi-coloured trainers and no teacher is saying a thing. I sometimes come to school with no uniform and get through the day.

David is not trying to achieve a balance between the pressure on him from racist teachers and his own desire to learn. It is in fact teacher neglect that has made him feel insecure about schooling. There were many African-Caribbean boys in all categories who complained that their biggest problem in school was not direct teacher racism based on the idea of a mythic challenge to teachers by the boys but, rather, an absence of authority. One of the more problematic notions to arise from the African-Caribbean students' good attendance record was that nearly all the teachers interviewed used it as a way of explaining the disproportionate exclusion rate. Teachers would make cynical remarks such as: 'The only problem with this student was that he came to school regularly'. They pointed to the fact that disaffected white boys would absent themselves, thus minimising their conflict with teachers, unlike African-Caribbean boys who attended regularly. I have never been convinced by this argument, especially when one asks what the purpose of the school is. Is it there only to teach a select group of boys who want to learn or is it a service for all children? Blaming good attendance was an easy means of escaping questions about the quality of classroom management, particularly when one took account of the uneven experiences of the children. I observed David Nelson in his Economics class and his English class. The classes were worlds apart. The Economics teacher managed the class well and David went to the front of the class where he produced excellent work. In English he went to the back and began playing cards in a classroom atmosphere that was virtually chaotic.

This analysis is supported by Alan Wilson, a year nine student who had just returned to school after serving his fourth three-day exclusion in less than three months:

TS: How would you compare Mr Francis with Mr Jones?

Alan: Mr Jones is a better teacher; Mr Francis didn't know what was going on nor did he really care. It's like some of those teachers

who turn a blind eye when they se
They don't really give a fuck. All
money for doing fuck-all. So wh
take advantage. The school is a l
still can take the piss.

The one school convention that mc
not break was regular attendance. I
with the high absence rate of the
African-Caribbean students had a
good as that of white students. D

TS: What is your attendanc

David: Excellent.

TS: Have you been tempt
don't like?

David: If there is a lesso
through the lesson. Th
moment. If you go or
There is the police an

TS: What does your

David: It's the most
hard for Black pe
whites because the

TS: Do you belie

David: Of cours

TS: What affec

David: At the
go back to be

School for Davi
that made him f
headteacher, '
input by Davi

terms of
Caribbean
counterpar
by the num
outside the
incident aft
were being r
in under two
was; 'Will a
rebuked by a
report him. T
harassment wl
boys did not
environment w
course, is the c
blind eye to mis
the others, while

Students like Da
exhibit a high de
schooling structu
Although they wi
own class, race ar
meeting ground o
police harassment.
schooling is to cr
process of hierarch
students is a more
emphasis within th
ideology, on pro-
effective at socialis
school could ever be
but it had to be on t
only by the school.

When David complai
away with what he wa
its obligations to educa

major influence on his socialisation. It is not the educational goals that he wants to undermine in his opposition to school, but he will fight for the space to continue his social activities, many of which have the same objectives as schooling. One example is the way in which his sense of dominant masculinity is affirmed within the school's ideologies and discourses. David and the other Innovators feel they can enjoy the luxury of complaining about 'bad schooling' because its goals do not influence their own agenda. They reject school on the level of their own relationship to the outside (capitalist) world. In spite of the fact that they know that the life of the ghetto hard man is far from glamorous by observing the lives of older friends and relatives, they construct fantasy futures and elaborate an ideology of phallocentric supermen. They create a specifically Black male anti-school culture which consists of 'aggressively' defending their pride from the slightest provocation from teachers or other pupils and wearing baseball hats and hoods instead of school uniform.

The majority of the innovators perceived the schooling process as repressive, exclusive and racist. Their struggle with Township was a contradictory one. They shared the objectives of schooling, but the means were defined by their own relationship to capitalistic structures outside school. They wanted school to provide a 'secure' space in which to conduct their own social relations, which most of the time ended up with exclusions. Unlike Fuller's Black girls, this attempt at a pro-education anti-school 'accommodation' was more likely to fail because of the teachers' expectations of challenge and the boys' attraction to their own sub-culture.

## Innovators and the fear of the 'white devil'

American researchers Fordham and Ogbu (1986) looked closely at the fear of 'acting white' as a significant influence upon the attitudes and achievement of African-American students. They stated that 'one major reason Black students do poorly in school is that they experience inordinate ambivalence and affective dissonance in regard to academic effort and success'. According to Fordham and Ogbu's theoretical framework, African-Americans experience a group identity or fictive kinship with other African-Americans. One aspect of this group identity is that members of the group are united in an oppositional social identity that is partly defined as not doing things that are associated with white Americans, who are viewed as their historical oppressors. Fordham and Ogbu (1986) argued against the cultural discontinuity theory of minority achievement, which claims that a major reason for underachievement of minority students is that they do not share cultural backgrounds, meanings, and understandings of time, space and purpose with those who teach them and grade them. Ogbu (1987) pointed out that if cultural discontinuity were a primary reason for underachievement, groups like immigrant Asians should experience low achievement, yet they do not. He distinguished caste-like minorities, who have suffered a long history of oppression and discrimination, from immigrant minorities, who may suffer current discrimination but who as newcomers lack the history of persecution of cast-like minorities. Cast-like minorities are most likely to experience fictive kinship, an oppositional social identity, and low achievement. It is they who fear being accused of 'acting white' because it would suggest that they are not 'good' members of their community. An important marker for acting white is speaking standard English: according to Phinney (1990) 'language has been considered by some as the single most important component of ethnic identity' (p505). Other attitudes and behaviours identified as acting white include listening to white music, studying, working hard to get good grades, actually getting good grades and putting on 'airs'.

The issue of acting white is tied to issues of ethnic identity. Theories of ethnic development suggest that accusing others of acting white may be part of a stage of ethnic identity in which the individual feels strongly identified with his or her own group and weakly identified with or even antagonistic towards the majority group (Cross, 1991; Phinney, 1990). For example Cross (1991) referred to the 'Blacker-than-thou' syndrome as part of the Immersion stage of Black identity development. Phinney (1990) observes that the stage of exploring one's ethnicity may 'involve rejecting the values of the dominant culture' (p503).

What has not been developed by these writers are the different ways gender interacts with the syndrome of acting white. The literature

(Fuller, 1980) and the evidence from the Innovators at Township indicate that acting white has connections to the way in which these boys construct their masculinity. For Black girls, although not immune from the syndrome, traditional academic knowledge is linked to power. This knowledge was not only meaningless to the male innovators in its connections to power in the job market but was also positioned as feminised and so inferior to the superior knowledge of the street kept safe by the anti-school peer group.

This tension was one key source in explaining the disaffection of many of the boys in Township with school. However, one must make certain qualifications before suggesting that this is a universal phenomenon. According to Bergen and Cooks (1995) it seems that the students who had the hardest time with regard to accusations of acting white or selling out were those in racially balanced schools. Students in racially balanced schools seemed to feel more polarised in terms of race, so they were under more pressure to choose sides/to choose whether to affiliate with white students in addition to their own ethnic group.

In Township School the innovators were in a predominantly Black context and their burden was not so much acting white but acting as 'a Black hyperheterosexual male' . This required rejecting some notions that could link them to the white world. However, the white presence was not large enough in Township to warrant this anxiety. It was the 'surveillance' from their Black peers that gave major cause for concern.

## RETREATISM

There were a minority of African-Caribbean students in my sample who can be classified as 'retreatist' (6 per cent). These are students who reject both the goals and the means of schooling but for whom these are not replaced by the subculture. In fact schooling is replaced with no significant alternative; their task is simply to reject work.

Joseph is a third year student. He spends most of his day walking around the corridors. He claims never to have been 'picked up' by his class teachers who regard him as a 'slow learner'.

TS: Why do you spend so much time outside lessons?

Joseph: It's just boring and the teachers that I have are weak and they can't control the class.

TS: Do you ever hang around with the 'Posse'?

Joseph: You must be joking. I hate them. They go around trying to bully students and get their dinner money. They just want to start trouble.

TS: Have you ever been excluded?

Joseph: No.

TS: Why?

Joseph: Because I'm not that rude when I'm around teachers.

TS: How long can you get away with not turning up to lessons?

Joseph: Weeks. Teachers sometimes see me on the corridor but they don't say anything. They don't think I'm a bad boy because I'm not aggressive.

Joseph is not only opposed to teachers; he also hates the sub-culture of the 'Posse'. It is because he is not visibly rejecting the schooling process that he avoids open conflict with teachers. He is never seen in a group but walks alone, missing work, because, as for the rebels, it has little value. The African-Caribbean retreatists are nearest in kind to the white boys who resist schooling in Township. Research from OFSTED has shown that white working-class boys are actually performing worst in school in terms of academic achievement and attendance, although not of course when it comes to punishment procedures like exclusions. Vivek Chaudhary reported as follows in *The Guardian*:

Last week Chris Woodhead, Chief Inspector of Schools, announced that girls are now more successful than boys in every subject except physics, and almost all ethnic minorities are achieving better examination results than white boys from poor inner city schools.

In practice, it is girls who have taken advantage of greater educational equality. It feels as if the general opening up of opportunities for women has filtered down into childhood.

Mothers encourage their girls to aim higher than they did. Young women are seizing the opportunities, now communication skills and team work are more prized than competitiveness and physical strength. Only the police and the military are left as occupations in which sexism, homophobia and racism have precluded women and minorities from making inroads – and even these are under pressure to make themselves more representative of modern life. Grant and Chaudhary (1996 )

Retreatists are never seen in groups of more than two and they resist schooling through subversion. They might walk the corridors pretending that they are on an errand for a teacher. In Township it was significant that this form of resistance was open to only a few Black boys, the irony being that even in a school which is predominantly Black it is still hard to be 'Black' and invisible.

Joseph was a bit overweight for his age and the teachers perceived him as 'soft and cuddly' – to quote his form teacher. The physically aggressive signals that teachers picked up from the Posse were not present in a student like Joseph. He was therefore more likely to be ignored because he was perceived as non-threatening. A new subcategory for Retreatism is 'invisible resistance'. It points markedly to the main cultural similarity in the way teachers perceived white and African-Caribbean response to schooling. However, it was hard for African-Caribbean boys in Township to use this category as a successful strategy of resistance.

# 6

# Rebels: It's all or nothing

'*The master's tools could never dismantle the master's house.*' –
Audre Lorde

Writing about the Black music scene in the seventies, Julien talks
about the alleged division between those who followed soul and those
who follow reggae:

> Reggae was more tied up with Black nationalism and certain
> rigidities of sex and race – tough masculine left politics. Soul on
> the other hand, allowed inter-racial relationships and challenged
> some of the structures of Black masculinity. Julien (1991, p2)

Although Julien has exaggerated this divide, he forgets the popularity
of Lovers Rock, a melodic ballad-based genre of reggae. There is
temptation by critics to link music genres with masculinities. Ironically
the old 'tough' followers of reggae have become the critics of the
Black sounds of the nineties, popularly known as Raggamuffin music.
Again the criticism is based on a masculinity that is too 'raw' and
'crude' compared to the past. There is a real danger in making these
connections because the reason often lies in nostalgia felt by an older
generation unable to respond to a changing world. Many Rastas were
angry at the new order and blamed the capitalist-materialist eighties for
the formation of Raggamuffin sub-culture. Ras Junior from the
Rastafari Universal Zion commented in *The Sunday Times* of
November 13, 1994:

> It was a cultural cul-de-sac. Ragga was highly influenced by things
> American, but American society is only all right for people who

have money. Materialism was the order of the day, based on how much money, guns and women you have. People realise that co-operation not competition is the way forward. (p16)

The key anti-school group in Township was a group of about ten boys in the year ten who called themselves the Posse. All were interested in the ragga culture that was popular with Black youths in most inner-cities. Although ragga lacked the political muscle of the Rastafari ideology of the seventies, the music, style and clothes served the same function as in most other sub-cultures. The Posse were creating a sub-culture of resistance to schooling which was essentially concerned with collective protection and survival. Brake (1980) explains why these groups develop:

> Sub-cultures arise as attempts to resolve collectively experienced problems arising from the contradictions in the social structure, and because they generate a form of collective identity from which an individual identity can be achieved... This is nearly always a temporary solution, and in no sense a real material solution but one which is solved at the cultural level. (1980, p86)

For the members of the Posse, Township presented a contradiction. It was a school that failed to engage critically with their own racialised masculinity, apart from seeing it as a threat. Yet for many, school was still a much needed formal structure in their lives. School has not provided a forum for learning or creating a positive identity, but it has given them what I call 'the security to rebel'.

Because of the complex nature of school resistance, it is important to divide the Posse into two sub-groupings; the Black nationalists and the 'hedonists'. Unlike the Rastafari framework, these are tentative affinities which help to give a source for school resistance. The Black nationalists are children who reject schooling in terms of a racialised perspective in which white racist teachers and a Eurocentric curriculum are working against the best interests of Black people. The 'hedonists' are those who reject both the means and the goals of schooling and replace them with the clothes, style and music of the sub-culture.

## Black Nationalists

Calvin is a fourth year pupil. His Dad died, leaving his Mum to raise five boys. He has a good many contacts and a strong network of friends outside school who are a lot older. This helps to bolster his reputation in the Posse as a man who does business with 'big people'. The teacher with whom he has most conflict is Ms Kenyon (Antagonistic):

Calvin: The worst teacher in this school is Miss Kenyon. She's a bitch; she's like a man – everyone says it. She's a joker – you just laugh when she gets mad. I always tell her she's a man.

TS: What does she say?

Calvin: She says, 'I don't care what you think'. I don't like her and she don't like me. She used to find me threatening. She talks to kids as if they're idiots, but she couldn't talk to me like that. She thinks she's vicious. She was also a racist; she pays nuff attention to white lads.

TS: Can you give me an example?

Calvin: Yeah, in her class all the Black people sit round one table, all the whites round one table and all the Asians round one table. She would then pay more attention to whites. Observe her class and you'll see.

I took his advice and observed several lessons. Calvin was right – there was a hierarchy of learning, but it wasn't based absolutely on race. Ms Kenyon refused to 'differentiate' her lessons for the benefit of the less able students. She assumed that all the children could read, so she spent little time actually reading the text in class but expected the children to do it for themselves. This became particularly evident when she taught Shakespeare. She was clearly what I call a 'fast track' teacher and the students in the slow lane were neglected. This did have a racial implication. Many of the white boys of low ability stayed away from her class but the African-Caribbean boys of similar level did turn up to her lessons. Therefore, Calvin, who was of average ability, found it easier to be lost with the low ability Black children in this class. It was really the inflexibility of Ms Kenyon that was the source of conflict with African-Caribbean children.

Calvin's resistance was always expressed in terms of a confrontation around 'talking' and inattention. In one class Calvin was sharing a joke with a group of African-Caribbean boys at the back of the class. Ms Kenyon's response was to seek confrontation in a battle of wills:

Ms Kenyon: Calvin, will you shut up. I don't know why you come to my lessons because you're not interested in doing any work.

Calvin: I would do if you didn't give us rubbish work. Look around, half the class haven't got a clue what you're on about.

Ms Kenyon: And you have, have you?

Calvin: The lesson is boring and so are you.

Calvin does not see a link between schooling and getting a good job. He has already set up his own small business as a 'mobile barber', cutting hair at people's homes. He said he could make up to £300 a week. He carries a mobile phone in school so that clients can make appointments.

TS: How important is it for you to own your own business?

Calvin: It is important for Black people to make money because white people don't take us seriously because we're poor.

TS: Is education important to you?

Calvin: Not really, I know what I need to know from the street. I'll give it three years and I bet no one will bother with school. There ain't no jobs for no one and they don't want to give jobs to Black people.

The figures (Table 7, page 74) on the job prospects of African-Caribbean boys compared to white boys supports Calvin's claims that few Black children will get work after they leave school.

Calvin has rejected the world of schooling and replaced it with his alternative lifestyle where he can make quick money and have contact with an adult world (even though it could be a criminal world) that takes him seriously. For Calvin school has become a place where Black people get exploited. It is also only for the naive, for those who are unaware of 'real' Black education, which will teach you how to make quick money and restore your pride. It differs from the race pride found in Mary Fuller's Black girls, who retained a strong sense of their own identity but accepted schooling as a necessary evil in order to succeed. Calvin feels that because of his network in the Black community, 'racist' Township has become irrelevant:

TS: Do you come to school to meet friends?

Calvin: You must be joking. Most of the people here are wankers. The only people I talk to are my brothers and cousins. The rest of them are wankers – they haven't been through what I've gone through.

Calvin has a contempt for what Dhondy (1978) calls the functions of school:

The reaction of Black youth to discipline, grading and skilling processes is substantially different and potentially more dangerous to schools. And it is precisely because the education of Black youth starts and continues within the communities of which they are still a part. (1978, p46)

This key point is supported by Ogbu (1988), who points to the intolerable pressure that local Black communities often place on young people: 'The ethos that values the collectivity over individual mobility has an important impact on the academic efforts and perceptions of Black adolescents.' (1988, p23)

Although Calvin exercises individualism in terms of his contempt of many of his peers and his desire to be his own boss, he looks towards the local Black community for inspiration, guidance and success. He has not distanced himself from the power of knowledge; it is school knowledge that he despises most. He firmly believes that knowledge can be used for collective action and the eventual betterment of the condition of Black people. It is proof that students in this category do not close off the possibility of pursuing an emancipatory relationship between knowledge and dissent. In order to define Calvin's relationship to the larger society, a sub-category for 'Black nationalism' has emerged, called 'community'. The only text for these students is survival. They feel that they have outgrown a schooling process designed to make them into social and academic failures. The rejection of the means and goals of schooling is replaced by a nationalism that sees them as 'victims' of a greater racist system.

## Hedonists

The Posse was not a sophisticated gang with rituals and initiation rights; they were a hard core of boys who applied different methods to challenge the school process. The group all shared an interest in some of the new changes in Black British music. At the time of this research, the new hybrid sound of ragga and jungle electro music was the defining feature of their style and interest. Many of them would exchange information and stories about 'Jungle dances' or 'Raves' that they were promoting or attending. The emphasis on sex, hyper-male sexuality and violence in this music has brought to the fore the argument that this has been the source for turning Black boys into aggressive males who then use this sub-culture to rebel against teachers and school.

The detractors point to the new Black popular sub-cultures as generating slaves to their own stereotypes. Robert Staples (1982) suggests that by internalising the mythology of Black sexuality, Black men have invested in the 'macho' role which trades off and perpetuates the stereotype and gives rise to exploitative and instrumental uses of sexuality. According to Staples, because Black men are...

> ...denied equal access to the prosaic symbols of manhood, they manifest their masculinity in the most extreme form of sexual domination. When they have been unable to achieve status in the workplace, they have exercised the privilege of their manliness and attempted to achieve it in the bedroom. Feeling a constant need to affirm their masculinity, tenderness and compassion are eschewed as signs of weakness which leave them vulnerable to the ever-feared possibility of female domination. (1982, p85)

The members of the Posse all felt that the schooling system had failed them. So was their status enhanced, as Staples suggests by a shift to extreme forms of masculine domination? Eric has a long record of exclusions, mostly over bullying other children. He had just come back from another exclusion, this time for aggressive behaviour and forcefully taking dinner money from a year six student. He says that most of the members of the Posse have outgrown school and find it difficult to be treated as 'little kids' when outside they hang out with 'big people':

TS: Why do you think that you've clashed so many times with the teachers?

Eric: I admit I've done some bad things, but what really annoys me is that they treat me like I'm a baby. They're always talking down to me. Kids are having kids and we know how to make money from early. Teachers are treating us like little kids, even when our parents don't treat us like this.

TS: Does this include the new headmaster?

Eric: Well, Mr Jones – he was born in Jamaica; he has got an understanding. But times have changed, he's seeing it in his time. Even though it might be harder in his day we're going through a different phase.

TS: Tell me about that change?

Eric: Kids from 13 upwards know about sex, they cuss, they sleep with loads of girls. They're doing more things than Mr Jones could ever dream about.

Eric operates a similar logic to the 'nationalists'. This time school is rejected not because it is too white and middle-class but because it can not meet his expectations as a 'man'. Although he is sympathetic to Mr Jones, he feels that Jones' brand of respectable conservative ideology is out of touch with his own perception of manhood. This is not based on ideas of 'responsibility' and 'caring', but is rooted in two actions – the ability to make money and the ability to make babies. Eric's father has eight children by four different women and is separated from Eric's mother. I asked him if he felt he was likely to end up the same way:

Eric: Well, at the moment I've got four girlfriends and although they don't know about each other, I'm smart enough to use a condom. I won't have any children until I make my money. If any of them have a baby for me I'll make sure that I give them money for my child.

Eric still perceives 'manhood' on a money/sex dynamic. He talks about his responsibilities as an extension of his dream to be wealthy. It is an immature vision, especially because he has no real job plans apart from a long shot of becoming a professional footballer. He provides a scenario which was typical of the boys in the gang. They felt that the schooling process assaulted the thing that was most precious to them – their 'manhood'. The teachers' ability to 'shame them up' and 'make them look small' was the reason for many conflicts. The other side of the dynamic was the fear that many teachers had of their 'size', 'presence' and 'styles of walking'. It was this interaction that they felt was the source of repression in Township and they responded with their own exaggerated sexuality. Delroy, like Eric, had a long record of exclusions. He was often seen on the corridor during lesson time, where he listened to music tapes with other members of the Posse. He has an essentialist perception of Black people which links them not with academic success but only with pleasure seeking:

TS: Which group of children would you say gets the most exclusions?

Delroy: Black.

TS: Why?

Delroy: Because that's the way Black people are.

TS: What do you mean?

Delroy: Well, if you look at Indians they work hard and own shops; Black people are into other stuff.

TS: What other stuff?

Delroy: They got more social life, they go out more. Black people aren't thinking about work, they've got other things on their mind.

TS: What other things have you got on your mind?

Delroy: Just getting out of school, meeting my friends and having a good time.

TS: Are you saying that Black kids in this school don't want to work?

Delroy: No, they just like to express themselves – show everyone who they are. A lot of my friends don't like to be told what to do. They hate being given orders. If a teacher tells them to do something and they don't respect the teacher, they're going to turn round and tell them to shut up.

Delroy reveals a standard western conflict between the body and the mind. The way in which these boys have been gendered within the school context has left them both alienated from 'caring' and 'responsible' notions of masculinity and victims of the commodification of Black culture. This is an argument that Gilroy (1993a) develops in his book *Small Acts*:

> The popularity of materialism and misogyny is partly a result of the fact that those images of Blackness are the mechanisms of the 'crossover' relationship. They are in a sense the most comfortable representations of Blackness. They are the images that the dominant culture finds easiest to accept, process and take pleasure in. So often the medium of their transmission is a discourse on Black masculinity that constructs Black men as both sources of pleasure and sources of danger to white listeners and spectators.(1993a, p228)

Gilroy (1993a) is pointing to the internalisation of stereotypes within the 'hedonist' group. This is a process of acting out an exaggerated manhood in response to the subjugation of your own. Victor, another prime mover in the Posse, feels that women teachers, in particular, wrongly perceive him as aggressive:

TS: What impression do you think teachers have of you?

Victor: Some say I'm too aggressive. I don't agree. Especially Ms Patel; she would say I'm aggressive when I shout. She kept on saying I was threatening her, which wasn't true. Because she's small and I'm big she thinks I'm going to harm her. She once said to me that I don't shout at teachers like Mr Arnold because they're men and they're big.

TS: Is this true?

Victor: No, I don't care what size they are. She thinks because I clench my fist that I am about to hit her. It's like no matter how I move my body she would claim I'm being aggressive.

TS: When did things begin to go wrong with you and Ms Patel?

Victor: From day one she couldn't control the class, so she asked me and another boy to help her. So we would tell the class to be quiet. She chose us because people would listen to us. And the class was quiet. When she started shouting at me I let the class do what they want.

Victor claims that he would be never be silent if a teacher accused him of doing something he had not done. He enjoys the classes of the three 'strongest' male teachers, Mr Avril (Supportive), Mr Lewis (Supportive), and Mr Davis (Supportive). He feels that they combine good classroom management with a good interaction with students. There was, in Victor, a strong desire to be a 'class clown' but at the same time he enjoyed the security of a tough male regime. His biggest clashes with teachers came in the 'aggressive' discourse he would have, usually around the wearing of his baseball hat. Even during the interview he wore his hat, knowing that it was against the school rules:

TS: Why do you wear your baseball cap when it's against the school rules?

Victor: I like my hat and I like the style. I listen to ragga and rap so that's the style. I can't help it, I just like wearing it.

TS: Do you think coming to school has any value?

Victor: When I don't feel like coming to school I really hate it. If I do come in then it's to meet my mates and have a laugh.

There are two key questions here. Firstly, why do the tough male teachers present the acceptable face of school? And secondly, why does everything else appear irrelevant outside of 'having a laugh'? I asked Ms Patel (Antagonistic) what she thought of Victor:

Ms Patel: As soon as he enters my class he sits with a group of other boys, and he and his friends immediately display total disrespect for me. He becomes talkative and noisy and totally ignores me when I try to encourage him to work. Consequently, he produces little or no work at all. He has also used school and lesson paper to make paper aeroplanes which, while standing on the windowsill, he throws out of the window. He frequently uses paper for silly graffiti. He generally uses the classroom as a playground and has engaged in playing 'games', including football with a paper ball or tennis ball, arm wrestling, fighting and generally running around. He has deliberately thrown his book and work-sheets on the floor and refused to work. When I tried to show a video, he displayed the same disrespect in that he chose to ignore me, talk to his friends and be a law onto himself. During this particular lesson he became very, very aggressive and very, very threatening with his body language and the tone of his voice. He shouted very loudly at me. In fact, he aims, in general to shout loudly to prevent me from being heard and having my say.

Victor is operating within the myth, or stereotype, of an African-Caribbean challenge. Ms Patel emphases his 'very aggressive body language' as something that particularly worried her. There is no evidence that she made this up or was imposing a wider racialised discourse on this student. It was part of his demonstration of power towards authority for which he had no respect. Victor knows that this 'performance' is feared by certain teachers and he enjoys his new-found power. For him school is a 'game', a 'playground' where only the teachers with big enough personalities and deep enough voices can get his attention. He has a need to operate on the level of 'appearance', 'style' and 'gesture'. This is much wider than simply a defence of ethnicity against Eurocentric norms. It reflects where the 'hedonists' find themselves in a society that has made 'schooling' and 'mental activity' the preserve of the white middle-classes.

The hedonists, unlike the Black nationalists, had totally rejected 'mental labour'. At least the 'Black nationalists' held on to the ideal that knowledge was positive and that it had emancipatory potential. The hedonists were similar to Paul Willis' (1977) 'lads' who rejected the primacy of mental labour, thus cutting themselves off from pursuing an emancipatory relationship between knowledge and dissent. Mac an Ghaill (1994) describes how the sub-culture can give students like

Victor a new status once they feel cut off from mainstream notions of knowledge and power:

> At the micro-cultural level, student peer groups, clothes, haircuts, trainers, sports bags, bikes and video games were the key signifiers that marked out gender and sexual status. Possession of these highly desired commodities served as an index of high status masculinity and femininity. Intense gender surveillance was a major student practice involving deeply felt and articulated cultural investments. (1994, p106)

Victor is not prepared to make all the 'existential' leaps necessary to become a school success. In particular he refuses to make the cultural distinction between a life outside school and the demands of a lifestyle inside school. In other words, his baseball cap stays on, and so do his continual clashes with teachers.

It has been argued that the schooling process is a mirror of the dominant culture of the society (Williams, 1961, Corrigan, 1979) and that school 'rebels' like those in Township are pivotal in challenging this white hegemony. This is an oversimplification of the way school resistance worked for African-Caribbean boys at Township. There is a need to look at how their own autonomous sub-culture worked not only against a schooling that reproduced the values of the white dominant society but also how it reproduced the very same values it was contesting. The tough, dominant virility which was present in the hidden curriculum and teacher attitudes was one way in which African-Caribbean boys were 'processed' in school. The other pressure came from their peer group and white students. Therefore African-Caribbean students were perceived as good fighters because of their race and reputation. Teachers and students, on the whole, expected white and Asian but not African-Caribbean students, to be bullied.

The sub-culture for the hedonist wing of the rebels was mainly an 'internalisation of stereotypes'. The Black nationalists were not too dissimilar in their reproduction of dominant masculinities, but they at least saw the value of knowledge within a Black collectivist framework.

This inability to – or desire not to – break from the 'collectivist' culture and reproduce the dominant culture as a form of rebellion is noted by Weis (1985):

> In differentiating themselves from the institution, students are, in a sense, differentiating themselves from the cultural mainstream. In so doing, they fall back on their own culture which is linked dialectically to dominant culture and developed in opposition to this culture. Genovese's comments are still relevant here. Blacks, he argues, 'learned to take the blow and parry it as best they could.' Shut out by white racism from part of the dominant culture's value system, they simultaneously resisted that system by necessity and by 'historically developed sensibility'. Blacks forged their own values (which are linked dialectically to dominant values) as a force for community cohesion. (1985, p155)

## Teacher attitudes to the Rebels

What were the teachers' attitude to the rebels? In particular how did the few Black teachers respond to the 'racialised' resistance that was characteristic of many rebel students.

Mr Walsh's ambivalence about culture comes from a reluctance to 'racialise' anything in school – be it the teachers' or the pupils' perspectives. Therefore we have a discourse that perceives Township as above racism and the African-Caribbean students' sub-culture as insignificant when it comes to a racialised opposition to schooling. He explains any differences in outcomes (for example, exclusion numbers) by blaming the parents. The teachers in the support category did not share the same ideological standpoint as those in the idealism category. Mr Howard could be described as a Black nationalist who felt that Black children needed to be taught by Black teachers:

> Mr Howard: In a survey I carried out amongst the heads of year I found that this all-white team couldn't relate to the problems of the Black children in the school. A white middle-class woman cannot empathise with a Black working-class boy – they are poles apart. She's interested in children coming to school, sitting in rows working away. In the real world we know that just doesn't happen.

In my experience the only solution that the heads of year have is to show them the door. They are excluded for a couple of days and come back. I'm appalled at the race barrier that exists between teacher and taught.

Mr Howard sees the conflict in Township as a racial one, in which middle-class teachers are unable to connect with the 'different' culture of African-Caribbean boys:

TS: How would you get teachers to relate better to African-Caribbean pupils?

Mr Howard: You need more teachers in school both Black and white, but more so Black, who can understand the street culture, who can empathise, relate to the Caribbean culture and understand how Caribbean people behave. Until we get that in inner-city schools, we will always be in the position where exclusions lists are disproportionately higher for Black children than other ethnic groups. What we need are more Black teachers. I'm not saying that white teachers aren't sympathetic or can't relate, but I think there is a cultural barrier in the way that Black people behave, which white people don't understand and don't want to understand.

Mr Howard states that African-Caribbean boys are different. This idea is based on their strong links with the Caribbean. He goes on to say that teachers and the school need to respond to this difference by being more sympathetic and employing more Black teachers. Mr Howard has a homogenised perception of these boys and he uses the same logic as those teachers who believe in the myth of an African-Caribbean challenge (Gillborn, 1990). It is the same framework which sees the boys as an alien mass whose cultural expressions differ from the white middle-class norm. The only difference is that Mr Howard sees the African-Caribbean boys as being the victims of the absolute racism of the white teachers. Therefore he shares an 'essentialist' notion of African-Caribbean culture. Not all the conflicts in Township can be explained in terms of white teachers misinterpreting cultural expressions of boys.

Mr Howard, although stressing his concern about teacher racism, has attributed to the boys 'special' qualities that not all of them possess.

Neither does he mention that among the excluded were boys who share the dominant middle-class ethos of the school. His support for a cultural perspective is based on exaggerating the boys' cultural 'difference' from white middle-class culture, whatever that might be. He has not begun his discourse with teacher racism. Instead he states that these boys are so 'different' that white or middle-class Black teachers can not relate to them. Thus a new or sub-category of 'Supportive' has emerged. I would describe this category as 'homogenous'. It incorporates a perspective that does not challenge the dominant ethos of the school. Mr Howard stresses the concept of an 'essential' difference in the culture of African-Caribbean boys, in order to explain their conflict with their teachers.

Even though Mr Howard's perspective had its limitations he still remained the only teacher to directly challenge the racist structures that were prevalent in Township. He was not popular among the white staff because they found him threatening. They disliked the way he would take up the perspective of the children – often against them. This point is made by the white head of year eleven, Ms Glasgow:

> Ms Glasgow: The school did recognise that many African-Caribbean boys seemed alienated from the schooling process. That's why we got Mr Howard to work with them individually and in groups, to try and make them feel part of the school and at the same time make them feel proud of the fact that they were Black.
>
> TS: You sound cynical. Was this a failure?
>
> Ms Glasgow: I'm saying the intention was wrong, I'm saying it didn't work.
>
> TS: Why not?
>
> Ms Glasgow: I think Mr Howard's approach was wrong, he actually fuelled it [their alienation]. Making them feel a 'them' and 'us'. So the kids thought, 'we've got someone on our side against them' [the teachers]. A more appropriate measure would have been a mentor scheme, where the kids could see that Black people have got a chance to go further – that they can get good jobs and good professions and there's nothing to stop you going all the way.

Sadly, there was a lot of aggravation between Mr Howard and the rest of the staff. He would question everybody in an accusing way. His approach was that white teachers were nothing because we can't understand. I think he needed to be more sympathetic. You can't expect people to change if your approach is antagonistic. It only gets their back up and they become worse. They look at you as a troublemaker.

Ms Glasgow defends Township by deracialising the conflict with African-Caribbean boys. Her vision of what is good for 'alienated' boys is to deny that the school may be contributing to the problem. Instead she recommends Black middle-class mentors who will uphold the ethos of the school, not challenge it.

## The threat to authority

Mr Lewis (Supportive), a white geography teacher who has taught for over 15 years, points to the different ways in which white and African-Caribbean students challenge authority, when he tries to explain the disproportionate number of exclusions among Black pupils:

TS: Why are so many African-Caribbean boys excluded?

Mr Lewis: I think that Mr Jones could have put out [excluded] certain Anglo-Saxons. What has been missed by most people is the aggravation caused by white boys in this school. There are a small group of white boys who are deeply racist and have a negative influence on the school. They do this through graffiti, victimisation of other boys and they've got away with it. I don't believe in many cases that we challenge certain white boys in this school.

TS: Why?

Mr Lewis: Because what they do isn't the one-off flare-up, because they are more subversive. I think we have an exclusion policy which is based on the one-off incident, which I think is wrong. African-Caribbean boys tend to be involved more with the one-off incident which is seen as more dangerous than other acts of anti-school behaviour. I think it is wrong to be excluded for a one-off violent flare-up.

This confirms Gillborn's (1990) analysis that the reason for most of the African-Caribbean exclusions in his study school was not the breaking of official rules but a teacher's interpretation of a boy's behaviour. A likely characteristic of a Supportive teacher is the ability to be flexible enough to make a distinction between serious threats to the good order of the school and one-off flare-ups that can be resolved without resorting to exclusions. The willingness to be flexible is a sub-category that emerges for Supportive teachers. Most of the Supportive teachers pointed to the weaknesses in the schooling process and teacher attitude when explaining the performance of African-Caribbean boys:

T.S: The group of African-Caribbean boys in year ten have been identified as trouble makers. Do you agree?

Mr Lewis: The problem there starts right back to year seven, whereby most of the boys had an unstable beginning in this school – where their forms were changed and their form teacher left. You can't say one year is better than another because of the boys; it's down to the staffing and the need for continuity.

TS: Do you think these boys respect a male teacher more than a female one?

Mr Lewis: It's not a macho thing. For kids it is about consistency and liking the boys. There are certain members of staff in this school who don't like the boys, and they can feel it. These boys need a professional approach, which means [teachers] always having work for the boys to do and delivering a lesson which the boys can understand. This is not a male attribute, it's simply giving the boys what they expect. I don't think female teachers can't do this and I know some male teachers who can't.

TS: How much is their schooling affected by Black popular culture?

Mr Lewis: I don't think they pick up anything from the popular culture that influences their attitude in school. I don't think they really understand a lot of it. They don't understand that a lot of these rap artists aren't rebels at all; they're making millions of dollars and living in style on Long Beach, New York. They don't understand the subtle ways of the media. They just repeat the slogans but have no idea what they're talking about.

Mr Lewis has trivialised the influence of Black popular culture on these boys. Even if it appears that they have only a superficial understanding of the media process, there is power in slogans alone. The feminist challenge from bell hooks (1990) is really about how 'uncritically' young Black men are influenced by the phallocentric core of Black male youth culture. Secondly, Mr Lewis has failed to recognise the sophisticated relationship that now prevails between white capitalism and Black youth as consumers. In fact recent developments (which I will explore in later chapters) have seen 'ordinary' Black youngsters subverting white capitalism and 'manufacturing' cultural expressions on their own terms.

Mr Lewis, although supportive, has undermined the impact of Black popular culture on these children. He has done the opposite to Mr Howard, for whom cultural differences were so great that African-Caribbean children could not succeed in a majority white teacher institution. Yet both view the students through what I call 'the lens of innocence'. For Mr Lewis African-Caribbean boys are so 'green' that the massive engine of white capitalism has no profound effect on their attitude to schooling.

Mr Howard also believes in the 'innocence of the Black subject' (Hall, 1988). It is a belief which claims that all Black people are in 'the same boat' – that is, subject to a reductive form of white racism, commonly known as 'institutionalised racism'. The weakness of this concept has been highlighted by Rattansi (1992):

> There has been, however, a tendency to use the concept in a reductive manner to imply that racist processes are the only or primary cause of all unequal outcomes and exclusions which Black students experience. (Troyna and Williams, 1986; see also Mason, 1982). The significance of the class and gender inequalities which are intertwined with the racism that Black students encounter is thus underplayed. This weakens the analysis and suggests inappropriate and possibly divisive policies which ignore discriminations and disadvantages common to white and

Black students, or which impinge in varying ways upon boys and girls. (1992, p35)

Another sub-category, called 'innocence', has emerged from the Supportive teachers at Township. It has not only made this category complex but has raised the issue of how much responsibility we should place on African-Caribbean boys in looking for reasons to explain their disproportionate exclusion numbers. The teachers in the 'irritated' category had no doubts that the students had to take most of the blame.

Ms Allen (Irritated), a white teacher desperate to leave Township, would regularly talk abusively about the boys she did not like – she called them 'shits' and 'little bastards' quite openly in the staff room. The children regularly had conflicts with her. The worst incident was when a boy head-butted her, breaking her nose. However, she refuses to see any racial perspective in the conflict, even though most of her clashes have been with African-Caribbean students:

> TS: Is there any group in this school that tend to give a significant amount of discipline problems?
>
> Ms Allen: As far as I can see there is no specific group, I would say the vast majority [cause discipline problems]. [However,] I can pin-point groups in this school who tend to be better behaved. For example, Asian and Chinese boys tend to be better motivated. However, that is not true of every person from these groups.
>
> TS: How would you explain the high numbers of exclusions of African-Caribbean boys?
>
> Ms Allen: Looking around, they are the most well-represented group in the school. There are more of them, so the most difficult ones are going to be from those groups. It is about certain individuals giving trouble, it has nothing to do with their race or racism within the school.

Ms Allen over-estimates the number of African-Caribbean boys in the school. There is a majority only if you include African students (see Table 2, page 69). In year nine (the year she has most conflict with) there are equal numbers of Black students and white. Ms Allen clearly 'feels' the presence of African-Caribbean students above their real number, suggesting that she is aware of a disproportionate cultural/race influence. Furthermore, she denies that racism has anything to do with the boys' school experience, yet she admits that African-Caribbean boys bring to school problems from outside:

TS: Do you think African-Caribbean boys have a different experience to other boys out of school?

Ms Allen: Yes I'm certain.

TS: So it does influence the way they behave in school?

Ms Allen: I'm sure it does, I wish it didn't.

There are two sides to Ms Allen. She is politically on the left – or as Mac an Ghaill would say (1994) an 'old collectivist', who has a strong sense of 'us' and 'them' in relations with the headteacher and who promotes the values of collectivism, egalitarianism and meritocracy:

Ms Allen: My politics are very left-wing – that's why I wanted to teach in schools like Township. I left my last school because I couldn't stand the head; and the kids in this all-white suburban school all looked the same – they had no personality. However, one kid really stuck in my mind, and that was a Black kid. He was a really smashing boy. He was naughty but nice, a real character. I thought, 'I want to go and teach more kids like him'. Sadly, I now teach too many kids that, deep down, no one wants to teach. There isn't too much personality here, but too much arrogance – arrogance is big in this place.

Ms Allen has made the link between arrogance and Black children. For her the majority of the children in Township are (mistakenly) African-Caribbean. This majority who are presenting discipline problems are not like the Black child she knew at her old school. It is her 'liberalism' which prevents her from saying explicitly that it is African-Caribbean children who give her the most discipline problems. She works within a stereotype of Black children that expects them to be more lively and have more personality than white children. This is supported by Mac an Ghaill (1988) when he examines some of the contradictions in the attitudes of liberal teachers in his study school:

It would seem that their caricature of the Afro-Caribbean students had developed exclusively in behavioural terms excluding a technical evaluation. Hence, the oppositional structure of this group consisted of an evaluative system of their temperament which varied from truculence to exuberance but did not include such technical categories as the measurement of academic achievement. (1988, p68)

Ms Allen is opposed to cultural expressions of the boys' sub-culture but she almost always refuses to articulate that it is African-Caribbean. She asserts that 'Black kids' have more personality than white kids and, by inference, that they are more arrogant. It is in her engagement with the machismo atmosphere of Township that Ms Allen shows how schooling influences her identity. She has moved from being a 'liberal' to a 'ringmaster' in order to survive:

Ms Allen: I think I'm a Circus ring master cracking the whip to try and make animals jump through hoops. A lot of them are rebelling against it. Its like a wild tiger – you can't really train it. I hate the job, I hate coming in here in the morning, being verbally abused – we all are. It's happening to all of us, it's only that some people are burying it. It's killing me before my time. I resent damaging my health – for people who don't appreciate it. We get no support from the senior management team, who are soft on discipline and expect us to work out our own salvation.

TS: After your nose got broken, why did you decide to come back to Township?

Ms Allen: Because I need the money. It's the only reason I'm here. There are a few nice kids that I'd like to help, but I'm not here due to any sense of duty towards the children. It's just keeping them contained in a circus ring – not real education, stopping them from escaping outside to damage the audience.

A sub-category for Irritated, then, is teachers who are 'cynical'. These teachers partly blame the school leadership, as well as the boys' culture, for the school's problems. They never blame themselves – rather they see themselves as victims of circumstance. Also characteristic of these teachers is that they see good and bad in the boys' cultural expression and are not totally antagonistic. Ms Allen is most directly opposed to the 'sexism' in the culture:

> TS: Does the cultural expression of African-Caribbean boys have any influence on their attitudes to you?

> Ms Allen: Yes, I think they've got to be hard where a woman is concerned. They're not going to do what a woman tells them. I do think this is encouraged by the music and macho culture that they are exposed to outside of school.

In contrast, she is opposed to Mr Jones' ruling that Black boys should not have patterns in their hair. She says: 'I agree with the boys; it makes no difference to their education or behaviour; it is the headmaster being trivial and even racist.' Such ambivalence between support and antagonism to the sub-cultural African-Caribbean expressions is demonstrated by Ms Williams (Irritated):

> TS: What do you think about the rule that forbids Black children to have patterns in their hair?

> Ms Williams: I totally disagree with the rule. I think something like hair, particularly for Black people, is an expression of their identity. We live in a society where if you're not as white in looks and so-called attitude then you're marginalised. Particularly for Black males, there is something about that style which is about them. It's been copied all over the place. This rule is a total intrusion on a person's freedom to express themselves.

> TS : What do you think is the logic behind the rule?

> Ms Williams: I think he wants them to conform to a particular norm. I think uniform is fine, but this is [going] too far. I really like some of the haircuts, they are great expressions, they show a certain flair and individuality – it also shows a great skill.

Ms Williams then qualifies her defence of the boys and gives a qualified criticism of other aspects of this sub-culture:

> Ms Williams: I firmly believe that Black youth sub-culture is the biggest influence on these kids. It isn't us or their parents but the street culture. We have certain children who come from back-

grounds where their parents lose control of their children too quickly. I think a lot of it is to do with stress – trying to cope with their lives and the changing lives of their teenagers. The powerful influence of the peer groups and the music and all the things that go – violent image, the sexist image and even racist image – is an easy alternative. They are aware of being Black and wanting certain things because of that, but it's not like it was in the seventies. Then we saw education, knowing the system and using it as the key to success. These children only have a superficial image of Blackness – they don't understand the system they are in and they don't understand how to use it to their advantage. It's all about image. They know about poverty and racism but they don't know how to tackle it.

Ms Williams recognises twin characteristics in the sub-culture of African-Caribbean boys. There are the positive elements that help to enhance racial pride, but this is contrasted with the 'violent' and 'sexist' aspects that reveal themselves in school. On this basis we have a new category that has emerged, which more accurately places the teachers in the 'irritation' group. The new category is 'ambivalence'; it captures the double response of being 'supportive' and 'antagonistic' to the dominant sub-culture in Township.

This 'ambivalence' is expressed in the comments of Mr Walsh (white). He feels that the African-Caribbean sub-culture has a negative influence on only a small percentage of boys. However, he has to admit that they have a powerful influence on the schooling process. He even contradicts himself when he says that the 'street culture' is insignificant and differs little from the white boys' cultural expression, but goes on to give specific examples of how this sub-culture disrupts schooling. There is a similarity between this view and that of Ms Allen, in that he is reluctant to point specifically to racism on the part of the teachers and the school in determining the performance of African-Caribbean boys. However, he is equally reluctant to give these boys any special racial category on the basis of their cultural expression:

TS: Do you think that African-Caribbean male youth culture in this school influences the boys to be resistant to schooling?

Mr Walsh: I think this question has an implicit nasty piece of stereotyping because all Afro-Caribbean children don't behave in the same way. Therefore to talk of an Afro-Caribbean street culture is in my view incorrect and it is stereotyping. Amongst our Afro-Caribbean children there are many kids who conform perfectly to school and are very successful and whose cultural norms differ little from white children's.

Mr Walsh suggests that the influence of the sub-culture is minimal because the majority of African-Caribbean children are conforming to the schooling process. However, he contradicts himself when he later goes on to explain the disproportionate influence of this sub-culture:

Mr Walsh: They may well wear a certain type of clothing (which may not interfere with the lesson) but it sends a signal – 'this is what I am'. They will spend a lot of time standing around doing their so-called business and seeing their friends. This will mean they will be late for their lessons – this could be even a quarter of an hour late. When they come into the lesson, that's the point at which they can get the class's attention. They like to make an entrance – that in itself disrupts the lesson. They will resent attempts to get them to concentrate on the work rather than talking about their own business. This means they're getting behind all the time and disrupting the lesson by asking for extra help. It is not so much an anti-school culture, it's more an 'anti-their-own-success-in-school' culture.

and home background:

Mr Walsh: I think the pressure to join the 'non-personal-success peer group' is strongest on African-Caribbean children and next strongest on African children. The pressure is best withstood by the Black children who have the strongest home background. It appears to me that more African children, compared to African-Caribbean children, have a stronger home background i.e. one that is setting very important goals for the child and is able to support him in carrying them out.

# 7

# How Britain became 'Negro' – Black masculinities go national

*The fundamental problem was, if I was going to continue to live in Britain, how was I to reconcile the contradiction of feeling British, while being constantly told in many subtle ways that I do not belong* – Caryl Phillips

## Introduction

It was shown in chapter 2 that, although teachers in Township School had an ambiguous attitude to African-Caribbean boys which made racism a contingent variable, they located the boys' sub-culture as the major threat to the schooling process. In this chapter, I try to identify the nature of this culture in the context of a wider historical develop-ment of Black culture in Britain and its Atlantic influences.

The process of becoming part of Britain and not an immigrant was really left to the children of the Caribbean migrants who came here in the 1950s. In America it was music, significantly the blues, which signified the drastic change from slavery to citizenship. In a similar way the music was to signal in Britain the shift from being a Caribbean immigrant to becoming a Black British citizen. This process would never be complete because of the characteristics of British racism. It would leave these children continually ambivalent about their new context. The responses to this 'condition' has been varied – some grasped for the cultures of the parents while others looked forward to creating something that was uniquely British. It was an acknowledg-ement that youth culture in Britain had, almost unconsciously, become

'Negro'. This was linked most powerfully to the rites of passage of boys into men. It was not only on the streets but in school that this new cultural dynamic was forged and tested.

## From Rastas to Raggamuffins: the changing dynamic of African-Caribbean male sub-cultures

Paul Gilroy (1992) outlines three tendencies in defining Black British youth culture. First, it is a culture that has to reckon with its position within international networks. Therefore it is a diaspora culture with influences from America, the Caribbean and Africa. Second, it is a culture that has been created from diverse and contradictory elements and, third, it has evolved through various stages, linked in different ways to the pattern of capitalist development.

In 1960 there were approximately 125,000 West Indians in Britain who had arrived since the war. British industry gladly absorbed them because there was a serious shortage of labour. These new immigrants from the colonies regarded themselves as 'English'.

However, between 1958 and 1968 the honeymoon was over, with Black people facing racist attacks and suffering discrimination, particularly in housing. It was the question of immigration and nationality that was the breaking-point, and it is still a key issue today. Peter Fryer (1984) points to this attack on the cultural citizenship of West Indian immigrants as the main weapon of racism against those early settlers:

> Between 1958 and 1968 Black settlers in Britain watched the racist tail wag the parliamentary dog. It was a sustained triumph of expediency over principle... The problem was not white racism, but the Black presence; the fewer Black people there were in this country the better it would be for 'race relations'... Step by step racism was institutionalised, legitimised, and nationalised. (1984, p381)

The importance of immigration legislation in 1962, 1968 and 1971 sent a message to Black people in Britain, that Blackness and being British were incompatible. It would be in the arena of nationalism that the children of Caribbean migrants, born in Britain, would have to struggle to carve out their space in a hostile society.

In education this new generation suffered and resisted an education system designed to keep the white working-class in their place. This system faced increasingly difficult issues concerning 'race' and achievement. In 1971 Bernard Coard's landmark book was published, *How the West Indian Child is Made Educationally Subnormal in the British School System,* in which he argued that Black children were labelled to fail and that schools needed to move away from a Eurocentric curriculum.

This new generation of Black children born in Britain developed what Farrukh Dhondy (1974) described as a 'culture of resistance':

> They are a breed most dangerous to capital, as they refuse to enter the productive partnership under the terms that this society lays down. They have turned the sale of their labour into a seller's market by refusing to do dirty jobs ...School has not succeeded in inspiring them with ambitions they know they will not be allowed to fulfil. Their ambition can be characterised as survival. They refuse to work as their parents' generation did. They need very little convincing about the slavery of that process, they are the children of it. Their culture is a day-to-day affair, an affair of the styles and fashions they collectively generate. They educate them-selves within the community, and carry their community into the school, where one may see them gathered around reggae, develop-ing the social image of their groups. (1974, p49)

Dhondy points to school as the reproductive organ of a system designed to produce another generation of compliant workers, who would staff London Transport, the hospitals and the assembly line. The 'Black explosion' in schools during the late sixties and seventies saw these children resisting this process of socialisation. In Dhondy's (1974) words:

> They expected that the machine that had processed white labour power and passed it through the sieve of the meritocracy, would do the same for the Blacks. It didn't. The Black population, in two distinct steps, carried their opposition to the forms and functions of schooling through the cohesion of their communities into the schools. (1974, p46)

Some schools tried to respond to the problem by introducing 'Black studies' programmes. This came out of political initiatives undertaken by some Black parents alongside Black nationalists e.g. the Hackney Black Parents Association. These programmes became a kind of 'special needs initiative' by schools and never touched the fundamental structural problems in the schooling process. As Dhondy (1974) observed:

> It is futile for a Black studies course to attempt to encapsulate their culture. Its only text is survival, and it is bound by a rejection of the disciplines of work that the society offers them, and can therefore be called a culture of resistance. It is a culture antithetical to the idea of schooling, and so finally unco-optable. (1974, p50)

It would be outside Britain that the forging of the new 'alternative' culture would seek inspiration. In this quest, schools faced more than just resistance in the classroom – they faced an ideological conflict.

## Black identity and the role of reggae

It was no coincidence that the intense resistance of Black children in British schools occurred at the same time as Black power uprisings in America and, more powerfully, the flourishing of the Rastafarian movement in Jamaica. The Rasta movement's influence increased steadily in Britain between 1970 and 1981, and its Pan-African, Ethiopianist ideology can be considered to have formed the core of a mass movement during the mid seventies. It began in the 1930s in Jamaica when followers of the Pan-African leader, Marcus Garvey, developed a movement that sought to reverse the colonial cosmology around them. Central to this new ideology was the idea that God was Black and that Africa was their true home, to which they would one day return. This desire for a new home came from their spiritual and psychological alienation from the imitation-British Jamaican society. As Rex Nettleford (1970) put it:

> To the Rastafarians who are Black, Jamaica becomes the Babylon which holds them in the captivity of a protracted diaspora. Here there is no pleasure of exile, only oppression and suffering at the hands of imperialist Europeans and 'their derivatives' (meaning the Jamaican brown men and privileged evolved Black members of

the middle classes). There is, too, among the oppressed Blacks, a deepening of the conviction that the Return is imminent, that redemption and freedom for the true (Black) Israelites is in the land of their forefathers – Africa in general and Ethiopia in particular. The Promised Land of Ethiopia awaits the Return (repatriation) of the 'children of the seed of Israel' and the ruler Haile Selassie fulfils in the twentieth century the prophecy that a 'king would arise out of Jesse's root' as 'God Almighty for his people and a liberator of all the oppressed of the earth.' The oppressed of the earth are all Black people whose forcible displacement (i.e. slavery) from their original habitat Ethiopia until this day, has caused the slaves to be resentful and at times revengeful of the cause of their enforced exile and ultimate privation. (1970, p41-42)

If Rastafarian philosophy was the content of this new movement, then its engine was reggae music. In the early 1970s it was the rise of singer Bob Marley that was significant in facilitating the popularisation of Rastafarian ideology in Britain and throughout the world. It gave reggae music a place in the lexicon of pop. Bob Marley's reggae was, like all reggae, a hybrid marked as much by its ties to American rhythm and blues as by its roots in Mento and calypso. One of the best known songs of Marley's middle period, 'Three O'Clock Road Block', for example, was extrapolated from Cole Porter's 'Don't Fence Me In.' Paul Gilroy (1987) argues that it was not only the Black communities that were influenced by Bob Marley; his music appeal was world-wide:

If Marley's excursions into pop had been the ground for this two-tone harvest, this era suggests that the lasting significance of his rise to prominence lies not at the flamboyant extremities of youth sub-culture where punks had reworked the themes and preoccupations of Rastafari around their dissent from and critique of Britishness, but in the youth-cultural mainstream. Here, the posters of Bob, locks flying, which had been inserted into his crossover product by Island, became icons in the bedroom shrines of thousands of young whites. In his egalitarianism, Ethiopianism and anti-imperialism, his critique of law and of the types of work which were on offer, these young people found meanings with which to make sense of their lives in post-imperial Britain. (1987, p171)

This is a key point. The impact of Jamaican music which was filtered through the Black presence in Britain was not a cultural side-show. During the seventies it gave energy to the main core of youth sub-culture in Britain. The well known movements such as punk rock and the flourishing of white reggae bands such as Madness and Bad Manners hijacked the Jamaican music of the sixties. However, the most interesting phenomenon of this period was the cultural mixing and contextualising, which took inspiration from the Caribbean and America and made it a distinctly Black British expression. This meant that Black youth cultures were developing around Britain and taking on the core problem of cultural definition and redefinition. It was a post-modern exercise – which more white scholars should have looked to as they struggled to grasp this abstraction. However, for those born in Britain of Caribbean parents, it was an everyday struggle of making a mark on a world that would leave you in its margins.

The struggle with the canon that said 'white equals British' was an attempt to decolonise a mental slavery which threatened to render this new generation as lost souls without any identity. The moral outrage that motors this decolonisation process is best captured by Frantz Fanon (1963):

> Decolonisation, which sets out to change the order of the world, is obviously a program of complete disorder... Decolonisation is the meeting of two forces, opposed to each other by their very nature, which in fact owe their originality to that sort of substantification which results from and is nourished by the situation in the colonies.
>
> ... In decolonisation, there is therefore the need of a complete calling in question of the colonial situation. If we wish to describe it precisely, we might find it in the well known words: 'The last shall be first and the first last.' Decolonisation is the putting into practice of this sentence. (1963, p36-37)

The identity struggle of African-Caribbean youths in the seventies was not a simple mimicking of the cultural expressions of the Caribbean; they used it to help re-make themselves in a culture that rejected their presence. Cornel West (1993) talks of this process as a quest for validation and recognition:

> This state of perpetual and inherited domination that diaspora Africans had at birth produced the modern Black diaspora problematic of invisibility and namelessness. White supremacist practices – enacted under the auspices of the prestigious cultural authorities of the churches, print media, and scientific academics – promoted Black inferiority and constituted the European background against which African diaspora struggles for identity, dignity (self-confidence, self-respect, self-esteem), and material resources took place. (1993, p17)

The response by Black youth to this 'post-modern condition' was to turn to the Black nationalist ideas within Rastafari. It was an ideology that would reconstitute and unify new world Black people. The word 'Babylon' became a popular term as a critique of white institutions and capitalism. Black people were seen as prodigal sons who had now returned to their culture. It was a text about redemption, and Black people in Britain were perceived as innocent victims confronted by white oppression. It is in this context that Mac an Ghaill's (1988) anti-school 'Rasta Heads' must be seen. This was an African-Caribbean gang in his study school who regarded their world as superior to and more 'relevant' than that of the school authorities:

> The Rasta Heads' visibility within the school was partly due to their generation of style. This included dress, hairstyle, posture, language and the wearing of Rastafari colours. The teachers had reacted against this, as it was perceived as a threat to their social control. There was a systematic attempt to prevent student identification with Rastafarianism. The wearing of dreadlocks, hats, Rasta badges or colours were banned. No distinction was made by the school authorities between those who identified with it spiritually and those for whom it was a more loose cultural association. (1988, p97)

It soon became a 'muscular religion', which had few prominent women members and projected an image of toughness. This macho image was an adaptation of the passive cult of Rastafarianism that had its origins in the Jamaican countryside. Mac an Ghaill (1988) talks of the overall rejection of schooling by the Rasta Heads:

One aspect of the visibility of the Rasta Heads was their overt rejection of the work discipline of the curriculum. But also of significance were the more subtle strategies of resistance that they had developed in their refusal to participate in the 'hidden rules' of classroom interaction. They rejected what Jackson (1968) describes as the unofficial three Rs – rules, routines and regulations – that students must learn if they are to be successful at school. (1988, p101)

The struggles of Black youths during the 1970s was based on a realisation that school was mirroring the same racist discourse that operated outside. It was not only processing these boys to take the place of their unskilled parents, it had also denied them any cultural space in the national consciousness. Their adoption and adaptation of Caribbean and Black American forms of cultural resistance led many to totally reject the schooling process. In this battle for minds, the position of the 'Black community' was key in providing and reinforcing an alternative consciousness. This was another important point in Dhondy's (1974) article:

They refuse the work that society allocates to them. School is their most immediate experience of state institution, if indeed it isn't borstal or jail. Their rejection of work is a rejection of the level to which schools have skilled them as labour power, and when the community feeds that rejection back into the school system, it becomes a rejection of the functions of schooling. (1974, p50)

It would be during the 1980s and 1990s that the notions of 'the real Black community' and 'positive images' would be seriously questioned. There would no longer be an uncontested consensus. The 'innocent' rhetoric around what constituted the Black community could no longer apply. It is into this new context that many of the second and all of the third generation of African-Caribbean migrants (the children in Township School) find themselves.

## The end of innocence and the new cultural hybridity

Music has been the key social/cultural indicator for those in the African diaspora. It not only marks the mood or tempo of an age but acts also as the major artery connecting African peoples across the globe. This was how the powerful ideology of Rastafari made its way into the hearts and minds of those in Africa and its diaspora. Therefore when 'the powerful march of Rastafari' (Gilroy, 1987) ended, this was expressed in radical changes in the music. Gilroy (1987) reveals how the economic and political changes in Jamaica during the eighties had a traumatic influence on the music:

> Michael Manley's socialist government was ousted by Edward Seaga's American-backed regime in 1980. This change had cataclysmatic effects on the relationship between music and politics there, transforming both the content of the music and the structure of the music business. The largely Rasta-inspired singers, songwriters and dub poets who had guided the music to its place as a vibrant populist force for change in the society were brushed aside and their place taken by a legion of DJs or toasters. Manley's own path to a populist socialist politics had been guided by the semantics and vision of Rasta reggae, a fact he acknowledged in a discussion (1983) of Bob Marley's art, 'the greater part' of which he recognised as the 'language of revolution'. Under Seaga, the singers' and songwriters' influence faded and they retreated from the revolution which their Rasta language demanded. The DJs took centre stage. (1987, p188)

Edward Braithwaite (1985) summed up this new era by saying: 'Things have changed. Jamaicans no longer relate to that kind of nativeness'. One of the major characteristics of the Rastafari movement was its critique of capitalism, which saw the labour process as oppressive. It attacked the police and state for their militarism. There was a prevailing sentiment that freedom was a place where the poor would triumph over the rich. This was an inevitable historical process whereby the Rastaman would finally conquer this materialistic earth.

This critique was beset by a contradiction that would sow the seeds for its own decline. When the early Rastas first set up the movement, they were outcasts, but it was from this that they drew their strength.

Babylon was down below in the changing 'madness' of Kingston, while the Rastaman lived peacefully in the hills, living off the land and withdrawn from the Babylon system. The movement grew and became an urban development in the poor areas of Kingston, and took on a new dimension when reggae music became its most vital source of expression. The Rastaman (on behalf of a number of singers) became an international superstar. He had joined the capitalist market-place, with its emphasis on 'image' and its consumer-led orientation. Rastafarians' close links with the commodity – reggae music – meant that when this kind of music no longer sold, the movement suffered a similar demise.

The decline of radical reggae was demonstrated by the shift from singers to DJs. The DJ was a kind of poet who spoke rhyming lyrics over the music bed of old reggae classics. The most controversial issue in this shift was the contents of the DJs' lyrics. They no longer proclaimed the Rasta ideals of social justice and Black redemption in Africa; reggae's mainstay was gun machismo and Black male sexual prowess. Gilroy (1987) illustrates this point when he describes the fortunes of 'Yellowman':

> The decline of radical reggae can be illustrated by reference to the career of Winston 'Yellowman' Foster, the most popular toaster of the early 1980s whose work took both Britain and Jamaica by storm during 1982. After two explicitly political sides chronicling the rise of authoritarian statism in Jamaica – 'Soldier Take Over' and 'Operation Eradication' – he opted for the safety of nursery rhyme, animal noises and anti-woman jive talk. (1987, p188)

This decline of a politically radical form of Jamaican music was replaced with a new sound that was less oppositional. At the same time Black British music was ready to develop its own unique sound. With the Rasta canon in decline, the British scene provided a loose pluralistic and diverse new culture. The language and politics of Rastafari had until then blocked these new possibilities. There was a new confidence in this generation of Black people, who began to create a position for themselves in England. They soon began to redefine England and Britishness through a new cultural pluralism. Whereas Rastafari had seen Britain as Babylon, the place of exile for the true sons of Africa, the new Black British DJs began to create a sense of belonging which went beyond the divisions of race and class. This was achieved through language. The trick was to disrupt the racial hierarchy: it was an act of decolonalisation. Gilroy (1987) analysed the lyrics of DJ Smiley Culture in his 1984 hit record 'Cockney Translation' showing how this it presents a view of language as truly interchangeable; therefore what it means to be a Cockney has a new meaning for Black youth. The song went into the pop charts and was popular with Black and white youths, particularly in London:

> Say Cockney fire shooter. We bus' gun
> Cockney say tea leaf. We say sticks man
> You know dem have a wedge while we have corn
> Say Cockney say 'Be first my son' we just say Gwaan!
> Cockney say grass, we say outformer man.......
> Cockney say Old Bill we say dutty babylon.........
>
> Cockney say scarper we scatter
> Cockney say rabbit we chatter
> We say bleach Cockney knackered
> Cockney say triffic we say wackaard
> Cockney say blokes we say guys
> Cockney say alright we say Ites!
> We say pants Cockney say stride
> Sweet as a nut... just level vibes. Seen.

Contrasting London Black patois, thus, with cockney rhyming slang signalled that Black working-class youth were cockney by birth and experience but were denied this identity because of the way racism excluded them from the national character. The song also alludes to the hybrid nature of African-Caribbean culture, which asserts a new kind of cultural politics. It defies the new racism and develops a political and cultural aesthetic that seeks to locate itself as both Black and English.

## Raggamuffins in the Jungle: towards a definition of Black masculinity

The Oxford dictionary describes a Ragamuffin as a person in ragged, dirty clothes. This was the label (now spelled Raggamuffin) that Jamaican and Black British youths used from the mid-eighties to describe their culture. It was not a term of self-degradation but an identity that glorified in the raw side of manhood, even to the point of being misogynistic. It also rebelled against a conservative mainstream.

As with Rasta, the image was linked to music, this time led by DJs, with its African-American version in what was earlier called hip-hop and later known as rap music. The African diaspora influenced the Black British context, as it had in the seventies. This time it was not a radical Black nationalist political agenda that was passed through this medium but the red hot subjects of sex and violence. This caused controversy in Black communities across the diaspora, and in some cases the State censored records. In Britain the Black community have debated this new music intensely: parents worry about its influence on their sons. In his study of the cultural politics of race and nation in Britain, Paul Gilroy (1987) argues that:

> Jamaica's DJs steered the dance-hall side of roots culture away from political and historical themes towards 'slackness': crude and often insulting wordplay pronouncing on sexuality and sexual antagonism. I am not suggesting a simple polarity in which all toasters (another word for DJs) were agents of reaction and all singers troubadours of revolution. The Jamaican DJ tradition had been involved in the spread of Rastafari during the late 1960s and early 1970s as recorded song... However the role and content of reggae changed markedly after 1980. (1987, p188)

Yet, paradoxically, though DJ 'slackness' as critiqued by Gilroy is conceived as politically conservative, it can be seen to represent in part a radical, underground confrontation with the patriarchal gender ideology and pious morality of fundamentalist Jamaican society. In its invariant coupling with culture, slackness is potentially a politics of subversion. For slackness is not merely sexual looseness – though it certainly is that. Slackness is a metaphorical revolt against law and order, an undermining of consensual standards of decency. It is the antithesis of Culture. Carolyn Cooper (1993) supports this aspect of the DJ tradition:

> To quote Josey Wales: 'Slackness in di backyard hidin, hidin from Culture.' Slackness as an (h)ideology of escape from the authority of omniscient culture is negotiated in a coded language of evasive *double-entendre*. Gilroy (1990) himself notes, but does not fully explore at the level of politics, the subversive potential in the ability to switch between languages of oppressor and oppressed. (1993, p141)

This brings me neatly back to my point about Raggamuffin: the post-modern creative drive in the culture of the diaspora is to subvert the oppressors' text/language by making it your own. Raggamuffin, or its shortened version, ragga, no longer means a man with dirty clothes; it is an assertion of self, achieved by shifting or subverting the cultural margins.

The development of ragga music from Jamaica and the African-American expression of rap music, although different styles of music, have been the most powerful influences on the landscape of Black British culture during the 1980s and 1990s. Its most powerful detractors are on two fronts: First, a political criticism that sees ragga and rap as displacing the political energies that were found in older Black cultural expressions, like the blues or Rastafari. The second is a feminist critique which sees rap as misogynistic and as glorifying a Black phallocentricism.

Greg Tate (1993) recognises the hugely expanded forum that rap (or hip-hop) music, as a popular form, has made possible. At the same time, he is frustrated by the commercial dictates and by the ever more exacting decrees of style politics:

> A lifetime of Tarzan and John Wayne teaches us that when the drums fall silent, the pink man should really begin to know fear. Conventional wisdom would have us believe that hip-hop predicted all but the day and time of the Los Angles rebellion. But what if hip-hop is not the expression of Black folks' rage, but only another momentary containment of it, or worse, an entertaining displacement? During the Gulf conflict, hip-hop's drums were

deafeningly silent. They went on to the beat of cash registers while the F-15s were taking out Baghdad's mothers and children until the break of dawn... Cornel West has called rap visionless, but what it is, even at its most progressive, is agendaless. It reacts better than it proposes, and we who feebly wait for hip-hop nationalists to salve our rage and pain, hoping they will speak with us or for us, are to blame for not developing our own ways to radically speak above the fray. Hip-hop should be an invitation for everyone to break the silence around injustice, but it has become an invitation to party for the right to demagoguery. As a successful counter-cultural industry, whose style assaults have boosted the profits of the record, radio, junk food, fashion and electronic industries, hip-hop's work is done. But as a harbinger of the Black revolution, hip-hop has yet to prove itself capable of inspiring action towards bona-fide social change. Now we'll see, like Bob Marley sang, who's the real revolutionary. After all, real bad boys move in silence. (1994, p1)

Tate's lessons, therefore, draws upon a perennial complaint among activist intellectuals – in this case, Black nationalists – about the inability of cultural movements to deliver the masses. The responsibility given to this music genre, in terms of providing social commentary and leadership, needs to be questioned. Its power in the market-place is unprecedented. However this must be balanced by the fact that rap was perceived, unfairly, as having to replace the structures of Black civil society. As Cornel West (1993) says, the rapper has taken over the role of the Sunday School teacher.

The feminist critics formed an unusual allegiance with Right wing groups who opposed obscenity, culminating in 1990 when the United States federal courts ruled that the rap group 2 Live Crew's album 'As Nasty as They Wanna Be' was banned. It was the first musical act to have an album deemed obscene in a US district court. It was alleged that the album portrayed women as objects for sexual assault and some critics claim that the lyrics promote violence against women. For instance, in the rap 'Dick Almighty' we hear these words:

I'll tear a pussy open cause it's satisfaction
The bitch won't leave cause it's fatal attraction
Dick so powerful she'll kneel and pray.

In the rap titled : 'Put Her in the Buck', the group teaches young males a new sexual technique, which is meant to be pleasurable to men but painful to women:

I'll break you down and dick you long
Bust you pussy and break your backbone.

Onyekachi Wambu (1994), writing in *The Voice* newspaper, accused Black musicians in Britain and America of debasing sex. He says:

The second reason why I worry about the new sex in Black music is because of the way it has become just another commodity. I think we have crossed the thin line between celebrating sex, in the tradition of the best Black music, and exploiting bodies to sell sex. (1994, p9)

Feminist writer bell hooks (1993) points to the nihilism and power-lessness amongst many Black men as a reason for this sexist expression:

I think a lot of misogynist rap is similar to crack (cocaine). It gives people a sense that they have power over their lives when they don't. It's like they have consumed the worst stereotypes white people have put on Blacks. (1993, p1)

She (1992) points to the embracing of patriarchy and phallocentricism as destructive not only in relationships with Black women, but also for Black males themselves:

If Black men no longer embraced phallocentric masculinity, they would be empowered to explore their fear and hatred of other men, learning new ways to relate. How many Black men will have to die before Black folks are willing to look at the link between the contemporary plight of Black men and their continued allegiance to patriarchy and phallocentrism? (1992, p112)

In contrast to hooks, Henry Louis Gates, Jnr, a university professor and author of several works on Black culture, has insisted that this crisis is also rooted in a lack of cultural understanding in addition to being racist. His claim is that 2 Live Crew's lyrics are part of a long-standing tradition of ritual insult practised by segments of the African-American population, and that these rhetorical exchanges are being taken out of context by 'watchdogs' from outside the culture, who understand neither the form and function of these rituals nor the people who perform them. Writing in the *New York Times* in defence of 2 Live Crew, Gates (1990) says:

> For centuries, African-Americans have been forced to develop coded ways of communicating to protect them from danger. Allegories and double meanings, words redefined to mean their opposites ('bad' meaning 'good' for instance), even neologisms ('bodacious') have enabled Blacks to share messages only the initiated understood...

> 2 Live Crew is engaged in heavy-handed parody, turning the stereotypes of Black and white American culture on their heads. These young artists are acting out, to lively dance music, a parodic exaggeration of the age-old stereotypes of the oversexed Black female and male. Their exuberant use of hyperbole (phantasmagoric sexual organs, for example) undermines – for anyone fluent in Black cultural codes – a too literal-minded hearing of the lyrics. (1990, p23)

He is referring to the street tradition called 'signifying' or 'playing the dozens', which is generally risqué and where the best signifier, or 'rapper', is the one who invents the most extravagant images, the biggest lies. In the face of racist stereotypes about Black sexuality, you can do one of two things: you can disavow them or explode them with exaggeration.

Debate on this issue within Black communities has been intense. Peterson-Lewis (1991) disagrees with Gates' analysis. She claims that many rap groups' treatment of sex is too entrenched in violence to allow their lyrics sanctuary under the category of satire:

> Through intended or unintended glorification of dysfunctional views about male-female relationships – carried out under the guise of fun-making – 2 Live Crew's lyrics not only desensitise

their audiences to violence against women, they also rationalise and reinforce a nihilistic mentality among those who already suffer from the effects of ghetto reality. Finally, their lyrics help to rationalise an already existent suspicion and distrust of Black males. The study of the media's potential to affect public and private behaviour and attitudes should continue unimpeded by the trivialist, particularist, spiritualist, and universalist arguments posited by those who wish to veil their economic aspirations under the label of art. (1991, p125)

Peterson-Lewis (1991) feels that to credit rap groups like 2 Live Crew with having the literary genius of satirists is to overstate their case. She argues that their obsession with sex is used as a violent weapon against women:

Overall, the lyrics lack the wit and strategic use of subtle social commentary necessary for effective satire, thus, they do not so much debunk myths as create new ones, the major one being that in interacting with Black women, 'anything goes'. These lyrics not only fail to satirise 'the myth of the hypersexed Black', they also commit the moral blunder of sexualising the victimisation of women, Black women in particular. (1991, p130)

African-Caribbean boys in London (as well as other groups) have not only been influenced by rap and ragga music from America and Jamaica respectively, they have also (as was the case in the seventies) contextualised this influence into their own music. The children of the first generation of Caribbean migrants had been strongly influenced by the importation of Jamaican reggae also known by the Rastafarians as Dread music. This was coupled with the funk music of Black America. In the mid eighties the funk sound of America was merged with the dreadlocks, or reggae influence, of Jamaica to produce the Funki-Dreds, whose main exponent was music producer Jazzie B. Paul Gilroy (1993b) describes this hybrid culture:

It bears repetition that Britain's Black settler communities have forged a compound culture from disparate sources. Elements of political sensibility and cultural expression transmitted from Black America over a long period of time have been reaccentuated in

Britain. They are central, though no longer dominant, within the increasingly novel configurations that characterise another newer Black vernacular culture. This is not content to be either dependent upon or simply imitative of the African diaspora and cultures of America and the Caribbean. The rise and rise of Jazzie B and Soul ll Soul at the turn of the last decade constituted one valuable sign of this new assertive mood. North London's Funki Dreds, whose name itself projects a newly hybridised identity, have projected the distinct culture and rhythm of life of Black Britain outwards into the world. Their song 'Keep On Moving' was notable for having been produced in England by the children of Caribbean settlers and then re-mixed in a (Jamaican) dub format in the United States by Teddy Riley, an African-American. It included segments or samples of music taken from American and Jamaican records by the JBs and Mikey Dread respectively. This formal unity of diverse cultural elements was more than just a powerful symbol. It encapsulated the playful diasporic intimacy that has been a marked feature of transnational Black Atlantic creativity. The record and its extraordinary popularity enacted the ties of affiliation and affect which articulated the discontinuous histories of Black settlers in the new world. The fundamental injunction to 'Keep On Moving' also expressed the restlessness of spirit which makes that diaspora culture vital. (1993b, p15-16)

Bob Marley, Smiley Culture and Jazzie B can be described in Gramscian terms as organic intellectuals who are important in showing the dynamic shifts in the way that that African-Caribbean culture adopts and adapts to changes in time and space. African-Caribbean local communities adopted and rejected the Rastafari hegemony at different speeds, usually depending on the socio-economic context. London has traditionally been a place where cultures have crossed and mixed. Its relative prosperity compared to the North and Midlands has allowed it to be an environment for cultural experimentation and the development of new styles. Its radical traditions within the Art colleges helped to produce punk rock and the New Romantics in the seventies. Increasingly, African-Caribbean youth culture in London developed its own style, of which the Funki-Dreds were one example. At the start of the nineties London continued to make American and Caribbean fusions. The best known to date is called 'Jungle' music.

Jungle can be identified as rave music with reggae and soul mixed into it. It has absorbed all the major dance music styles since the reggae of the seventies and created a distinctive Black London music. As with Ragga music there has been a debate around its name. Critics object that it is racist to link Black music with the popular racist term 'jungle'. Yet this is surely a classic example of what Gates (1990) calls 'signifying', whereby you deconstruct the language and make it work on your terms. Writing in *The Voice* (1994), independent record producer Peter Harris describes how jungle music, although influenced by America and Jamaica, is a distinctive sound of Black London:

> The Americans have got R & B and rap sewn up, the Jamaicans have pretty much got reggae sewn up, so we wanted to make something here that they (Americans and Jamaicans) would have to come to us for. Because of our feel we find that bigger companies are approaching us to do jungle mixes of their tracks to appeal to a younger market. (1994, p13)

What are the ideas that come from a music that takes the best of other music forms and moulds them into one entity? The rave scene in the eighties saw Black electro dance music colonised by a white youth culture. The so-called rave scene, with its links to huge warehouse parties and the drug ecstasy, either excluded Black youths (thanks to white bouncers) or obliged them to join strictly on assimilationist terms. Jungle music was a Black reaction to this subtle racism, as the *Observer* magazine (1994) declared:

> For many, jungle, a hybrid of ragga and rave, has signalled the end of racial harmony on the dancefloor. Charged with bringing crack into clubland, it represents white club owners' fear of Black youth. But to followers, it's the old story of demonising Black sub-culture before exploiting its commercial fallout. (1994 p27)

In truth, jungle could only ever have developed from Britain's inner cities. Just as rap music grew out of Black urban poverty in New York, jungle expressed the growing frustration and resentment in the capital's council estates. Its assertiveness has indeed placed the music at odds with the 'colour blind' naiveté of the rave scene. Tracks like 'Potential Bad Boys Warning', with its gun shots and thinly veiled threats of violence, may leave little to the imagination. Chris Simon, a jungle music producer, commented in *Face* magazine (1994):

> Jungle is our street sound. Just as hip hop became the sound of America's streets, jungle will take hold in every British city that's fucked up. That's why no one in the media wanted to touch it. It's a street thing. It's about enjoyment for people who might not have much to go for in life. (1994, p95)

The seventies in Britain did see the establishment of what could be called 'a Black British youth culture', but (unlike the post-modern nineties) African-Caribbean youths in Birmingham and London were forced to make a choice between reggae or soul music. This would then define your tribe: soul music meant you followed the Black music of America and tended to go to night-clubs like Crackers in London's Wardour Street, where Black and white would mix in the non-political dance music of the seventies. The only option was the heavy rhythms of reggae. The attitudes of its followers were deeply 'Black' and in-fluenced by Rasta. There were few white people in these clubs, which were often seen by the police as a threat to law and order.

The big shift in African-Caribbean youth culture during the mid-eighties was the break with the big tribes of soul and reggae. The confidence that has come with understanding and taming Britain has generated the freedom to have a whole range of diverse cultural expressions. There is a sense in which white groups feel less threatened by different Black expressions. These differences do not seem to threaten Black group identity as much as they seemed to in the past. There is now the courage for fragmented cultures and spaces.

Alongside these fragmented cultures, there is also, paradoxically, a much narrower and more fixed umbrella for Black culture, which is less tribalised than its seventies counterpart. It is now virtually impossible to tell junglists, ragga boys and girls, and those from the hip hop nation apart in terms of their badges of identity and the clothes they wear. Regimentation and tribal chauvinism has given way to cross fertilisation under a standard banner. People have drifted apart, and yet come together. To that extent Black youth culture in Britain's inner cities is much more varied and interesting than it was in the seventies.

Now dozens of pockets of new voices and interests emerge yearly – bohemians, Black rockers, Black Muslims, nationalists, Khemetics, free spirits – all with their distinctive stories and angles on life.

## The cultivation of an African-Caribbean sub-culture

In this section I want to outline the ways in which African-Caribbean boys in Township School formulated notions of Black identity. Black identity has its historical roots in the 'negritude' movements developed in Africa and the United States in the 1920s. It had its zenith during the sixties, with the civil rights movement and the rise of 'Black power'. In Britain it has traditionally signified the rise of a collective Black identity in opposition to racism. In this context Black is constructed as a political colour and as an alternative to the imposition of a racist structures. Stuart Hall (1982) identified the link between the need for identity and class struggle:

> Sometimes, the class struggle in language occurred between two different terms: the struggle, for example, to replace the term 'immigrant' with the term 'Black'. But often, the struggle took the form of a different accenting of the same term: e.g. the process by means of which the derogatory colour 'black' became the enhanced value 'Black' (as in 'Black is Beautiful'). (1982, p59)

Identity politics has been about the shift of the Black self to a position free from the stigma of racism. It is through the media of language and music that local Black cultures in Britain are formulated. This popularity in language and music signifies a connection with the Black diaspora in the United States. Les Back (1991) shows in his study how the diasporic connections in Black identity help formulate a particular African-Caribbean youth culture in South London:

> I argue that young Black people plot the interconnections within the African diaspora through the cultural construction of Blackness. Blackness is not just defined in terms of Caribbean origins but through making connections with the entire diaspora. The prime medium through which this identification takes place is expressive Black musical culture. (1991, p151)

It was difficult (compared to my generation in the seventies) to label Black children in Township School according to the music they listened to. Eric, a fourth year student, says:

> I like jungle, soul, ragga and old-time reggae. No one in this school is into just one type of music. I play [work] as a DJ at the weekends and if I don't carry a wide selection of music then the crowd will get vex [annoyed].

Back (1991) stresses the importance:

> ...of understanding how Black young people navigate their notions of identity across national boundaries to connect with New World African diasporas and the critical transformations which are taking place in English/British national identity. This analysis contrasts with the literature that characterises Black youth as suffering from a crisis of identity... I maintain that while Black young people may experience a tension between the ways their identities are socially defined, they are also actively resolving the racist identity riddle, i.e. that Blackness and Englishness are mutually exclusive identities. (1991, p152)

This conclusion was supported by what most of the boys said when I asked them to describe their race and ethnicity:

> Jeff: I am a Black, English, Jamaican who has African roots and likes rap music.

Unconsciously, Jeff has taken me through most of the diaspora in one sentence. He never described this as a state of confusion. For him his hybrid identity was a matter of fact.

## Hair raising roots and routes to Blackness

According to Mercer (1994):

> From a perspective informed by theoretical work on sub-cultures (Stuart Hall and Tony Jefferson, 1976; Hebdige, 1979), the question of style can be seen as a medium for expressing the aspirations of Black people historically excluded from access to official social institutions of representation and legitimation in

urban, industrialised societies of the capitalist First World. Here, Black peoples of the African diaspora have developed distinct, if not unique, patterns of style across a range of cultural practices from music, speech, dance, dress and even cookery, which are politically intelligible as creative responses, to the experience of oppression and dispossession. Black hairstyling may thus be evaluated as a popular art form articulating a variety of aesthetic 'solutions' to a range of 'problems' created by ideologies of race and racism. (1994, p100)

One of the sites of conflict and alienation for African-Caribbean boys in Township School was the ban on certain Black hairstyles, made by the new Black headteacher, who linked haircuts styled with patterns, with an antagonistic attitude to school. This allowed some white teachers to openly devalue a key aspect of the ethnicity of African-Caribbean boys. As one teacher firmly told a boy in the corridor: 'Don't come back to school with hair looking like that; you know the rules – no ethnic haircuts.'

Hair has never simply been a biological fact for Black people; it is what can be called a social and political cultivation. The time, energy and money invested in hair care in Black communities now makes it the biggest Black commercial enterprise in Britain. Hair has become a medium of significant statements about self and society and the codes that bind them. Hair is a raw material, constantly processed by cultural practices. In this sense it also provides a map of the changing formations of Black sub-cultures.

The historic importance of hair care has its 'roots' and 'routes' in the white racism which surrounded slavery. Racism can be described as an ideological code in which physical characteristics are given negative social meaning. This was seen most clearly in eighteenth century portrayals of 'Black sambos' with huge broad noses and 'woolly' hair, and the perception of Black people as savage and ugly helped to justify slavery. The issue was taken up by the descendants of African slaves, even after emancipation. Therefore it is not uncommon to hear African-Americans and African-Caribbeans talking about 'good hair' when they describe a Black person's hair which is not too curly, and describing curly hair as 'tough', 'nappy head' or 'Nigger head'. In

Township School it was the African-Caribbean boys, not the white boys, who would tease boys who let their hair grow without any of the new 'stylisation'. This is a key point because the new styles of haircut in Township School would produce their own cultural hegemony which marginalised boys who did not conform – a point I develop later.

Historically, Black people's hair has been devalued along with the colour of their skin. In the context of the New World plantation societies, hair remained a powerful symbolic currency that indicated one's place in the racial hierarchy. Under this system the African attributes were devalued and the European elements could facilitate upward social mobility. As Mercer (1994) observes:

> In the complexity of this social code, hair functions as a key ethnic signifier because, compared with bodily shape or facial features, it can be changed more easily by cultural practices such as straightening. Caught on the cusp between self and society, nature and culture, the malleability of hair makes it a sensitive area of expression. It is against this historical and sociological background that we must evaluate the personal and political economy of Black hairstyles. (1994, p103)

It is in this sense that all Black people's hairstyles are political: they are invested with social and symbolic meaning. The two most graphic styles this century have been the Afro and Dreadlocks. Both have been seen as an epistemological break with the dominance of a white ethos. They both made a statement against the so-called 'artifice' of Europe in favour of the so-called 'natural' of 'Africa'. The Afro was an attempt to find 'solutions' to the devaluing of the Black physique, by just letting the hair grow 'naturally'; the same could be said about the Dreadlocks which came from Jamaica. However these 'solutions' were loaded with contradictions. They helped in the sixties and seventies to redefine Blackness and shift it away from its white bias. On the other hand in a relatively short time both styles were depoliticised and incorporated into the mainstream. They soon became a fashion statement in which Afros and Dreadlocks became another form of 'artifice'. Both styles were meant to be leading the war against Eurocentric artifice but in reality they were just as far from nature as straightened hair with a hot comb. As Mercer says:

Both these hairstyles were never just natural, waiting to be found: they were stylistically cultivated and politically constructed in a particular historical moment as part of a strategic contestation of white dominance and the cultural power of whiteness. (1994, p108)

These styles were another form of artifice, and they were also an example of how much of the discourse around Black nationalism is another expression of European romanticism. The eighteenth and nineteenth centuries were influenced not only by the philosophy of Hume and Hegel, who saw Africa as outside history and in a savage 'state of nature'. There was also the notion of the 'noble savage' popularised by Rousseau, who saw nature as good and beautiful. It was this Romantic notion that the 'Black power' protests of the sixties and the Rastafarian movement of the seventies imitated. Africa was seen as an ideal, or imaginary, landscape. The counter-hegemonic tactic of inversion appropriated a particular romantic vision of nature as a means of empowering the Black subject. By remaining within a dualistic logic of binary oppositionality to Europe and artifice, it can be argued that the break with European 'thinking' was a limited one. The key point is that all Black hairstyles are 'cultivated' and 'made' as political constructions. They speak of how Black people have been 'positioned' historically and how they 'position' themselves.

The paradoxes around the Afro and Dreadlocks provide significant clues to the workings of Black diaspora sub-cultures. There can be no claims to a pure African identity. The process of interculturation has left those in the Black diaspora affected by a variety of influences. In cultural terms what we have is not the retention of actual African artifacts but the reworking of a neo-African sensibility. The Afro and Dreadlocks are perceived by modern day Africans as creations of the diaspora. Ironically, it has been the influence of the hybrid music of Bob Marley that has given this style to present day African youth. The culture of the African diaspora is shaped by engagement with a dominant white culture together with an expressive link with neo-African styles and traditions – clearly illustrated by the development of reggae music and its Rastafarian philosophy (already discussed here). The sub-culture of the African-Caribbean boys at Township has been 'made' from within this framework. Mercer gives a succinct description of what he calls 'Black stylisation':

Diaspora practices of Black stylisation are intelligible at one 'functional' level as dialogic responses to the racism of the dominant culture, but at another level involve acts of appropriation from the same 'master' culture through which 'syncretic' forms of cultural expression have evolved. Syncretic strategies of Black stylisation, 'creolising' found or given elements, are writ large in Black codes of modern music like jazz, where elements such as scales, harmonies or even instruments like the piano or saxophone from Western cultural traditions are radically transformed by this neo-African, improvisational approach to aesthetic and cultural production. In addition there is another turn of the screw in these modern relations of interculturation when these creolised cultural forms are made use of by other social groups and then, in turn are all incorporated into mainstream 'mass' culture as commodities for consumption. Any analysis of Black style, in hair or any other medium, must take this field of relationships into account. (1994, p114).

The Black hairstyles worn by the African-Caribbean boys at Township School were much more self-consciously rooted in the diaspora than the Afro or Dreadlocks. The new styles make no overt attempt to be 'natural'. They incorporate an awareness of the contradictory conditions of interculturation. It is this self-consciousness that underscores their ambivalence and in turn marks them off as stylised signs of Blackness. This is best illustrated by the Funki-Dred style dreadlocks shaven short at the back and sides. Here was a style that expressed the 'funk' of America and the 'dread' of the Caribbean. The Mode Retro fade was the most popular – really a return to the sixties style of short back and sides. In Township this style was imitated by the white students who came to school with the short back and sides made popular by American GIs after the Second World War. So who, in this post-modern melee, was imitating who? The new styles have come in a variety of forms; some are mixtures of more than one tradition while others are retrievals from the past.

How, then, did the various hairstyles work as political and ethnic signifiers? How did they link with the various categories (attitude to school) of African-Caribbean boys? How did the staff react to these styles?

One of the ways the 'rebels' in Township School showed their defiance was to break the rules against haircuts with patterns, while the 'conformists' avoided stylised haircuts or simply sported (acceptable) short back and sides. The 'rebels' were also more likely to have Funki-Dreds or styles that copied rap and ragga musicians.

Those who did not conform at least to short back and sides were often ridiculed for being backwards when it came to fashion. The nature of this taunting was often racial/sexual, with words like 'nappy head', 'nigger head' 'batty man' (homosexual) and 'pussy'. This fits with Back's (1994) observation about how white apprentices' lack of power is linked with being feminine:

> My starting point is the complex ways in which gender and power are articulated in working-class cultures and the varying masculinities this produces. Where men are economically dependent on the sale of their labour, the expression of maleness provides a means to exert power; power is associated with maleness, its absence with feminisation. Such dualism appears in the feminisation of young male apprentices (Cohen 1988). (1994, p172)

The boys who suffered this 'feminisation' were not always 'conformists'; often they were boys who could not afford the frequent trips to the barber required for the latest stylised haircut. Although I have prioritised a semiotic reading of Black hairstyles and politics, the boys in Township School help us to see the other priorities of the Black hairdressing industry, exploiting consumers and creating gendered differentiations which are not always positive.

### Teacher reaction to Black hairstyles

On the whole, the predominantly white staff were not committed to preventing boys having patterns in their hair. It was not an issue with the former (white) headteacher and most of them felt that the new head's ruling was petty. However, they still claimed that the main reason for African-Caribbean boys having a disproportionate exclusion rate was their sub-culture. If Black hairstyles were a significant ethnic/cultural signifier, why did so many white teachers feel indifferent about them?

Staff reaction to Black hairstyles was based on two attitudes. The first was based on ignorance – Black hair was considered to be what I call a 'barren site'. I witnessed a PE teacher telling one student who was combing his hair in the changing room to hurry up because he had no hair to comb. The notion that curly Black hair needs no cultivation or treatment indicates a racist perception that Black men need the minimum of grooming.

The other attitude, shared by most of the Black teachers, was that the patterns looked good as a work of craft and added to the boys' self-esteem.

There are complex reasons for Mr Jones' objection to the patterned hairstyles of Black boys. He is making a wider cultural and political gesture, wanting the boys to adopt middle-class grooming which will help 'cultivate' them into a style appropriate for a career when they leave school. It is an attack on what he sees as the failure in African-Caribbean working-class culture in Britain to equip young men with drive and ambition to be socially mobile. Many were the times I heard Mr Jones telling an African-Caribbean boy to 'smarten up and look to me as a role model of how to make it'. The mission of Mr Jones is to save African-Caribbean boys from the 'street'. It can be seen as a racist discourse because he undermines the cultural expressions of African-Caribbean boys but not those of white boys. On the other hand, it could be taken as practical paternalism towards children in need of guidance. However, the point Mr Jones has missed is that teachers at Township continued to demand exclusions of African-Caribbean boys based on petty reasons and their own inadequacies – the fundamental reason why more African-Caribbean boys came into conflict with teachers. Black hairstyles, therefore, had a dual influence. They helped confirm a positive ethnic identity but were also a key factor in the display of an African-Caribbean masculine sub-culture that became an alternative to schooling.

For the boys at Township School, whether conformists or rebels, there was a realisation that one could derive cultural strength from the restlessness of not belonging. They had a contradictory attitude to Britain and being British: they loved and hated it at the same time. This 'nowhere land' was the inspiration for much of the dynamics of Black

British youth subculture since the mid seventies. Not feeling completely 'British' meant that the culture was open to many outside influences, mainly from the Caribbean and Black America. The triangle was completed by the local experience of working-class London, Birmingham or Liverpool. From the musical forms of lovers rock to jungle, something distinctly 'Black and British' has been carved out.

This culture has had different functions for different groups of Black boys in school. The first is that it has become an alternative to mainstream schooling and in some cases living. The mid-seventies adoption of Rastafarian influences, similarly, offered their many Black youths a source of strength after an extremely negative experience of school. The current ragga/rap style of youth culture does a similar job for some Black boys at Township. This alternative culture is often perceived by the school and the student as being incompatible or oppositional.

In a second model, certain cultural styles and patterns are adopted as natural; an affirmation of identity. In other words these boys perceive their sub-culture not as a weapon against the mainstream but as part of their identity. Yet they found themselves facing the same kinds of surveillance and opposition as the group who interpreted cultural styles as cultural wars.

The third group are boys who feel that they have to completely deny or reject affiliation with any Black cultural expression because it would not 'help them progress through school'. In some cases they would actively oppose all Black youth culture, linking it with crime and anti-school culture.

## Township School and Black masculinity

If hooks' interpretative model of phallocentrism can be applied to Township School, there must be evidence of what Mercer calls the 'dual dilemma' – in other words a 'machismo' based on the misdirection of negative resistance.

Mike Henry (rebel) is a core member of the Posse. He has one of the worst exclusion rates in the school, mainly for violent clashes with teachers and students. He was very much aware of how much power his 'tough image' had in Township:

TS: Do you belong to a gang or posse?

Mike: We have a group in school, but the real gang meets outside school – called the Jungle City Boys. Some kids from this school belong to this gang. We go around doing graffiti and mucking around. We go looking for girls.

TS: How do other students see you?

Mike: I think they see me as tough because I try not to act as a wimp.

TS: How would you describe a wimp?

Mike: Someone like my cousin Jeff Taylor. He avoids going to tuck, he avoids going to lunch – even though he wants to go. Another one is Dennis; he came in the first year with the reputation as a bad fighter. He's just a pussy, a woman who walks away from fights. And he's always grovelling to the teachers. I hate him.

TS: What do you feel teachers think about you?

Mike: They're always going on about my size. I know some of the weak teachers are really frightened of me. They are even scared of my Dad. One day I had a big argument on the stairs with Mr Fletcher (Antagonistic). He told me that if I threatened him that he would get his own mafia on me. I told this to my Dad who came down to the school. When Mr Fletcher heard he had come, he ran out of school, jumped in his car and ran off. My Dad would never hurt anyone; he just wanted to talk to the teacher about my behaviour. I think they are scared of Black people.

Like some other African-Caribbean boys at Township, Mike perceived being pro-school as unmanly. Jeff Taylor is not a real man because he does not get into trouble with the teachers. It is in a sexual framework that Mike describes his position and how he has been positioned. He dismisses conformist students as 'pussies' because they do not adopt his confrontational approach. He complains that the teachers are always referring to his size – a persistent problem for many African-Caribbean boys that illustrates the white teachers' obsession with Black bodies. This division of 'mind' and 'body' is what Connell (1989) calls 'differentiated masculinities'. He argues that:

The differentiation of masculinities occurs in relation to a school curriculum which organises knowledge hierarchically and sorts students into an academic hierarchy. By institutionalising academic failure via competitive grading and streaming, the school forces differentiation on the boys. But masculinity is organised on the macro scale – around social power. Social power in terms of access to higher education, entry to professions, command of communication, is being delivered to boys who are academic 'successes'. The reaction of the 'failed' is likely to be a claim to other sources of power, even other definitions of masculinity. Sporting prowess, physical aggression, sexual conquest may do. (1989, p295)

Mike has gathered many of his ideas about Black masculinity from both inside school and outside, through music as is evident from this comment:

TS: What have you got on your bedroom walls?

Mike: On my wall I have all my sporting certificates, and then on another wall I have music artists like Ninjaman.

TS: What do you like about Ninjaman?

Mike: I like the way he cusses other DJs. He's got his kind of style and he speaks a lot of badness. He speaks about guns and killing people. Kids like the way he swears. Most Black boys in school rate Ninja because he doesn't care what he says. He's a rebel.

TS: What do you think of the calls to have this kind of music banned?

Mike: A lot of white people are scared of Black people, of the hard image of the rappers. That's why it shouldn't be banned.

The causal explanation that links listening to the music of Ninjaman with becoming a disruptive pupil, cannot be 'proven' . In fact, as Mike has said, Ninjaman was popular amongst most of the African-Caribbean students, which of course included the conformists. However such cultural icons had most influence on those students who felt powerless in the schooling process. The Posse included students who were poor readers, those who had disruptive home lives and students who felt aggrieved because of teacher racism. Ninjaman, the icon of Black masculine phallus, is the inspiration for these students' partial rejection of a schooling culture. As Willis (1977) found in relation to white working-class boys:

> Most essentially this counter-culture is organised around the colonisation of symbolic spaces within the school, space left unpatrolled by the school authorities. The nature of this colonisation is the introduction of meanings and social ambience which subverts the school... This involves the development of a system of practices and a set of evaluative criteria, opposed to those sanctioned by the staff and aimed at maximum distancing from them. (1977, p35)

hooks would argue that some of the African-Caribbean boys 'colonised the symbolic spaces' within the school with the hallmark of destructive Black machismo. There was little evidence that teacher racism alone led these boys to adopt a culture of resistance to schooling. What was strongly evident was that many African-Caribbean boys were forced to deal with a disruptive home, ineffective teachers (of whom some were racist) and a market place ready to commodify and sell Black patriarchal and phallocentric images to young Black men.

## Conclusion

African-Caribbean local cultures have developed out of an engagement with a British nationalism which excluded and ignored the Black presence in Britain. Therefore the movement from Rasta to Ragga is a politically creative discourse which struggles with questions of identity, but at the same time it is changing and influencing the 'white' landscape of Britain. Paul Gilroy (1982) identifies three tendencies in defining modern Black British youth culture. First, it is a culture that has to reckon with its position within international networks: it is a diaspora culture with influences from America, the Caribbean and Africa. Second, it is a culture that has been created from diverse and contradictory elements and, third, it has evolved through various stages, linked in different ways to the pattern of capitalist development. It is this shift from being a critique of capitalism to being its servant, that has thrust Black diaspora youth culture into its greatest crisis since slavery. As Black males re-define the world on their terms, they have encountered criticism, primarily for the link between the contemporary plight of African-Caribbean men and the patriarchy and phallo-centricism within their sub-culture. This was taken up strongly by most of the teachers at Township School. This kind of African-Caribbean sub-culture has become a contradictory omen, which has survived the madness of popular British nationalism but at the same time has left Black boys uncertain about how they should act as males.

Sub-cultures worked on two levels in Township School. They confirmed a rich complex ethnicity, which benefited the African-Caribbean boys in establishing their social identity. This ethnicity was not 'fixed' or 'natural'; it was an artifice which incorporated multiple influences from around the diaspora as well as reworking themes from the past. In this sense clothes, music and hairstyles become ethnic and political signifiers. It is from this position that a 'politics of resistance' acquires its roots. The sub-cultures around the Black power era of the sixties and the Rastafarian movement of the seventies are important examples of how Black youth have retained their self-esteem and challenged the authority of white dominance.

On the negative side, however, hooks' (1992) model of Black phallo-centrism shows that both on the level of street sub-culture and in the scholarship of Black nationalism there is a self-destructive discourse that seeks to replace a white dominant patriarchy with a Black phallo-centrism. She says:

> Black men and women who espouse cultural nationalism continue to see the struggle for Black liberation largely as a struggle to recover Black manhood. In her essay 'Africa On my Mind: Gender, Counter Discourse and African-American Nationalism', E. Frances White shows that overall Black nationalist perspectives on gender are rarely rooted purely in the Afrocentric logic they seek to advance, but rather reveal their ties to white paradigms: 'In making appeals to conservative notions of appropriate gender behaviour, African-American nationalisms reveal their ideological ties to other nationalist movements, including European and Euro-American bourgeois nationalists over the past 200 years. These

parallels exist despite the different class and power base of these movements.' (1992, p106-107)

It is in this sense that the ethnic signals from some of the boys, namely the rebels, offers a destructive way of thinking. Its only logic is the offensive language of misogyny, homophobia or hyper-heterosexuality.

The question of how this negative aspect of sub-culture influences schooling must be seen in the context of a schooling system that seeks to make African-Caribbean boys intellectually powerless and/or bodily powerful.

# 8

# The case of two masculinities

*Follow me and you'll be a success* – Mr Jones, Headteacher at Township

In Township School there was a range of Black masculinities but two models dominated the psyche of Black boys and the discourses of the teachers. I have called these the 'McDonald model' and the 'Yard man' model. These are not necessarily accurate representations of real lives; rather they are ideals and discourses which push and pull the soul. They are dominant models which position Black boys into the madness of being either/or and nothing else.

Calling the conformist ideal the McDonald model was based on an article I wrote for *The Voice* (April 23, 1996). Commenting on the appointment by the Government of newsreader Trevor McDonald to lead their 'Better English Campaign', I argued that he should also take on the language and power issues that surround so-called proper English. The government had picked a 'Conformist' figure to propagate the notion that the key problem with English is that young people are not using it properly. What about the way language carries certain discourses which makes one group powerful and another powerless? I argued that:

> Trevor needs to stop being the 'nice Black Englishman' and turn his campaign into an assault on the oppressiveness of the English language and campaign to clean it up. How, in too many instances, 'Black' is unnecessarily linked to the negative, how the language used to describe disabled people like 'invalid' has a history that sees disabled people as freaks or cursed by God.

Methinks these objectives would be too political for the acceptable face of Mr McDonald. Sewell (1996)

Reaction to these comments, particularly from the Right, was absolute outrage. Somehow I had touched a national nerve. Trevor was the Black man that the white majority considered our best role model. To criticise this ideal was seen as a major assault on the conformist model of Black masculinity: the neutered male that does not bite but can carry the standard of England, including her language. The *Twickenham Informer*, a local newspaper, showed a picture of me next to a smiling Trevor McDonald, under the headline: 'Only one of these chaps can be regarded a gent'. During the week after the article appeared I received a sack full of racist mail. A paragraph of one letter encapsulates how Black masculine oppression works through two oppressive discourses, one 'conformist' and the other 'rebellion':

> At least Trevor tries to mix with his friends, behave decently, indeed he probably behaves better and speaks better than most of us whites, so if that is not enough to help raise our opinion of Blacks, what the hell is, or would you prefer him to drag himself onto the set in dreadlocks, unshaved, sweating, baggy shirts and trousers, mumbling in pidgin English, and ending every sentence with Yeah Man? (a man from Dorset, 1996)

So Black masculinity must either be like Trevor McDonald or else it becomes a caricature of the street rebel. Most boys in Township hated both extremes. Neither related to their real lives and experiences. They were imposed masculinities which came from teachers and peer groups. Eric, one of the hedonists, rejects school because of a number of complex reasons, some to do with his home background. However, it was the inability of many teachers to perceive him as anything other than a street rebel that led to multiple conflicts. One teacher told me that because Eric's Dad wore gold and drove a 'flash' car, he was giving his son the wrong signals. It showed that he supported petty crime and saw school as a waste of time. No one in the school had any detailed information about Eric's Dad. What was obvious, though was the 'disrespect' that this teacher showed Eric: Eric had just come back to school after a long period of truanting and the teacher's first words to him were: 'What are you doing back here? I'd thought you'd be in prison by now'.

It is often too easy when making observations of this kind to be naive about the real context. Eric had been involved in crime both in school and outside. This boy was no angel. However, he did want to do well in school but found that the attitude of his teachers changed from the time he was thirteen. He relates this to 'looking big and muscular for my age'. His form teacher confirmed this and said that too many teachers began to 'patronise' a boy who was both physically and mentally mature. Eric felt that he got on better with teachers who showed him 'respect'. We can sympathise with Eric, who, because of his home background, had experiences which matured him quickly even at 15. He needed teachers who appreciated this and did not speak to him as if he were a seven year old – which many did because of their own insecurity. They had a 'Street hood' perception of Eric, which denied the complex picture of his background and needs. He was not asking teachers to compromise their standards; he needed them to be flexible and respectful of his individual need.

The ways in which teachers and peer groups police these two oppressive masculinities, is clearly explained by Foucault (1980):

> In thinking of the mechanisms of power, I am thinking rather of its capillary form of existence, the point where power reaches into the very grain of individuals, touches their bodies and inserts itself into their action and attitudes, their discourses, learning processes and everyday lives. (1980, p39)

Foucault described disciplinary power as not just an abstract concept but one that functions in all actions, particularly at the level of the body. Foucault (1977) argued that this disciplinary power emerged with the advent of modern institutions and extended throughout society, such that we can see a continuity of power relations in schools, hospitals, prisons, factories and other institutions. Foucault says:

> A certain significant generality moved between the least irregularity and the greatest crime: it was no longer the offence, the attack on the common interest, it was the departure from the norm, the anomaly; it was this that haunted the school, the court, the asylum or the prison. (1977, p299).

Foucault talks about eight major techniques of power, namely: surveillance, normalisation, exclusion, classification, distribution, individualisation, totalisation and regulation. It is my contention that in Township School these were the techniques of power that forced African-Caribbean boys into one of two 'ideals' or 'norms' of masculinity which they were in most cases unhappy inhabiting. The McDonald man and the Yard man were the swords of Damocles held over their heads.

## Surveillance

There was evidence in Township to support the notion that African-Caribbean boys experienced greater scrutiny from their teachers compared to other ethnic groups. This was confirmed by one white teacher who said:

> TS: Are there any groups of boys that you find particularly threatening?

> Ms Brookes: The Black boys are a lot bigger than the white boys. I have to keep an extra eye out for them because they will either beat up first years or try and nick something.

The notion of being watched was an experience that African-Caribbean boys felt operated continually in other sites.

> Victor: It's like white people have got eyes in the back of their heads. Everytime I go into a shop up Oxford Street, you can see the salesperson getting nervous. Sometimes they don't hide it and just stare you out like you is some criminal or tea-leaf.

Victor's comment indicates how the wider perception of African-Caribbean youth as muggers and violent informs a particular image in school. Any expression of 'Black Culture' could be perceived as a threat. Headteacher Mr Jones ignored the wearing of pony-tails by white boys but heavily policed Black boys who wore patterns in their hair because this did not conform to his idealised image of a successful Black male.

Surveillance came also from many white boys in Township, who felt that 'acting Black' was being anti-school and was fuelled by a masculinity that they envied.

Township School was set in a part of the city where one could experience racist attacks, and yet it was known for close relationships between Black and white. This paradox came out in the youth sub-cultures of the school. As Hebdige (1983) noted, the impact of African-Caribbean youth culture on white youth was ambiguous but not pro-gressive – as, for example skinheads in the sixties incorporated Jamaican music to bolster their white nationalism. However, it is admiration of a phallocentric Black masculinity that most disturbs the psyche of white youths – as remarked by Back (1994) in his essay, 'The 'White Negro' revisited':

> For white young men, the imaging of Black masculinity in heterosexual codes of 'hardness' and 'hypersexuality' is one of the core elements which attract them to Black masculine style. How-ever, the image of Black sexuality as potent and 'bad' is alarm-ingly similar to racist notions of dangerous/violent 'Black muggers'. When racist ideas are most exposed, in situations where there is intimate contact between Black and white men, stereo-typical ideas can be reproduced, 'dressed up' as positive characteristics to be emulated. White identification with Black people can become enmeshed within the discourse of the 'noble savage', which renders Blackness exotic and reaffirms Black men as a 'race apart'. (1994, p179)

Black phallocentrism has a mirror effect on the Black male subject. He positions himself in phallocentric terms and this is confirmed by the obsessive jealousy of other groups. African-Caribbean boys are not passive subjects in the face of racialised and gendered stereotyping. They are active agents in discourses which appear to be seductively positive but are in essence racist. This leads to a strong confirmation of an identity that has its source in the dislocation of Black and white masculinity.

bell hooks shows how white men seeking alternatives to a patriarchal masculinity turned to Black men, particularly Black musicians. Norman Podhoretz (1963) in his essay 'My Negro Problem – And Ours' talks about white male fascination with Blackness, and Black masculinity:

Just as in childhood I envied Negroes for what seemed to me their superior masculinity, so I envy them today for what seems to be their superior physical grace and beauty. I have come to value physical grace very highly and I am now capable of aching with all my being when I watch a Negro couple on the dance floor, or a Negro playing baseball or basketball. They are on the kind of terms with their own bodies that I should like to be on with mine, and for that precious quality they seem blessed to me. (1963, p6)

In Township there was evidence not only that teachers made particular surveillance because of their wider 'mythic' perception of an African-Caribbean challenge but also that this came from Black boys themselves as they policed each other. White boys, too, looked to the Yard man ideal of Black masculinity as a model for their own development.

## Normalisation

Foucault (1977) highlighted the importance of 'normalising judgement' or normalisation in the functioning of modern disciplinary power. He explained that such normalising judgement often occurs through comparison, such that individual actions are refered 'to a whole that is – at once a field of comparison, a space of differentiation and the principle of a rule to be followed' (p182). In Township this 'normalising' was racialised and can be defined as: invoking, requiring, setting or conforming to a standard – defining the normal' In our case this normality was either McDonald man or Yard man.

It would be mistaken to think that the whole process of teaching was not to invoke sets of norms. What is at issue here is that African-Caribbean boys come under a certain 'colour of normalisation' that expects students to perceive even harmless cultural expressions like bopping as a sign of defiance.

My analysis at Township showed that that Black masculinity is a subordinated masculinity shaped by many contradictions. The internalisation and incorporation of the dominant definitions of masculinity have arisen in an attempt to contest conditions of dependency, racism and powerlessness. Phallocentrism is an attempt to recuperate some degree of power and influence under the subordinated conditions created by racism. Staples (1982) calls this the development of the 'Macho' or 'dual dilemma'. Mercer (1994) describes this process as a:

> ...form of misdirected or 'negative' resistance, as it is shaped by the challenge to the hegemony of the socially dominant white male, yet assumes a form which is in turn oppressive to Black women, children and indeed, to Black men themselves, as it can entail self-destructive acts and attitudes. (1994, p143)

The normalisation did not work negatively only for the Rebels. It was also detrimental to the self-esteem of the Conformists, who paid a heavy price for trying 'to make it'.

## Exclusion

Of all the categories or techniques of power, exclusion was the most relevant to African-Caribbean boys at Township (and across the nation). The category of 'exclusion' is used here to mark the obverse of normalisation – the defining of the pathological. Foucault refers to exclusion as a technique for tracing the limits that will define difference: defining boundaries, setting zones. Exclusionary techniques are pervasive in pedagogy, as demonstrated in Tyler's (1993) genealogical research which found that, even in preschool settings, the dispositions and behaviours of some children are constructed as 'better', while others are quickly excluded or constructed as 'other'.

Ms Williams, a Black teacher at Township School, shifts the responsibility for exclusions away from teachers and directly on to the 'machismo' sub-culture of the boys. She says:

> Many African-Caribbean parents find it hard to accept that the reason for the disproportionate number of excluded African-Caribbean boys rests solely on the fact that African-Caribbean boys are more likely to do things that warrant exclusion.

> My evidence for this is based on the attitude and behaviour of the African-Caribbean boys who I went to school with and that of those in this school. Though it pains me, as an African-Caribbean myself, to admit that the exclusion of African-Caribbean pupils is based solely on the attitude of the pupils themselves, I feel even

more strongly that to deny this fact is more destructive in both the short and the long term.

The African-Caribbean community is so obsessed with trying to prove that teachers and schools are racist, instead of trying to work out strategies to ensure success for African-Caribbean pupils despite the system. Then it will be energy and time well spent. What is less documented are the reasons why African-Caribbean males feel the need to misbehave in ways that will ensure ultimate exclusion. This image is based on their physique, the way they speak and also on their perceived culture: the rap, the dress, the films, the posters. In fact this image is totally incorrect. African-Caribbean males are actually very insecure.

Although Ms Williams has underestimated the influence of teacher racism in Township School, she confirms hooks' analysis that marginalised masculinity, when subject to racism, leads some African-Caribbean boys to adopt a phallocentrism they feel has been denied to them.

The reasons given for many of the exclusions of African-Caribbean boys in Township concerned their 'violent' and 'aggressive behaviour'. In too many cases this behaviour was open to 'interpretation' by teachers and not a clear breach of school rules. Mr Lewis is critical of this mechanism and suggests that there are too many exclusions:

> Mr Lewis: The problem with this school is that there are too many exclusions for what appears to be petty matters. One can't help wondering why it is that in one class a boy behaves brilliantly and in another he is clashing with the teacher. Boys need to have a safe and consistent experience in class with teachers who respect them and can motivate them. The exclusion button is pushed too easily in this school... it's not the answer. Also teachers are missing the subtle defiance and racism of many of the white kids. They cause just as much vandalism as anyone else and are less likely to be challenged over school uniform.

There is something fundamentally wrong with an institution that is 'excluding' its members, even temporarily, at the rate of two to three a week. Township had no targets or programmes to reduce this number and so sustained a policy that saw high African-Caribbean exclusions as inevitable.

## Classification

The author of this book is immensely concerned least he is adding to the pathology of African-Caribbean boys – by yet again making them the subject of a study. According to Foucault (1977), classification occurs when groups are differentiated from one another. This can be accomplished by classifying 'them' or by classifying 'oneself'. Two aspects of classification appeared to be important in Township. The first was the category 'African-Caribbean' and the second was the issue of Knowledge and Curriculum.

There was a sense in Township that the term 'African-Caribbean', although a positive category to describe a certain group of Black boys, was used only in a negative context. Township, even with a Black headteacher, had limited celebration of African-Caribbean culture and the term: 'African-Caribbean was usually only used in a context of discipline or the identification of a suspect.

There is also a popular tendency to classify Black boys as an 'endangered species' (Kunjufu 1985). The evidence in Township was never this stark. There was a range of boys, and they operated at different levels. In terms of exam results they slightly out-performed the white boys. Studies are not showing effort made and the success achieved by many African-Caribbean boys who do not get excluded. Recent figures (1996) have shown how white boys are just as disillusioned with schooling but are talking with their feet. This highlights the role of class as well as race in explaining poor performance. This book shows the real difficulty there is in making bland classifications for any group of children. Many of the Township boys went on to a college of Further Education (see Table 7, page 74) to complete their studies and not on the street to become muggers.

One can not deny that classification is an important and productive mechanism for producing knowledge. However, in its application and construction of particular notions of normality, its repressive potential is also clear. There was no attempt at the level of the curriculum to relate knowledge to the experiences of the boys. The implication was that there was a hierarchy of knowledge with the standard Eurocentric curriculum at the top, and the 'knowledge' that the boys had was devalued or wholly rejected. This particularly annoyed Eric:

Eric: When I asked my history teacher why we keep having to learn about Henry VIII, he said because that's the way life is. I was tired of seeing white faces in all my books. We know nothing about the Caribbean or Africa. We don't even know about Black people who lived in England. We might as well be all white.

## Distribution

Foucault also argues that the distribution of bodies in space – arranging, isolating, separating, ranking – contributes to the functioning of disciplinary power.

Township operated mixed-ability teaching and no streaming until year 10, when students were grouped by ability in maths and English. African-Caribbean students commented on the racial divide that existed in some classes. I observed a prevailing tendency for African-Caribbean boys to go to the back of the class:

TS: Why do you sit at the back of the class?

Devon: I like to sit at the back because I can talk to my friends.

TS: What do you think of those who sit at the front?

Devon: They are boffins who the teacher always likes. If you check it, most Black youth will go to the back. We just leave the rest to stay at the front.

There was an issue here of self-esteem – to be at the back of the class, is reminiscent of Black people in pre-civil rights America being compelled to sit at the back of buses and here are boys who, even if they have high ability decided to go to the back of the class. This distribution of bodies was different in classes where the teacher was perceived to be supportive of African-Caribbean students. For example Devon, despite what he has said, sat in the front for Mr Lewis' class, where he produced good work and made positive contributions to discussion.

The use of distribution as a technique was particularly pronounced in the physical education site, with its sanctioned and very visible manipulation of bodies. Mercer and Julien (1995) talk about the 'paradoxical' way this has worked for Black boys:

A central strand in history is the way Black men have incorporated a code of 'macho' behaviour in order to recuperate some degree of power over the condition of powerlessness and dependency in relation to the white male slave master. The contradiction that this dialectic gives rise to continues in contemporary Britain once we consider images of Black males in political debates around 'law' and 'order'... This paradoxical situation is played out in other areas of popular culture such as sport. Classical racism involved a logic of dehumanisation in which African people were defined as having bodies not minds: in this way the super-exploitation of the Black body as a muscle machine could be justified. Vestiges of this are active today in schools, for instance, where teachers may encourage Black kids to take up sport because they're seen as academic underachievers. But on the other hand there are concrete advantages to be gained from appearing to play up to such general expectations. (Mercer and Julien, 1995)

There was no evidence in Township that Black boys were particularly encouraged into sports as distinct from academic rigour. In fact many of the PE teachers felt that they had an advantage over other teachers because they had a chance to get to know the boys on an informal level. Travelling for miles on Saturday morning to an away match broke down some of the formal strictures in teacher-student power relations.

A more interesting distribution of bodies among the students themselves was found in the playground. Football was dominated by Black boys, with a token presence of white boys. This could be explained by two cultural factors. Many white boys used the break times as an opportunity to leave the school and truant. Secondly, there was a distribution of bodies such that the Asian boys tended to play hand tennis, chase or play computer games indoors with the younger students.

There was no evidence to support the notion that Asian boys did not like football. On the contrary, it was a major interest and they enjoyed playing football during organised PE sessions. What they were not permitted to do was play in the main game of football with the African-Caribbean boys. I asked Dennis, a year 10 African-Caribbean boy, if he thought the Asian kids were good at football:

Dennis: No way, if they played with us they'd get mashed down. We're just too tough for them. Some of them are good goalies, like Rajinder. But they are really like girls. Plus none of them can run. They got no speed. If the Black kids were to play the Asian kids then we would leave them crying for mercy.

The Asian kids also believed in a kind of superiority in African-Caribbean athleticism and sexuality. This was one reason why they were content to play hand tennis at break time. Ali says:

Ali: Black kids are the best fighters in this school. They are also the best footballers and they've got the most women.

TS: How do you feel about that?

Ali: Well I suppose I'm jealous but there are plenty of good footballers who are Asian. They don't get a chance to see it.

TS: Why do you think the Black boys are better at football?

Ali: I think it's because they are bigger and they can bully us around.

The two quotes illustrate how bodies are ranked and separated not by the teachers but by the students themselves, as they each buy into negative images of the other. Dennis had failed to account for the many African-Caribbean boys who do not like football and the many Asian boys who were good at it. Ali admits that his admiration was based on jealousy but he still perceives African-Caribbean boys as a threat.

## Individualisation and Totalisation

Schooling by its very definition is about conformity. There was evidence to show, however, that African-Caribbean students at Township experienced an extra pressure from teachers and their peers not to be an individual but to act according to the stereotypes of their ethnic group. When applying the concept of individualisation we see how this technique of power can work against African-Caribbean boys.

If individualisation means giving individual character to oneself, then totalisation is its opposite. It means the specification of collectivities, giving collective character. There is, however, a close relationship between these two concepts and one needs to understand both sides of the coin.

In Township, 'individualisation/totalisation' power play was clearly operating when students assigned certain behaviours as acting white and others as acting Black. African-Caribbean students provided the following indicators of acting White:

SPEECH:
talk proper
don't talk slang or curse
talking with no 'street accent'
using big words

MUSIC:
listen to White music, classical music, heavy metal or rock music

DRESS:
don't wear training shoes
always wearing school uniform
wear shoes from Clarks

SCHOOL:
you suck up to the teachers
grovelling to teachers
get good grades
always do your work
bunk off lessons

OTHER BEHAVIOURS:
you only date white girls
have lots of white friends, hang around with white people
act stuck up
Speak like Trevor McDonald

Apart from 'bunking off' lessons most African-Caribbean boys perceived white children to be conformist and African-Caribbean children to be essentially rebellious. Therefore any African-Caribbean child not acting like the collective (totalisation) was regarded as someone who acts white. It is another example of dual masculinity, where there are only two extremes the (acting white) McDonald man and the rebellious Yard man.

## Regulation

While all the previous techniques of power could be seen to have regulating effects, this category was used specifically to code incidents in which regulation was explicit. Hence, regulation is defined as 'controlling by rule, subject to restrictions, invoking a rule, including sanction, reward, punishment.'

In Township the majority of African-Caribbean boys were excluded not for breaking explicit rules but for 'crimes' that were open to interpretation, for example, violent and disruptive behaviour. What was key in the perception of many teachers was that African-Caribbean boys were the ones who broke most of the school regulations or had the propensity to do so. The irony for most of these boys was that their convictions were rarely for breaking any 'explicit' rule. They were trapped by techniques of power which had regulating effects.

Put simply, African-Caribbean boys were in a double bind that principally involved their teachers and their peers. They suffered a disproportionate amount of disciplinary power, which their teachers (prison guards, courts, psychiatrists, police) justified by their imagined perception of Black masculinity.

In the next chapter I explore ways of cleansing the soul of these 'false imaginings' and breaking down powerful obstacles that occur not only at the level of school but are linked also to the construction of 'self'.

# 9

# Towards Solutions:
# practical strategies for teachers
# and students

Inward stretch, outward reach – *Rex Nettleford*

This chapter attempts to connect the important theoretical work on normative masculinities and schooling to the practical everyday world of the classroom. What can we, as teachers and administrators, do to ensure that African-Caribbean boys get an education that is rich, fulfilling and free from racial/sexual injustice? The practices of both teachers and students need attention. The research in Township showed that both parties need to reflect seriously on themselves. It is really a question of ownership: teachers being willing to own their racialised/sexualised perceptions of Black boys and, equally, Black boys coming to terms with the normative notions of masculinity that act as an oppressive and repressive agent on their schooling.

In Township the process of schooling brought two negative forces into collision. It was not only Black boys who were to blame for conflict but also many of the teachers, who resorted to 'blaming the victim' rather than dealing with their own prejudices and shortcomings.

How can we reduce the number of exclusions of African-Caribbean boys? What can administrators, teachers and the children themselves do to counter the complex oppressive and repressive schooling process that these boys face every day? This chapter tries to answer some of these questions, indicating approaches that could usefully be taken by 1. the school, 2. the teachers and 3. the students. The students are –

deliberately – the main focus of this section. Teacher attitude and race has been tackled well by other authors, notably Richardson (1990) and Mac an Ghaill (1988). There is a wealth of race awareness literature for teachers but little that gives practical ideas for working specifically with Black boys. Much of what this chapter offers has been gleaned by good classroom practice and in-service training sessions. Here are ideas and strategies that have worked with particular groups of Black boys and their teachers – not a universal answer to the complex problems outlined in previous chapters. The following ideas, that have worked for me in a given context, are arranged under three major headings: 1. School and policy issues; 2. Teachers; and 3. Students.

## I. SCHOOL AND POLICY ISSUES

### The making of a policy that acknowledges privilege and values 'difference'

Too many multicultural and antiracist policies are tokenistic documents which no one owns. There is a need to probe the silence and get behind the policy text. In many cases schools are embarrassed about even making reference to antiracism. They may adopt a more strident tone over issues like sex discrimination and bullying but become opaque when it comes to the vexed issue of race and racism. Sarah Neal (1995) sums it up well:

> A prevailing feature which characterised the case studies' equal opportunities policy texts was their extensive and shared use of 'condensation symbols' (Edelman 1964), 'slogan systems' (Apple, 1977) or 'essentially contested concepts' (Gallie, 1956).

> Condensation symbols refer to terms or phrases that contain a particular emotional impact and positive associations while at the same time retaining an elasticity which means that they are open to different and often competing interpretations. (Neal, 1996, p6)

This symbolic antiracism would never be able to speak to the 'messy' everyday world of 'real' schools. As Blase (1991) has argued:

> Political theorists have argued that rational and systems models of organisations have failed to account for complexity, instability and conflict in organisational settings. They contend that such models also ignore individual differences, for example, in values, ideologies, choices, goals, interests, expertise, history, motivation and interpretation – factors central to the 'micropolitical perspective. (Blase, 1991)

So how are we going to make antiracist policies more relevant to the real world of schools? The first requirement is that constructing a policy becomes a democratic activity and involves the whole school. We need a new language for antiracist and multicultural issues because, I would argue, the old words have been contaminated by the symbolic antiracism of the left and the destructive responses of the new Right. The new language will need to be powerful and not water down real issues of oppression, power and privilege. Words like 'diversity' still carry weight and so do 'fairness' and 'justice'. A major new development for a school like Township should be to draft a policy for social justice. The process would involve a committee of students and teachers, who would table their concerns and issues so that a 'real' policy came out of the struggles within the school. A working party of students and teachers, meeting separately and together, would draft the policy and monitor its progress. The importance of student involvement in this context is stressed by Anderson and Herr:

> ...regardless of how well meaning, educational institutions cannot move from 'soft' definitions of multiculturalism to more sophisticated ones without an understanding of the role the educational institution plays in the identity struggles of its students. The interface of dominant institutional norms and the struggle of students to form an identity constitutes a micro-political struggle, which takes place under the noses, but outside the consciousness, of most educational institutions. In addition.... when various voices within the students are not legitimated by the larger institution, even the students themselves lose access to those parts of themselves that might challenge institutional assumptions and explanations, thereby effectively 'silencing' themselves. (1994, p45)

The second requirement is that the document relates to the complex and changing notions of race and its interplay with other contingent subject positions. This would involve taking on the concerns of students from the full range of communities represented in the school, including the white working class. The Burnage report is emphatic in its advocacy of an antiracism that positively engages all students:

> Since the assumption is that Black students are the victims of the immoral behaviour of white students, white students almost inevitably become the 'baddies'. The operation of the (doctrinaire 'moral') antiracist policies almost inevitably results in white students (and their parents) feeling 'attacked' and all being seen as 'racist', whether they are ferret-eyed fascists or committed antiracists or simply children with a great store of human feeling and warmth who are ready to listen and learn and to explore their feelings towards one another (Macdonald et al, 1989, p347)

The third requirement of a policy is that it should inspire research, review and self-reflection so as to keep policy in line with the changing context of school.

## Conflict resolution

Conflict resolution is a constructive approach to interpersonal and intergroup conflict that helps people with opposing positions work together to arrive at mutually acceptable compromise solutions. The term also refers to the body of knowledge and practice developed to realise this approach. Conflict resolution programmes can encompass a variety of strategies. They roughly fall into two categories: programmes in which the disputants work among themselves to settle their differences and programmes in which a mediator (an uninvolved, impartial 'third party) helps the disputants to reach agreement.

Conflict resolution programmes are characterised by: active listening, where participants summarise what each has said to ensure that it has been fully understood; co-operation between disputants; acceptance of each other's differences; and creative problem solving, which takes into account each disputant's position. The programmes should emphasise learning from experience, with teachers serving as facilitators and coaches. Through role-playing and a variety of team projects, students learn how to deal with anger and how to work with others at win-win solutions. Schools with mediation programmes use students as mediators so they can learn from experience how conflicts can be resolved peacefully.

A good model of a conflict resolution programme would operate on three levels:

**Lessons in conflict management**: At least once a week Personal and Social Education lessons deal with conflict resolution. Schools with acute problems need to time-table more time. Lessons cover intergroup relations, co-operative learning and dispute resolution techniques. As well as setting aside these dedicated lessons, classroom teachers are encouraged to infuse conflict resolution skills into other subject areas. This could incorporate History, Geography and Science (How does nature resolve conflicts?).

**Peer mediation**: Mediation provides schools with an alternative to traditional disciplinary practices. The students involved, whether as mediators or disputants, learn new ways of handling conflict. In mediation, trained students help their classmates identify the problems behind the conflicts and find solutions. Peer mediation is not about establishing who is right or wrong. Instead, students are encouraged to move beyond the immediate conflict and learn how to get along with each other – an important skill in today's world. Peer mediators ask the disputing students to tell their stories and ensure that points are clearly made and understood.

Certain problems such as assault and other criminal activities are unsuitable for peer mediation, but common situations involving name-calling, rumours, bumping into students in the hallways and bullying have been successfully resolved in this way. So far peer mediation has operated mainly at secondary level. However, children as young as five can and should be taught conflict resolution techniques. We do this as parents, when we encourage siblings who have been fighting to share their toys and make friends.

**Training**: For any conflict resolution programme to be effective there must be: a training course for teachers; mediator training for interested students, parents and staff; and 'outreach seminars' to help all students become aware that non-violent techniques are available at the school for resolving conflicts. Although this may well require some funds, parents might be willing to be trained, so that they can help in future programmes on a voluntary basis.

## Curriculum policy and planning

That erasing stigma improves Black achievement is perhaps the strongest evidence that stigma is what depresses it in the first place. This is no happy realisation. But it lets in a ray of hope: whatever other factors also depress Black achievement, poverty and a wider social isolation may be substantially overcome in a schooling atmosphere that reduces racial/gender and other vulnerabilities, not through unrelenting niceness or ferocious regimentation but by 'wiseness' – by seeing value and acting on it. Goffman (1963) used 'wise' to describe people who do not themselves bear the stigma of a given group but are accepted by the group. These are people in whose eyes the full humanity of the stigmatised is visible, people in whose eyes they feel less vulnerable. For the boys in Township School these were the teachers they 'respected'.

One factor which makes schooling unwise is the basic assimilationist offer made by schools to Black boys. You can be valued and rewarded in school and society, the schools say to these students, but first you must master the culture and ways of mainstream Britain and, since mainstream (as it is represented) is essentially white, this means you must give up many characteristics of being Black – styles of speech and appearance, value priorities, preferences – at least in mainstream settings like school.

Accordingly, curriculum change and adaptation would be 'wise'. The particulars of Black life and culture – art, literature, political and social perspective, music – must be presented in the mainstream curriculum of British schooling, not consigned to special days, weeks, or even months of the year, or to special topics, courses and programmes aimed essentially at Black children. Such channelling carries the disturbing message that the material is not of general value. And this does two 'unwise' things: it wastes the power of this material to alter our images of the British mainstream – continuing to frustrate Black identification with it – and it excuses in white people and others a huge ignorance of their own society. The true test of democracy, Ralph Ellison (1952) has said, 'is... the inclusion – not assimilation – of the Black man.'

Barbara Ellis (1996) argues that there are no subjects in the curriculum that cannot incorporate an African-Caribbean perspective. I have expanded her model and in the process I have discovered/recovered a more inclusive curriculum, which can be taught to all children (see page 194).

## ART

- African influences on Art
- graffiti
- using natural materials (dyes, shells)
- history of art/ popular fashion
- design
- philosophy and values of art from the black Diaspora

## GEOGRAPHY

- map of the Caribbean
- Critical geography – deconstructing the negative
- migration
- urban development

## PHYSICAL EDUCATION

- Black contribution to sport now
- history and struggles of famous Black sports people
- encouraging boys to look at alternative sports like fencing and horse riding

## MATHEMATICS

- Egyptian/African counting systems
- maths for life – economics, informal saving schemes (known as the pardoner)

## HISTORY

- The Arawak Indians
- thematic history which looks at concepts like 'the sea' and shows how historically it has been a transmitter of culture. Look at the development of areas like East London, Bristol and Liverpool
- Resistance to slavery
- Famous Black figures
- Colonialism
- Migration to Britain
- Local history Black perspective.

## RELIGIOUS EDUCATION

- Caribbean religions
- African religious systems and expressions
- history of the Black church in America and the UK.

## DRAMA

- Work of Black dramatists
- images of black people in British and American television.

## TECHNOLOGY

- influence of new technology on local populations
- intermediate technology
- use of local materials in developing countries' technology.

## ENGLISH

- Caribbean Language and dialects
- African writers
- Popular/classic writers from Diaspora
- Critical study of lyrics of popular Black music
- Language and power.

## MUSIC & CULTURE

- origins of raggae
- African music
- origins of calypso
- famous singers from the diaspora
- black music influences on the development of popular music styles.

## SCIENCE

- history and contribution of Black scientists
- medicines and herbs from Africa and the Caribbean.

## PSE

- racial identity development or deconstruction
- conflict resolution.

## 2. TEACHERS

The eighties and nineties will be known as the time when teachers faced unprecedented attacks on their professionalism and ability to maintain standards. This section is not intended to add to the criticism. Rather, I wish to share good practice and outline strategies by which teachers can be more effective in situations of difficulty. Teachers should be encouraged to engage in action or practitioner research on issues of social justice policy. Equal opportunity and antiracist issues should be the subject of professional development days.

In the summer of 1996 I worked with an inner-city school on tackling their escalating rise in exclusions of African-Caribbean boys. Instead of preaching at the teachers I invited them to consider a number of issues about their school which could be the source of the problem. They did an exercise in groups, in which they had to: 'Design a school which aims at getting as many African-Caribbean boys excluded as is legally possible', considering discipline, ethos, policies, curriculum, parents, teacher attitudes and communications. These are the points made in response by two of the groups:

### Group A

- An attitude that connects African-Caribbean boys with a wider 'criminal' profile of Black men
- All the staff are white
- No antiracist policy
- Curriculum not adapted
- No parental involvement except of a negative kind
- Didactic style of teaching
- Inappropriate expectations
- Inflexible discipline, non-negotiable/confrontational
- No pupil rights
- Resources: images do not reflect the community
- Body language /syntax/tone of voice/ misinterpretation
- Mismatch between teacher encouragement and reality in school

## Group B

- Totally Euro-centric rigid application of the National Curriculum
- Reverse discrimination that does not give children wide access to a broad knowledge
- Streaming policy
- Reading tests
- Ignoring parents' need to interact
- Rigid uniform: restrictions on hats, trainers and hairstyles
- Employing only white staff
- Vocational counselling that pushes boys into non-professional jobs

The teachers found this exercise useful and many confessed that it was not far removed from what went on in their school. In our feedback discussion it became clear that any change made in the curriculum based on social justice would have to be of benefit to all pupils. Any changes must be not for ideological reasons, to benefit a so-called Black perspective, but to benefit the whole school while addressing the specific problem of the exclusion of African-Caribbean boys. Next, the devised plan of action to tackle attitudes and poor practice set teachers practical targets to reduce the number of African-Caribbean exclusions. They decided on a combination of behaviour management programmes for teachers, peer group conflict resolution strategies with students, and programmes to increase the self-esteem of African-Caribbean boys.

## Teacher attitude

Hardiman and Jackson (1996) have produced a model of racial identity development which can help teachers to evaluate their own strengths and shortcomings on the issue of social justice and race. What makes this such a powerful tool is that it requires the 'individual' to make the self-reflecting journey on issues that are generally, at best, hidden by slogans or, at worst, totally ignored. The same model can used by students, Black and white, for confronting the crises and anxieties in their own development.

The students in Township could never conform to some master narrative that enclosed their identity – there is no essential Black or white identity. The purpose of the following exercise is to deconstruct those essentialists masks that makes us feel comfortable under labels such as 'Black', 'White', 'English', 'Jamaican', 'Male' or 'Strong'.

## RACIAL IDENTITY DEVELOPMENT

|  | NAIVE |  |
|---|---|---|
| PASSIVE ACCEPTANCE |  | ACTIVE ACCEPTANCE |
| PASSIVE RESISTANCE |  | ACTIVE RESISTANCE |
|  | REDEFINITION |  |
|  | INTERNALISATION |  |

At a conference in Texas in 1996 Hardiman and Jackson were asked to explain each of these categories with examples to support their case. They came up with the following:

**Naive**: a state of no social consciousness, usually from birth to age 3, when children accept what they see. Only with the development of social consciousness comes the potential for race awareness.

**Passive Acceptance** is an unquestioned acceptance of 'knowledge' which has been 'normalised'. White teachers might for example believe that Europeans discovered Africa. The world is seen from a point of view according to which everybody who differs from oneself is abnormal. In relation to racism, then, the victim will be blamed for all problems.

**Active Acceptance** is usually linked to overt expressions of racism, of the kind made by far Right wing groups. Such extremists tend to be a minority but the increase in racist attacks on Black students suggests that they have become more active and more violent. No teachers in Township came into this category, but some were (at times) too close for comfort.

**Passive Resistance** describes the 'social worker' liberal mentality – one fashioned by a 'missionary' consciousness. It asks: 'How can I help you be more like me?' There is no real respect for difference: the aim is to assimilate the 'other'. Unlike Passive Acceptance, Passive Resistance acknowledges social injustice but it advocates an 'assimilationist' resistance strategy. So a passive resister would be Mr Jones, believing as he did that conforming to conservative Caribbean culture was the best way to resist racism.

**Active Resistance** is difficult for many white teachers because this category acknowledges that racism exists 'within me'. This usually provokes a degree of shame or guilt about being white: one actively resists that consciousness which gives your race power and privilege.

**Redefinition** recognises that racial domination is a system that positions or constructs everyone who falls within its orbit. Focusing on ideas about whiteness and the various constructions of white racial identity can offer avenues of thought and action to those working to understand and dismantle systems of racial domination. However, in a society habituated to dominant ideologies of white supremacy it is often easier for people described as 'white' to see themselves as simply 'normal' and therefore without a radicalised identity.

The final category is **Internalisation**. If redefinition is a deconstruction of white racial identity then internalisation is the reconstruction of 'self' – a 'self' of parts which may have nothing to do with 'race' but is linked to factors such as class, caste and geography.

It follows that whiteness is ultimately about learned behaviour and social consciousness. Seeing a distinction between the idea of 'white' as a visible 'racial' type and as a way of thinking and acting in the world is an important step towards exposing the emptiness of the category. This leads to a political choice: to reject whiteness and its privileges, repudiate whiteness as an ontological category (a definition of being) and refuse to act white.

According to Hardiman and Jackson, one way forward has been to embrace diversity in all its seemingly inexhaustible combinations of form and content. Another is to look at positive coalitions which could transcend race, such as class or gender allegiances.

One useful exercise is for teachers to use Hardiman and Jackson's model without the prescribed racial dimension, using instead the word 'English'. Reflect first under the heading 'Childhood', recalling the incidents, memories, relationships, influences in one's life from age one to twelve.

Secondly, consider and respond to each category. The outcome of the exercise should be a range of internalised or deconstructed notions of 'Englishness'. So teachers not only examine their own constructions of race and nation but also take race off its lofty throne and consider other factors that could be making schooling unjust.

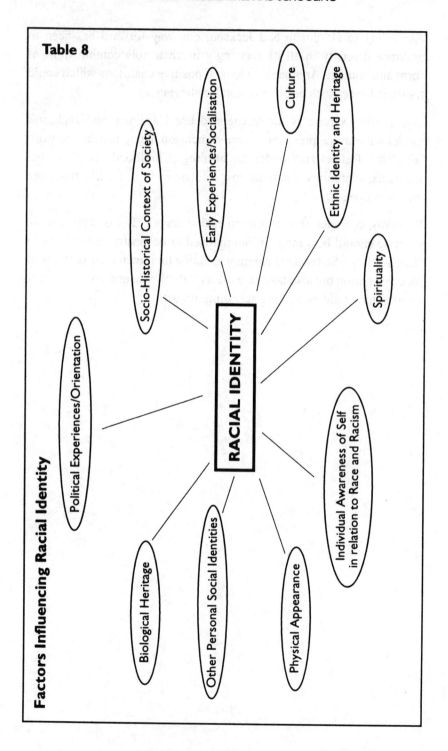

**Table 8**

**Factors Influencing Racial Identity**

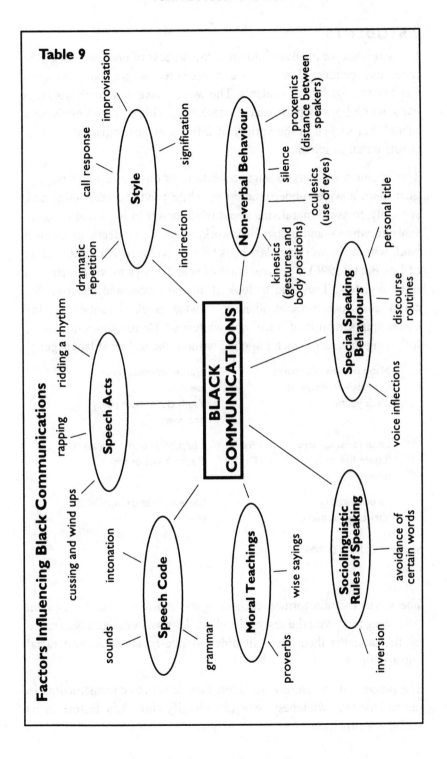

Table 9

Factors Influencing Black Communications

## 3 STUDENTS

It is vital that we involve children in the process of understanding how race and gender identities are constructed – not only African-Caribbean boys but all students. The work I have done with working-class white boys is particularly interesting. This involved devising a model that looked at the variety of influences that impacted on their construction of identity.

This requires teachers to engage white boys on two levels: firstly, to give them a wider understanding of white privilege and power and, secondly, to avoid moralising about white power in ways that make no sense to white – and particularly working class – students. In my own work with white working class boys I have developed some of the ideas of Les Back (1996). I got one class of year 10 boys to write their own 'race register'. They had to look at all the forces and tensions that could construct a racist identity – what Back describes as 'the conflicting semantic of 'race' and whiteness' He illustrates this in the following diagram, which I applied without the technical language:

| | | |
|---|---|---|
| National racist discourse<br>Criminalised images of<br>Black youth | | Egalitarian educational<br>ideology<br>Youth club/school policy<br>document |
| Local racist folklore<br>'Estate has gone<br>downhill' | WHITE<br>YOUTH | 'Neighbourhood nationalism'<br>'Racism's out of order' |
| Parental inputs<br>Racist talk at home | | Close friendships with Black<br>peers |

*Source*: Les Back (1996)

The students brainstormed each category and then shared their own 'race registers' with the rest of the class. This was vital data, generated by the students themselves in order to interrogate their own racial constructions.

The process of redefinition for white boys is akin to deconstruction. In deconstructing 'whiteness' one can identify three key factors in its social construction:

- Whiteness as a race privilege relationship to dominant groups. An example of this might be 'the old boy network'.

- Whiteness as a standpoint. This is seen in the normative way that whiteness assumes a patriarchal world-view. The white middle-class nuclear family is portrayed as the ideal unit.

- Whiteness as a set of cultural practices. Is there a white culture? An example of this is the linking of English/American nationalism to being white.

Once these planks have been removed, the sense of knowing who you are racially collapses. Many white children who reach this position decide to take on the characteristics of other cultural groups. In Britain and America we have seen the mass appropriation of Black youth sub-culture by white children. Some students may adopt aspects of Black culture in order to fill the vacuum. This leaves the question: What does it mean to be white? unanswered.

## African-Caribbean boys' routes to self-discovery

I have used Hardiman and Jackson's categories as a tentative framework in work with African-Caribbean boys in two schools. The outcome, given here in a composite breakdown, shows that the framework can be effectively applied to Black students as well as white.

**Passive Acceptance** is the category for the African-Caribbean boy who has internalised all the negative images of himself, passive in this context meaning unconscious. These are the many boys who unconsciously believed the negative perceptions that prevail among teachers and in the wider society. It was illustrated by two of the dominant beliefs among the African-Caribbean boys in Township School: that it was the Black children who gave the school a bad name and, secondly, the buying by some boys into the Black male hypersexual image as a normative value.

**Active Acceptance** describes the students who carried the 'burden of acting white', the rebel students who felt that to conform to schooling was a form of betrayal of a radical Black consciousness. They linked

Black culture/masculinity only with an anti-school and anti-education stance. In other words they played host to their own oppression.

**Passive Resistance** would be the category for the innovators in Township who were unable to operate a limited form of resistance sufficient to satisfy their peers and at the same time avoid confrontations with teachers. Black girls have been able to achieve this balancing act more successfully than Black boys.

**Active Resistance**: Into this category fall the failed passive resistors and those who were able to see the workings of racism in teachers and the institution. These students begin to fight against all the aspects of consciousness that are working against them. They begin to see the racialised way in which school operates and actively to fight against it.

**Redefinition** demands of African-Caribbean boys that they re-think Black masculinity. To deconstruct Black masculinity, they must ask themselves: what does it mean to be a Black male?

**Internalisation** is what bell hooks calls 'Black ego recovery'. It comes only after you have decolonised your mind. For young Black men it means understanding how racism is connected with other oppressions. It may even require making coalitions with other groups, be they racial or gender groups.

In my research in Township I discovered three aspects of the 'Black ego recovery'. Firstly, the abandonment of Black nationalism – not of Black pride but of the theoretical framework rooted in the European Enlightenment. Secondly, the need to resist a mind/ body split, which should have the same subversive implications it had for feminist theory. Thirdly, the need for Black youth subculture to shift from an 'uncritical' reportage in learning and play to a more creative framework that explores new avenues and opens fresh spaces.

When talking to African-Caribbean boys about these issues I would illustrate the process of 'ego recovery' in terms of a popular icon that they know or can relate to. The racial development profile can be used to explain the development of the life of major Black figures such as Malcolm X. A good exercise would be to show an edited version of Spike Lee's film and get the students to plot Malcolm X's racial development in terms of the profile. One of the key problems with this type of exercise is clarity of expression and for that a different register would be required for students.

## Presenting Racial Identity Development to Black Students

TRUSTING (toddlers)

| | |
|---|---|
| PASSIVE | ACTIVE |
| ACCEPTANCE | ACCEPTANCE |
| (parents, sports stars) | (Black kids who are |
| | ashamed of themselves) |

| | |
|---|---|
| PASSIVE | ACTIVE |
| RESISTANCE | RESISTANCE |
| (awareness that the | (awareness that the |
| world/school has | world/school has |
| a problem about your | a problem about your |
| race) | race) |
| Do little or nothing | Kick against everybody |
| | Demand that school |
| | and teachers change |

A NEW RHYTHM

(Doing well at school without taking any
bullshit. What does it mean to be a Black male?)

A CHANGE FROM WITHIN
(Look at Malcolm X, don't be limited by the narrow lens
of being a race victim, don't split your mind from your
body, don't be afraid to be an individual and follow your own
instincts. DuBois (1903) refered to a double
consciousness, an awareness of who I was and what I was capable
of achieving regardless of the prevailing beliefs of society.)

## Exploring Racial Development profiles through popular culture

The gangster lifestyle as represented in rap music has come under intense assault, not only from the white establishment but from Black feminists and concerned Black parents. The only times I witnessed the boys in Township in a mood of self-reflection about this gangster lifestyle was when one of their heroes fell. When rappers suffered from the contradictions and self-inflicted wounds inherent in their lifestyle, it became the topic of discussion during registration. These discussions were soon resolved by the boys accepting that a rapper who was shot or jailed must be honoured for his street credibility.

However there was one exception. This was the gangster rapper Tupac Shakur, the only artist in the history of popular music to have an album, 'Me against the world' (1995), rise to number one while he was still in prison. What made the strongest impression on the boys in Township School was not his jail sentence but the fact that he had decided to give up his gangster lifestyle.

Tupac Shakur was Black America's most famous tough rapper. The gangster lifestyle in rap was always about the expression of rage, frustration and hopelessness. It was a strategic option adopted by some young Black men in the materialistic 1980s as the most effective way to go through life and get 'paid'. These rappers simply gave voice to a mood that was already playing itself out in certain aspects of Black urban culture. In the process, however, the gangster lifestyle became romanticised and celebrated. It was no longer a life to avoid or dread but one to which Black youth could aspire. Bad was indeed good and 'good' was for the weak.

When interviewed about this gangster style, rappers said confidently that they were only reflecting reality. It was an easy way out because they were not just holding up a mirror to nature. It was more like taking the mirror and smashing it over the heads of rival gangs and women. Gangster rap was no longer a matter of reporting reality but the creation of a fantasy gangster world which fed into the real world and made it more extreme.

Tupac Shakur survived a shoot-out and when he was in jail for violence and accused of rape, he decided to give up his old life, one where gangsters rarely get old. A year later he was shot dead. In his own words (1995):

> When you do rap albums, you got to train yourself. You got to constantly be in character. You used to see rappers talking all that hard shit, and then you see them in suits and shit at the American Music Awards. I didn't want to be that type of nigga. I wanted to keep it real, and that's what I thought I was doing. But now that shit

is dead. That Thug Life shit... I did it, I put in my work. I laid it down. But now that shit is dead... I'm going to start an organisation called Us First, I'm going to start to save these young niggaz, because nobody else wants to save them. Nobody ever came to save me. They just watch what happened to you. That's why Thug Life to me is dead. If it's real, then let somebody else represent it, because I'm tired of it. I represented it too much. I was Thug Life. I was the only nigga out there putting my life on the line. (1995, p55)

The story of Tupac Shakur is the story that Black ego can be recovered. Teachers could use his story as a basis for looking at Blackness, racism and masculinities. His shift from a gangster style to a new perception of Black masculinity has important theoretical implications. First, he wanted to be free from the restrictions of Black nationalism that prevented him from cultivating contacts with white friends:

I was letting people dictate who should be my friends. I felt like because I was this big Black Panther type of nigga, I couldn't be friends with Madonna. And so I dissed her, even though she showed me nothing but love. I felt bad, because when I went to jail, I called her and she was the only person that was willing to help me. (1995, p55)

This part of Tupac's Black ego recovery was his realisation that the whole concept of Black Nationalism really is restrictive. He realised that the world is too large and varied to limit oneself to any race. This point was also stressed by tennis star Arthur Ashe in his autobiography (1993). In the last chapter he writes a personal piece to his young daughter, advising her on the best path to success:

You must also learn to feel comfortable in any company, as long as those people are good people. Travelling the world as a tennis player, I discovered that deep friendships with an infinite variety of people are not only possible but can definitely enrich one's life beyond measure. Do not hem yourself in, or allow others to do so. I am still dismayed when I go to some college campuses and find out that in the cafeteria, for example, Black students, by choice, sit separately at a table with only other Black students. Whether from force of habit, thoughtlessness, or timidity, this practice is usually a waste of time – time that should be used by these students to get to know people of other cultures and backgrounds. This mixing is an essential part of education, not something extraneous to it. I hope you will summon the courage to forge friendships with as many different people as you can. Some African-Americans may tease or even scorn you, and some other people may rebuff you, but I want you to persevere anyway. (Ashe, 1993, p321)

Black ego recovery must tackle the complex process by which Black fictive-culture translates itself into the notion that to be good in school means one is 'acting white'. It needs to give Black youths the desire and the confidence to feel comfortable about their identity (however shifting) without feeling restricted by a narrow nationalism. Glenn Loury (1993), a Black American academic, talks about this challenge to the 'Black psyche':

I now understand how this desire to be regarded as genuinely Black, to be seen as a 'regular brother,' has dramatically altered my life. It narrowed the range of my earliest intellectual pursuits, distorted my relationships with other people, censored my political thought and expression, informed the way I dressed and spoke, and shaped my cultural interests. Some of this was inevitable and not all of it was bad, but in my experience the need to be affirmed by one's racial peers can take on a pathological dimension. Growing into intellectual maturity has been, for me, largely a process of becoming free of the need to have my choices validated by 'the brothers.' After many years I have come to understand that until I became willing to risk the derision of the crowd I had no chance to discover the most important truths about myself or about life. I have learned that one does not have to live surreptitiously as a Negro among whites in order to be engaged in a denial of one's genuine self for the sake of gaining social acceptance. This is a price that Blacks often demand of each other as well. (Loury, 1993 p6-7)

Loury is clear that Black ego recovery is not about a Black 'Amen' corner where children are deprogrammed from a white perspective to a Black one through so-called positive images. It is a wider and harder project, that demands a willingness to risk derision as one breaks from the restrictive confines of 'race' and 'nation'. Loury goes on to expose the limitations of a personal identity that is wholly dependent on racial contingency:

> Thus, and ironically, to the extent that we individual Blacks see ourselves primarily through a racial lens, we sacrifice possibilities for the kind of personal development that would ultimately further our collective, racial interests. We cannot be truly free men and women while labouring under a definition of self derived from the perceptual view of our oppressor, confined to the contingent facts of our oppression. In *Portrait of the Artist as a Young Man*, James Joyce says of Irish nationalism: 'When the soul of a man is born in this country there are nets flung at it to hold it back from flight. You talk to me of nationality, language, religion. I shall try to fly by these nets... Do you know what Ireland is?... Ireland is the old sow that eats her farrow.' It seems to me that, too often, a search for some mythic authentic Blackness works similarly to hold back young Black souls from flight into the open skies of American [British] society. Of course there is the constraint of racism also holding us back. But the trick, as Joyce knew, is to turn such 'nets' into wings, and thus to fly by them. One cannot do that if one refuses to see that ultimately it is neither external constraints nor expanded opportunity but rather an indwelling spirit that makes this flight possible. (Loury, 1993, p10)

These theoretical possibilities must also be taken up by teachers, Black and white, and worked at within a curriculum that is open to both Black boys and white. The notions of 'masculinity', 'race' and 'nation' influence teachers and pupils from all backgrounds.

Tupac Shakur comments on the Western division of mind and body, which was a trait of his former Thug Life. He is aware that these diversions exist in the psyche of white people and are adopted into the lifestyle of many Black youths – an attitude that suggests that physicality is everything for the Black man:

> I'm not trying to make people think I'm faking it, but my whole life is going to be about saving somebody. I got to represent life. If

you saying you going to be real, that's how you be real – be physically fit, be mentally fit. And I want niggas to be educated. You know, I was steering people away from school. You gotta be in school, because through school you can get a job. And if you got a job, then that's how they can't do us like this. (Shakur, 1995, p55)

Black ego recovery must be about healing the body and mind wounded/divided by slavery, colonialism and cultural racism. It has been left to what Gramsci calls the organic intellectuals, such as Bob Marley and the radical tradition in rap music, to keep Black youth sub-culture as intellectually dynamic as anything emanating from university. This point is supported by hooks:

One of the central tenets of feminist critical pedagogy has been the insistence on not engaging the mind/body split. This is one of the underlying beliefs that has made Women's Studies a subversive location in the academy. While women's studies over the years has had to fight to be taken seriously by academics in traditional disciplines, those of us who have been intimately engaged as students or teachers with feminist thinking have always recognised the legitimacy of a pedagogy that dares to subvert the mind/body split and allow us to be whole in the classroom, and as a consequence wholehearted. (hooks, 1994b, p193)

In my model I would like to take the best of theory and practice of the African-centred academies and apply it, not to separate schools but to mainstream institutions. Black ego-recovery has to take place within the world in which we work and play. It is more than a matter of giving African-Caribbean boys new textbooks that feature Black characters and pictures. It presupposes a commitment by staff to a form of emancipatory teaching, as distinct from a white patriarchy dressed up in Black nationalism.

## THE 'RESPECT' FACTOR

The Runnymede Trust report (1996), *This is where I Live* was commissioned after disturbances in Brixton, south London involving African-Caribbean youths in December 1995. The report found that young African-Caribbean men had to show respect at home but that on the street they demanded it. Sometimes there was pressure to engage in petty crime in order to keep the respect of friends. This reinforces my notions of normalising masculinities that were faced by the boys in Township School.

According to the Runnymede report:

> Truancy is not a problem for this group. But white teachers' misinterpretation of young Black male behaviour, often results in sanctions and these sometimes have long-term effects if they contribute to the young men's reputation as trouble-makers. In particular problems and confrontations arise from the tendency to question requests and instructions. It's not necessarily insolence, but a desire to be treated with respect, which means being given reasons not just orders. (1996, p34)

A third of the youths interviewed had been excluded. Others had been subjected to bad school reports, detentions, suspensions and labelling as troublemakers. Among the key recommendations of the report were help for pupils to avoid conflict with teachers, conflict management training for school staff, and mentoring schemes.

In terms of 'respect', the boys in the Runnymede Report and in Township School do have a point. They object to situations in which teachers resort to insensitive and in some cases racist undermining of a student in their attempts to maintain or regain power. This understandably causes antagonism. Teachers will only shift towards more positive interactions if they change their behaviour as follows:

### • Listen carefully when students speak

Remain open-minded and objective. Consider the messages of students carefully. Avoid interrupting them or offering unsolicited advice or criticism.

### • Respect students' personal space

Students may feel threatened and become agitated if their personal space is constantly violated. This does not mean, however, that teachers should ignore the rules.

### • Use friendly gestures, not aggressive ones

Avoid pointing the finger. Open hands with upturned palms are less threatening.

### • Use the student's preferred name

Ask each student how he would like to be addressed in the classroom and then respect that preference.

### • Get on their level physically

If they are seated, try kneeling or bending over, rather than standing over them.

### • Ask questions rather than make accusations

Assume that the student is a responsible person. 'Are you ready to begin?' is less confrontational than: 'Put your magazine away. It's time to start class', especially when spoken in a concerned and kind tone.

### • Deal with problem behaviour in private

Reprimanding or 'shaming' students in front of their peers causes unnecessary embarrassment. Speaking to them privately respects their dignity and self-esteem.

### • Avoid negative comments on cultural styles

Students should be allowed to dress themselves and their hair within the agreed limits of a school's dress code and to move as they please if this does not encroach on the space of others.

The respect factor is not only important when teachers are relating to students. What is also crucial is that students learn that there is an appropriate behaviour for a particular context – the idea that all situations do not deserve the same response. One exercise that I successfully used with groups of Secondary year ten and eleven (14 and 15 year old) students was called 'Respect is due'. The students are given the following situations and then have to complete the exercise. This would be to choose two of the incidents, and then: 'Say how you would normally react when faced with this situation. Secondly, think of a different response which is positive but helps you to retain your self-respect'. The boys would then share their responses and the teacher would have a chance to talk about how students could re-model their behaviour so that they can balance the need for justice and dignity.

## RESPECT IS DUE
WHAT DO I DO WHEN...

1.  I'M IN CLASS AND A BOY/GIRL CALLS MY MOTHER A SLAG.

2.  WE ARE CHANGING LESSONS AND I'M IN THE CORRIDOR AND A BOY RUSHES INTO ME AND KNOCKS ME TO THE GROUND. ALL MY FRIENDS START LAUGHING. I FEEL SHAME!

3.  I'M TALKING WITH A FRIEND AT THE BACK OF THE CLASS AND A TEACHER SAYS 'BOY/GIRL, SHUT UP YOUR MOUTH IS LIKE THE BLACKWALL TUNNEL' – THE WHOLE CLASS STARTS LAUGHING.

4.  IT WAS MY TEACHER'S BIRTHDAY AND A BOY DECIDED TO GIVE HIM SOME FLOWERS. WHEN HE GAVE IT TO HIM THE OTHER BOYS CALLED HIM 'A BATTY MAN'. WHAT DID YOU DO?

What was interesting about the boy's response to the exercise is that they found the re-modelling process extremely difficult. They either said they would do something that sounded crass or comical otherwise their second reaction was not that far from their first. Here is a sample:

Dennis:

> For incident 1, if I was in class and a boy or girl called my mum a slag and they (weren't joking) my usual reaction would be to get up out of my seat, approach them and beat the f--- out of them.

> A different response that would make me feel a little better and keep me out of trouble would either be to curse their mum back or ignore them and wait for them after school.

Alan:

> For incident 3, if I was talking to a friend at the back of the class and a teacher told me to shut my mouth because it is like the Blackwall Tunnel, my natural response would most likely be to shout back and say 'your mother's mouth is like the Blackwall Tunnel.'

> Another way to handle it and keep my self-respect and dignity and keep out of trouble would be to ignore them and talk louder and then say 'I'm not a barking dog, I understand the words. 'Be quiet'. If this does not work I would say 'Have some manners'.

Joe:

> For incident 4, if a boy in my class gave a male teacher a bunch of flowers, I would curse him all day and every time I see him I would call him names like gay and batty man.

> Another way would be to advise him not to give male teachers presents while students were there.

## Black mentors

It is often suggested that African-Caribbean boys would be less disaffected with school if they had 'appropriate' Black male role models who could act as mentors. Mentoring schemes of this type have had mixed results.

African-American academic Spencer Holland was invited to the UK in 1995 by Diane Abbott MP to share the findings of his 'Project 2000', a Black male-mentor scheme that was having dramatic positive effects on the academic performance of Black primary school children in the poor areas of Washington DC. Holland discussed his project with parents, teachers and LEA officials in the London Borough of Hackney, which, like Washington, had disproportionally high exclusion rates from schools of Black boys. Holland's theory was that because the majority of six-year-old Black boys in Hackney came from households with single mothers, they began to reject school because they linked learning with being 'anti-masculine'. According to Holland, this was exacerbated because all their teachers were women:

The boy does not find it appropriate to be copying a woman. In 1988 we conducted an experiment in a local elementary school. We wanted to find what would happen if we put all the six-year-old Black boys alongside a Black male mentor. These men were all volunteers and from a variety of backgrounds. Their job was to act as a classroom assistant to the female teacher. Soon the teachers were saying that their classes had improved, the boys were following the male lead and began doing well. Today these boys did much better than expected. Research showed that at a comparable school not involved in the project the students performed below their required level. (Holland, 1995)

Holland believes that the real advantage that this exclusive Black male cadre has over women is that they are able to teach the boys about their maleness. This is the crux of what is so problematic about Holland's project and why it met so much resistance from teachers in Hackney. For a start, Holland has oversimplified the reasons for the poor performance of African-Caribbean boys. The issues around too much 'female' input into the lives of Black boys compared to the 'safe' hands of a man, is dangerously sexist. It overlooks the ethnographic evidence (Sewell, 1995) that exclusion rates in England were disproportionately high for Black boys from both single and two parent families. Secondly, the boys themselves talk not in terms of women teachers and men teachers but of 'good' and 'bad' classroom teaching. Thirdly, criticism of Holland's thesis is open to criticism when he asserts that a Dad's Army of mentors is the only effective strategy. Research has shown that the more individual attention that children get the better they perform, irrespective of the gender of the teacher. There is also a methodological problem with Holland's research. To support his claim that Black men are the only effective mentors for Black boys, he should verify it by setting up a pilot scheme with both men and women working with young Black boys. I would argue that the improved performance of Black boys would be just as likely if the classroom assistants were female. As the leader of Hackney Education Authority, Gus John, observed:

I have no problem with the idea that mentoring could enhance pupils' learning. I have a problem with the thesis which says that it is impossible for a woman to teach boys values and attitudes that get them focused upon learning. I find this part of the thesis most difficult to accept. You are training men to stand next to female teachers and present an alternative authority figure to these kids. (John, 1995)

## Role models and 'supervics'

The early literature on race and education explained Black underachievement in terms of racial pathologies that blamed the victim. The flipside to this has been the literature inspired by Black Nationalism which has turned the so called victim into a suffering saint – what I call the 'Supervic'. There are three major components of this resurgence which have triggered heated debates within the halls of academia and on the streets of Black Britain and America. They are: first, the cultural and intellectual movement known as Afrocentrism; second, the growing interest and influence of Louis Farrakhan and the Nation Of Islam; and third the provocative and popular lyrics of certain sub-genres of rap music. All three of these trends share two characteristics: they all contain an oppositional edge which offers respite from the oppressive realities of racism. At the same time, however, each trend represents a very male-centred definition of the problems confronting the Black community and proposes pseudo-solutions which further marginalise and disparage Black women. A masculinised vision of Black empowerment and liberation resonates through the literature on Afrocentrism, the lyrics of male rappers, and the symbolic characterisation of Louis Farrakhan as the redemptive Black patriarch.

Molete Asante is the scholarly daddy of Afrocentrism. With his male-centred vision, his book *Afrocentricity* (1980) surveys a pantheon of Black activist-intellectuals and does not find a single Black woman's contribution compelling enough to discuss in any detail. He concludes after an attack on homosexuality that 'the time has come to redeem our Black manhood through Afrocentric action'.

There is within the Afrocentric discourse a problem of being a supervictim. Super because Black men are total victims of white evil. The solutions are found within the Black community not outside. Drawing on a slightly modified language of biological determinism and essentialism, many Afrocentrists endorse 'traditional' sex roles for

Black men and women as being the natural ones. So male-headed nuclear families are synonymous with strong functional families. Those who reject or challenge the prescribed gender roles are dismissed as inauthentic and/or Eurocentric.

It is Afrocentrism then, that is the basis of the call for Black male role models as a solution to Black boys underachieving in school. The underlying assumption is that we need strong Black patriarchs to give moral direction to the floundering female-headed households which have disestablished the Black community. Ironically, this is also the point at which the politics and positions of some cultural nationalists, liberals and right-wing conservatives seem to converge. Consistent with the view that the problem with Black people is culturally based, and centred around an alleged crisis in Black manhood, their arguments are again framed by the use of certain race, class and gender coded terms which blame poor people for their own oppression. Personal characteristics such as low self-esteem, lack of self-awareness and pride and, most of all, lack of discipline are cited as the sources of the larger social problems confronting the Black community, from drugs and gangs to teenage pregnancy.

In addition, the gendered nature of this discussion of the 'problem with Black people' becomes obvious when one examines who is generally targeted, implicitly or explicitly, as its root cause. Black women, especially single mothers, are routinely vilified as the culprits.

There is actually no shortage of good Black male role models. In fact it is the lofty position of 'race' that has become an additional burden for many students. The survival of modern schooling must be achieved outside of a context that perceives Black boys as Supervictims. When I went back to Township School to share this research with the boys, I asked a group of them to devise a model of a school which deliberately excluded them. They were to identify ten factors that would make them most vulnerable to exclusion and arrange these in order of importance. Their top ten were:

1. Teachers who were afraid of children and couldn't control their classes.

2. Teachers and headteachers who were not consistent.

3. Boring lessons.

4. Teachers who would pick on Black kids because of their hairstyle.

5. Intelligent children being called 'boffins' and getting beaten up.

6. Teachers not explaining their lessons clearly.

7. Teachers not showing Black kids respect.

8. No heating in classrooms.

9. No Black history.

10. Ancillary staff being racist.

If you look at the top three points, it is clear that all are to do with having good, caring and professional teachers who make their lessons enjoyable and are able to manage their classrooms. The boys have not directly mentioned 'race' until point number four; they are indicating a range of other factors related to quality teaching and management. This is not to deny the existence of racism but rather to challenge a thesis that looks at race in isolation from several other factors.

The struggle for Black boys is not only against the madness of racism but against the equal madness of flawed solutions. The child who has the best handle on survival moves beyond racist narrow provincialism and embraces human possibility. All teachers and parents need to make this the key plank of their teaching.

## Summary

Stephen Ball (1987) warns against the danger of approaching school with 'the abstract tidiness of conceptual debate' when it comes to looking at the 'messiness' that exists inside school. This is particularly true when the complex notions of ethnicity, racisms and gender are added. I hope I have not been too prescriptive in this chapter. Schools may wish to pick, choose and edit my suggestions in the light of their particular situation.

What is certain is that the tension that exists between the schooling process and African-Caribbean boys can be resolved. The problem primarily is one of social justice. This means that there will be no meaningful way forward until white (and many of the Black) teachers come to terms with their own racial identity development. It is no use blaming the victims all the time.

Equally, African-Caribbean boys need to move through a racial identity development process, to secure their dignity and self-esteem in a process that I would call Black ego recovery. The process is underpinned by the necessity for young people to be able to name their experience and not be host to their own oppression. It acknowledges that negative peer pressure and teacher racism are not only a huge obstacles to good schooling but also massive barriers to self-development.

## CONCLUSION

African-Caribbean boys are not men but children. There is a real danger when looking at the complex issues of masculinities and schooling, that we forget that the focus is on schoolboys under the age of 16, who are the responsibility of parents and the State. The journey from childhood to manhood is processed through school. The reality of teacher attitudes and peer group pressure compels children to adopt certain normative values. For African-Caribbean boys in Township School this process was racialised. The peer group imposed both positive and negative influences; it was at once a cauldron of new vibrant Black culture, vital to the creation of an African-Caribbean identity in a hostile world, and a trap into a perception of Black boys as a force only of rebellion and never of conformity and creativity.

In Township School the teachers were so preoccupied with their own survival that they failed to address vital issues of race and sexuality. They did not see their task of education as an emancipatory practice whereby repressed voices are released. Instead all emphasis was on control and exclusion. The largest category of teachers were the irritated, who with their survivalist mentality denied their own perplexity. In entrenching themselves in this survivalist mentality they failed to challenge their own socialisation, so were unable to see how their own practice could lead to racist stereotyping.

Accordingly, many of the teachers at Township School failed to see how they were instrumental in the formation of dominant discourses and they continued to police their Black students. They did so by criticising the African-Caribbean family for its lack of patriarchy and the boys because of their size and physicality. They failed to demonstrate any conception of teaching and learning as a dialogic relationship in the classroom.

Teacher racism in Township School was complex and contextual. It could be argued that Mr Jones, the African-Caribbean head, perpetuated a racist discourse in his attitude to the hairstyles of his African-Caribbean pupils. It was ultimately out of his Caribbean idealism that a discourse emerged which was biased against the African-Caribbean boys. However, his critique of the boys also revealed how they had themselves reappropriated many Black masculine stereotypes in the context of their sub-culture.

There were many examples of the way African-Caribbean boys in Township School contested their feelings of powerlessness through phallocentric responses. This was shown in the way that the Rebel students positioned the Conformist boys as sexually deficient or unmasculine when they chose not to contest the school processes. However, the Rebels also offered a critique of the ideal pupil status that dominated the thinking of the head and his deputy. It was a critique that not only rejected the discipline of school but rejected also the poor standards of teaching and the cynical attitudes of some teachers.

This research reveals that African-Caribbean young men have to face the racist discourse and structure of the school. It also shows how these boys have to deal with a number of empty spaces along with the well-founded expectation of unemployment. Their response is varied and complex. Surviving modern schooling has indeed become an art for these boys. Some have chiselled out the craven image of Conformity and have sold their souls in the process. Others have cut out a rebel phallus that has lost touch with their minds and inner selves.

In suggesting that African-Caribbean boys are too sexy for school, I am referring to their normative attraction for peers and the media and, equally, the way that teachers perceive them as threatening. Answers are not easy, but schools that are prepared to recognise and examine this power-play have made a significant step towards improving their educational provision for Black boys.

# References

Aggleton, P. (1987) *Deviance*, London Tavistock.

Alcoff, L. (1988) Cultural feminism and post-structuralism: the identity aims in feminist theory. *Signs*: 13 405-36.

Allcott, T. (1992) 'Anti-racism in education: the search for policy in practice.' In D. Gill, B. Mayor and M. Blair (eds) *Racism and Education: Structures and Strategies*. London, Sage.

Anderson, G. and Herr, K. (1994) 'The Micropolitics of student voices: moving from diversity of bodies to diversity of voices in schools.' In Marshall C (ed) *The New Politics of Race and Gender*. Lewes, Falmer Press

Asante, M. (1994) in 'Detroit's African-centred Academics disarm skeptics and empower boys'. *Black issues in Higher Education* Feb 24 vl 10 no 26. Virginia, Cox Matthews and Associates, Inc.

Ashe, A. (1993) *Days of Grace*. London, William Heineman.

Austin, D.J. (1984) *Urban life in Kingston Jamaica. The culture and class ideology of two neighbourhoods*. London, Gordon and Breach

Ayers, W. (1990) Small Heroes: in and out of school with 10-year-old city kids, *Cambridge Journal of Education*, 20(3), 269-276.

Back, L. (1992) PhD thesis: Youth, Racism and Ethnicity in South London, University of London.

Back, L. (1994) The White Negro revisited. In A. Cornwall and N. Lindisfarne (eds) *Dislocating masculinity, comparative ethnographies*. London, Routledge.

Baldwin, J. (1965) *Nobody Knows My Name*, London, Corgi

Ball, S.J. (1987) *The Micro-Politics of the School: Towards a theory of school organization*. London, Routledge.

Banton, M. (1959) *White and Coloured: The Behaviour of the British people Towards Coloured Immigrants*, London, Jonathan Cape

Becker, H.S. (1952) 'Social class variations in the teacher-pupil relationship'. *Journal of Educational Psychology*, 25 April.

Becker, H. (1957) *The Outsiders*, New York: New York Free Press

Bhabba, H. (1986) Introduction to 1986 ed of *Black Skin, White masks* by Frantz Fanon. London, Pluto Press.

Blumer, H. (1969) *Symbolic Interactionism*, New Jersey: Prentice Hall.

Bogdan, J. and S. Taylor (1982) *Introduction to qualitative research methods: a phenomenological approach.* New York, Wiley.

Bondi, L. (1993) 'Gender and dichotomy', *Progress in Human Geography* no 16.

Bourdieu, P. (1976) The school as a conservative force: scholastic and cultural inequalities in: *Schooling and Capitalism, a sociological reader* (eds) Milton Keynes, Open University Press.

Brake, M. (1980) *The Sociology of Youth culture and Youth sub-cultures*, London, Routledge and Kegan Paul.

Brah, A. ( 1992) Difference, Diversity and Differentiation in J. Donald and A. Rattansi (eds) (1992) *'Race', Culture and Difference.* London Sage OUP

British Sociological Association (1973) Statement of Ethical Principles and their Application to Sociological Practice, London, BSA.

Bryman, A. (1988) *Quantity and Quality in Social Research*, London: Unwin Hyman.

Burgess, R.G. (1984) *In the Field: An Introduction to Field Research*, London: Allen and Unwin.

Cashmore, E. and Troyna B. (eds) (1982) *Black Youth in Crisis*, London Allen and Unwin.

Cohen, P. (1992) 'It's racism what dunnit' Hidden narratives in theories of racism. In J. Donald and A. Rattansi (eds) *op cit.*

Cohen, L and Manion, L (1981) *Perspectives on classrooms and schools.* London, Holt Reinhart and Winston.

Cohen, L and Manion, L (1986) *Research Methods in Education.* Beckenham: Croom Helm.

Collin, M (1994) Jungle Fever: The *Observer* magazine (26 June 1994) London.

Connell, R.W. (1987) *Gender and Power.* Cambridge, Polity Press.

Connell, R.W. (1989) Cool guys, Swots and wimps: The inter-play of masculinity and education, *Oxford Review of Education* 15 (3), 291-303.

Cooper, C. (1993) *Noises in the Blood: Orality, gender and the 'vulgar' body of Jamaican popular culture.* London, Macmillan.

Corrigan, P. (1979) *Schooling the Smash Street Kids.* London, Macmillan.

Denning, M. (1992) The Academic Left and the Rise of Cultural Studies, *Radical History Review* 54, 21- 48.

Derrida, J. (1976) *Of Grammatology*, trans G. Spivak. Baltimore: John Hopkins U. Press.

Dex, S. (1983) 'The second generation: West Indian female school leavers' in A. Phizaclea (ed) *One way ticket*. London, Routledge

Essence (1994), *Girls and rap*. August 1994. Colorado U.S. A, Essence Communications

Fanon, F. (1967) *Black Skin, White Masks*. London, Grove Press.

Fanon, F. (1963) *The Wretched of the Earth*. New York, Grove

Faraday, A. and Plummer, K. (1979) Doing Life Histories, *Sociological Review* 27(4), 773-798.

Figueroa, P.E. (1974) 'West Indian school-leavers in a London borough, 1966-67' Unpublished Ph.D thesis, University of London, L.S.E.

Fordham, S. (1988) 'Racelessness as a Factor in Black Students' School Success: Pragmatic Strategy or Pyrrhic Victory?', *Harvard Educational Review*, vol 58, no. 1

Fordham, S. and Ogbu, J. (1986) Black Students' School Success: Coping with the 'Burden of Acting White' *The Urban Review* vol 18, no.3

Foster, P. (1990) *Policy and Practice in Multicultural and Anti-Racist Education.* London, Routledge.

Foster, P. (1993) 'Methodological purism' or a defence against hype? Critical readership in research in 'race' and education. *New Community* 19 (3): 547-552. London.

Foucault, M (1972) *The Archaeology of Knowledge.* London, Tavistock

Foucault, M (1973) *The Order of Things.* New York, Vintage Books

Foucault, M (1982) *Discipline and Punish.* London, Peregrine Books

Frederickson, G.M. (1981) *White Supremacy: A comparative study in American and South African history.* New York, Oxford U.P.

Freire, P. (1981) *Pedagogy of the oppressed.* New York, Continuum.

Fryer, P. (1984) *Staying Power: The history of black people in Britain.* London, Pluto Press.

Fuller, M. (1980) 'Black girls in a London comprehensive school', reprinted in M. Hammersley and P. Woods (eds) (1984), *Life in School: The Sociology of Pupil Culture* Milton Keynes, Open University Press.

Gates, H Jr. (1987) *Figures in Black: Words, Signs, and the 'Racial' Self.* Oxford University Press.

Gates, H Jr. (1990) 2 Live Crew, decoded. *New York Times*, Tues June 19 A23, New York.

Gilroy, P. (1987) *There Ain't No Black in the Union Jack: The cultural politics of race and nation.* London, Routledge.

Gilroy, P. (1992) *The end of anti-racism*, in J. Donald and A. Rattansi (eds), op. cit.

Gilroy, P. (1993a) *Small Acts: Thoughts on the politics of black cultures.* London, Serpent's Tail.

Gilroy, P. (1993b) *The Black Atlantic: Modernity and double consciousness* London, Verso

Gillborn, D (1990) *Race, ethnicity and education.* London, Unwin Hyman.

Gillborn, D. and Drew, D. (1993) The politics of research: some observations on 'methodological purity', *New Community* 19(2) 354-360

Gillborn, D. (1994a) Transcipt of talk on black male exclusions, Lewisham Civic Suite. (19 May 1994)

Gillborn, D. (1994b) synopsis of paper: Racism, Identity and Modernity: Beyond pluralism/towards critical antiracism. At the International Sociology of Education Conference on Pluralism, Values and Curriculum Change 2-3 January 1995, Sheffield.

Glaser, B.G. and Strauss, A.L. (1967) *The Discovery of Grounded Theory: Strategies for Qualitative Research.* Chicago, Aldine Press.

Goodson, I. and Walker, R. (1988) Putting Life into Educational Research. In RJR. Shaman and RIB. Webb (eds) *Qualitative Research in Education: Focus and Methods.* Lewes, Falmer Press.

Green, P.A. (1983) 'Teachers' influence on the self-concept of pupils of different ethnic origins', PhD thesis, University of Durham.

Grossberg, L. (1994) Bringin' it all Back Home – Pedagogy and Cultural Studies. In H.A. Giroux and P. McLaren (eds) *Between Borders. Pedagogy and the Politics of Cultural Studies.* New York, Routledge.

Gurnah, A. (1984) The politics of racism awareness training. *Critical Social policy,* 11pp 6-20.

Hammersley, M. (1984) 'The researcher exposed: a natural history,' in R.G. Burgess (ed), *The Research Process in Educational Settings: Ten Case Studies.* Lewes, Falmer.

Hall, S. (1988) The toad in the garden: Thatcherism among theorists . In C. Nelson and L. Grossberg (eds) *Marxism and the Interpretation of Culture.* London, Macmillan.

Hall, S. (1990) 'Cultural Identity and diaspora'. In J. Rutherford (ed) *Identity, Community, Culture, Difference.* London, Lawrence and Wishart.

Hall, S. ( 1991) Old and new identities, old and new ethnicities. In A.D. King (ed) *Culture Globalization and the World System*, Hampshire, Macmillan.

Hall, S. (1992) New ethnicities. In J. Donald and A. Rattansi (eds), *op. cit.*

Hardiman and Jackson (1996) lecture notes at the National Conference on Race and Ethnicity in American Higher Education, San Antonio, Texas May 30-June 4.

Harpin, L. (1994) Jungle: *The Face* ( No 71 August 1994) London.

Harris, P (1994) Out of the jungle: *The Voice* issue 456 July 1994 London, Voice Communications.

Hebidge, D. (1982) *Subculture: The meaning of Style.* London, Routledge.

Hebidge, D. (1988) *Hiding in the light: On the Images and Things.* London, Routledge.

Henriques *et al* (1984) *Changing the Subject.* London, Methuen.

Hitchcock, G. and Hughes, D. ( 1989) *Research and the Teacher: a qualitative introduction to school-based research.* London, Routledge.

Hoch, P. (1979) *White Hero, Black Beast: Racism, sexism and the mask of masculinity.* London, Pluto Press.

hooks, b. (1992) *Black Looks: race and representation.* London, Turnaround.

hooks, b (1993) *Hard-core rap lyrics stir backlash.* New York Times, August 15, New York.

hooks, b. (1994a) *Outlaw Culture, resisting representations.* London, Routledge.

hooks, b. ( 1994b) *Teaching to Transgress: Education as the practice of freedom.* London, Routledge.

Husserl, E. (1965) *Phenomenology and the Crisis of Philosophy,* New York, Harper Torchbooks.

Jeffcoate, R. (1979) *Positive Image.* London, Writers and Readers

Junior, R. (1994) 'The end of Ragga' *Sunday Times,* November 13 1994.

Keddie, N. (1971) 'Classroom knowledge', in M.F.D. Young (ed), *Knowledge and Control.* London, Collier/ Macmillan

Keddie, N. (ed) (1973) *Tinker, Tailor: the myth of cultural deprivation* 2 Hammondsworth, Penguin.

Lacan, J. (1977) *Ecrits: A selection.* London, Tavistock

Loury, G. (1993) Free at last? A personal perspective on race and identity in America. In G. Early (ed) *Lure and Loathing: essays on race, identity and the ambivalence of assimilation.* New York, Penguin.

Lowenthal, B. (1994) 'Who's callin' who a bitch'. *The Sunday Times* 8 Feb p12

Mac an Ghaill, M. (1988) *Young, Gifted and Black: Student-Teacher Relations in the Schooling of Black Youth.* Milton Keynes, Open University Press

Mac an Ghaill, M. (1994) *The making of men, masculinities, sexualities and schooling.* Buckingham, Open University Press.

Macdonald, I. Bhavnani, R. Khan, L. and John, G. (1989), *Murder in the playground: The Burnage Report.* London: Longsight Press.

Malik, R. (1994) August 24-31 The new Avengers in *Time Out,* London, Time Out.

McCarthy, C. (1993) After the Canon: Knowledge and ideological representation. In C. McCarthy and W. Critchlow, *Multicultural Discourse on Curriculum Reform in Race, Identity and Representation in Education.* London, Routledge

Mead, G.H. (1934) *Mind, Self and Society.* Univesity of Chicago Press, Chicago.

Mercer, K. (1992) Back to My Routes: Postscript to the 80s. In D. Bailey and S. Hall (eds) *Critical Decade: Black British Photography in the 80s.* Ten-8 (3) (spec. issue), 32-39.

Mercer, K. (1994) *Welcome to the Jungle: New positions in black cultural studies.* London, Routledge.

Merton, R (1957) *Social Theory and Social Structure.* Chicago, Chicago Free Press.

Miles, R. (1978) *Between two cultures: The case of Rastafarianism.* Working Papers on Ethnic Relations, no.10. SSRC Research Unit on Ethnic Relations, University of Aston in Birmingham.

Mirza, H.S. (1992) *Young, Female and Black.* London, Routledge

Mouffe, C. (1993) Liberal Socialism and Pluralism: Which Citizenship? In J. Squires (ed) *Principled Positions: Postmodernism and the Rediscovery of Valued.* London, Lawrence and Wishart.

Mullard, C. (1982) 'Multiracial education in Britain: from assimilation to cultural pluralism, in Tierney, J. (ed) *Race, Migration and Schooling.* London: Holt, Rinehart and Winston.

Neal, S. (1995) A question of silence? Antiracist discourses and initiatives in Higher Education: Two case studies. In M. Griffiths and B. Troyna (eds) *Antiracism, Culture and Social Justice in Education,* Stoke-on-Trent, Trentham Books.

Norquay, N. (1990) 'Life History Research: memory, schooling and social difference.' *Cambridge Journal of Education* 20 (3).

Ogbu, J. (1978) *Minority Education and Caste: The American system in cross-cultural perspective.* New York, Academic Press.

Peterson-Lewis, Sonja (1991) A feminist analysis of the defenses of obscene rap lyrics. In Jon Michael Spencer, *The Emergency of Black and the Emergence of Rap.* Durham North Carolina, Duke University Press.

Phillips, A. (1993) *Democracy and Difference.* Cambridge, Polity Press

Podhoretz, N. (1963) 'My Negro Problem and ours'. Commentary

Powell, K. (1995) Tupac Shakur, April (ed), New York, Time Warner.

Pring, R. (1978) Problems of Justification in Pring, R. (ed) *Theory and Practice of Curriculum Studies.* London, Kegan Paul.

Pring, R. (1992) Education for a Pluralist Society. In M. Leicester and C. Taylor, *Ethics, Ethnicity and Education,* Lewes, Falmer Press.

Rampton Report (1981). *West Indian Children in our Schools.* London, HMSO.

Rattansi, A. (1992) Changing the Subject? Racism, culture and education in J. Donald and A. Rattansi (eds) (1992) *'Race', Culture and Difference.* London, Sage and Open University Press

Riley, K. (1986) 'Black girls speak for themselves' in Weiner, G. (eds) *Just a Bunch of Girls,* Milton Keynes, Open University Press.

Rist, R. (1970) Student social class and teacher expectations: the self-fulfilling prophecy in ghetto education. *Harvard Educational Review* 40, 411- 451.

Rist, R. (1977). 'On understanding the process of schooling: The contribution of labelling theory', in J. Karabel and A.H. Halsey (eds) *Power and Ideology in Education.* New York, Oxford University Press.

Ross, A. and Rose, T. (eds) (1994) *Microphone Friends: Youth music, youth culture.* London, Routledge.

Rutherford, J. (1990) A place called home: In J. Rutherford (eds) *Identity, community, culture and difference.* London, Lawrence and Wishart.

Sewell, T (1995) The Relationship between African-Caribbean Boys' Sub-culture and Schooling, Unpublished Phd thesis, Nottingham University.

Sewell, T (1996) Mind your language Trevor, *The Voice* Newspaper, issue no 699 23 April, London.

Shaw, C. (1994) *Changing Lives.* London, Policy Studies Institute.

Skeggs, B. (1991) Challenging masculinity and using sexuality, *British Journal of Sociology of Education,* 12 (1), 127-40.

Staples, R. (1982) *Black Masculinity: The Black Man's Role in American Society.* San Francisco: Black Scholar Press.

Squires, J. (ed) ( 1993) *Principled Positions: Postmodernism and Rediscovery of Value.* London, Lawrence and Wishart.

Swann, M. (1985) *'Education For All' Final Report of the Committee of Inquiry into the Education of Children from Ethnic Minority Groups* Cmnd 9453. London, HMSO

Tate, G. (1994) Introduction in A. Ross and T. Rose 9 (eds) *Microphone Friends: Youth music, Youth culture,* London, Routeledge.

*The Twickenham Informer* (1996 17 May) Letters to the Editor

Troyna, B. (1993) *Racism and Education: Research perspectives.* Buckingham, Open University Press.

Troyna, B. (1987) 'Swann's Song': the origins, ideology and implications of Educational for All, in Chivers , T (eds) *Race and Culture in Education: Issues arising from the Swann Committee Report.* Windsor, NFER-Nelson.

Walkerdine, V. (1990) *Schoolgirl Fictions.* London, Verso.

Wambu, O. (1994) 'Inner Vision', *The Voice* 11 Oct p6

Wellman, D. T. (1977) *Portraits of white racism*, Cambridge, Cambridge University Press.

West, C. (1993) The New Cultural Politics of Difference. In C. McCarthy and W. Crichlow (eds) *Race Identity and Representation in Education*. London, Routledge

Willis, P. ( 1990) *Common Culture: symbolic work at play in the everyday cultures of the young*. Milton Keynes, Open University Press.

Willis, P. (1977) *Learning to Labour: How Working Class Kids Get Working Class Jobs*. Farnborough, Gower.

Woods, P. (1986) *Inside Schools*. Ethnography in Educational Research. London, Routledge.

Wright, C. (1985) School processes – an ethnographic study, in: S. Eggleston, D. Dunn and M. Anjali (eds) *Education for some: the educational and vocational experiences of 15-18 year old members of minority ethnic groups*. Stoke-on-Trent, Trentham.

# Index